ARKHAM ASYLUM
ISBN 1 85286 256 4

Published by
Titan Books Ltd
58 St Giles High St
London WC2H 8LH

Published under license from DC Comics Inc.
First British edition November 1989
10 9 8 7 6 5 4 3 2 1

Printed and bound in Canada

aRKHAM
aSYLUM

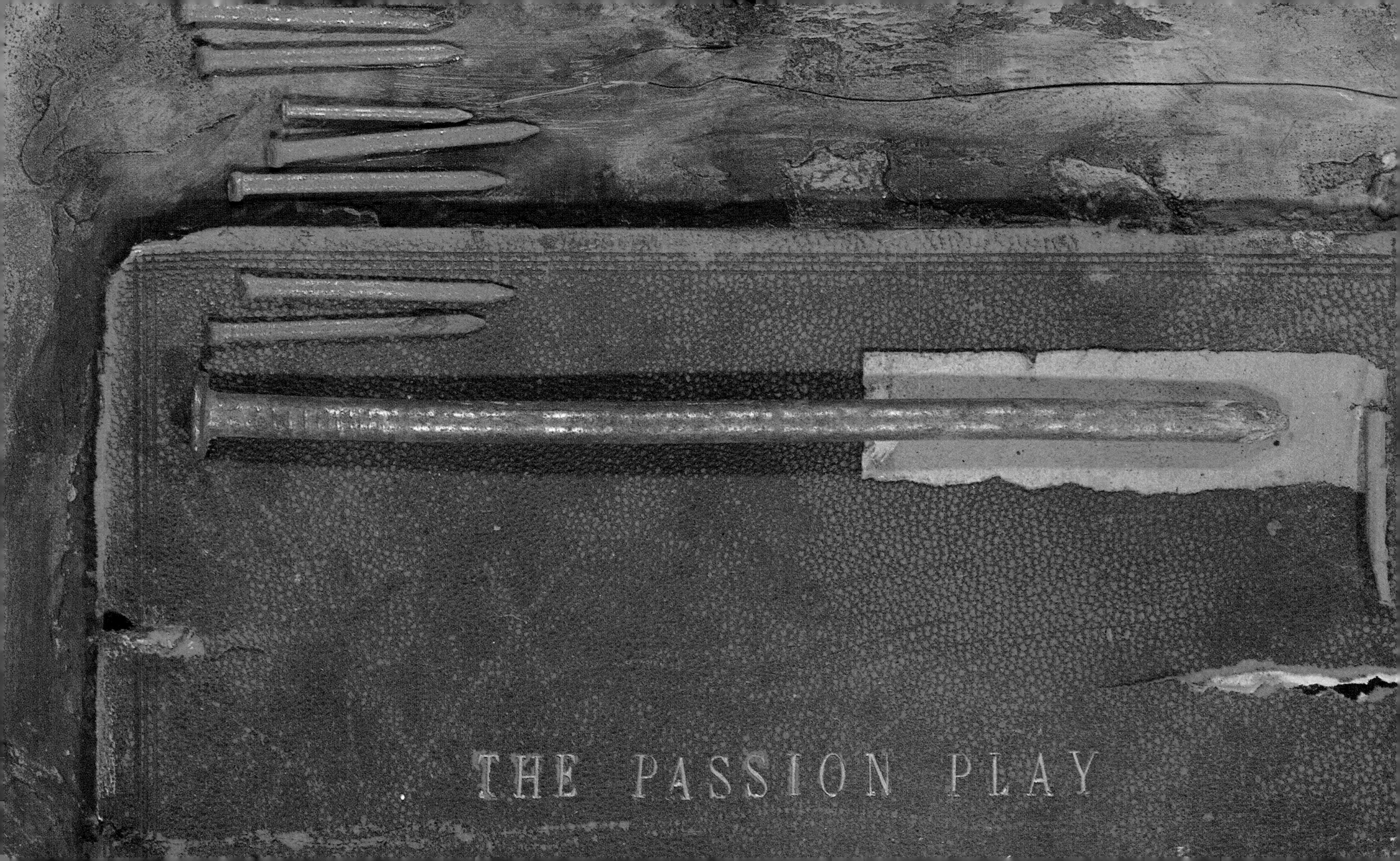
THE PASSION PLAY

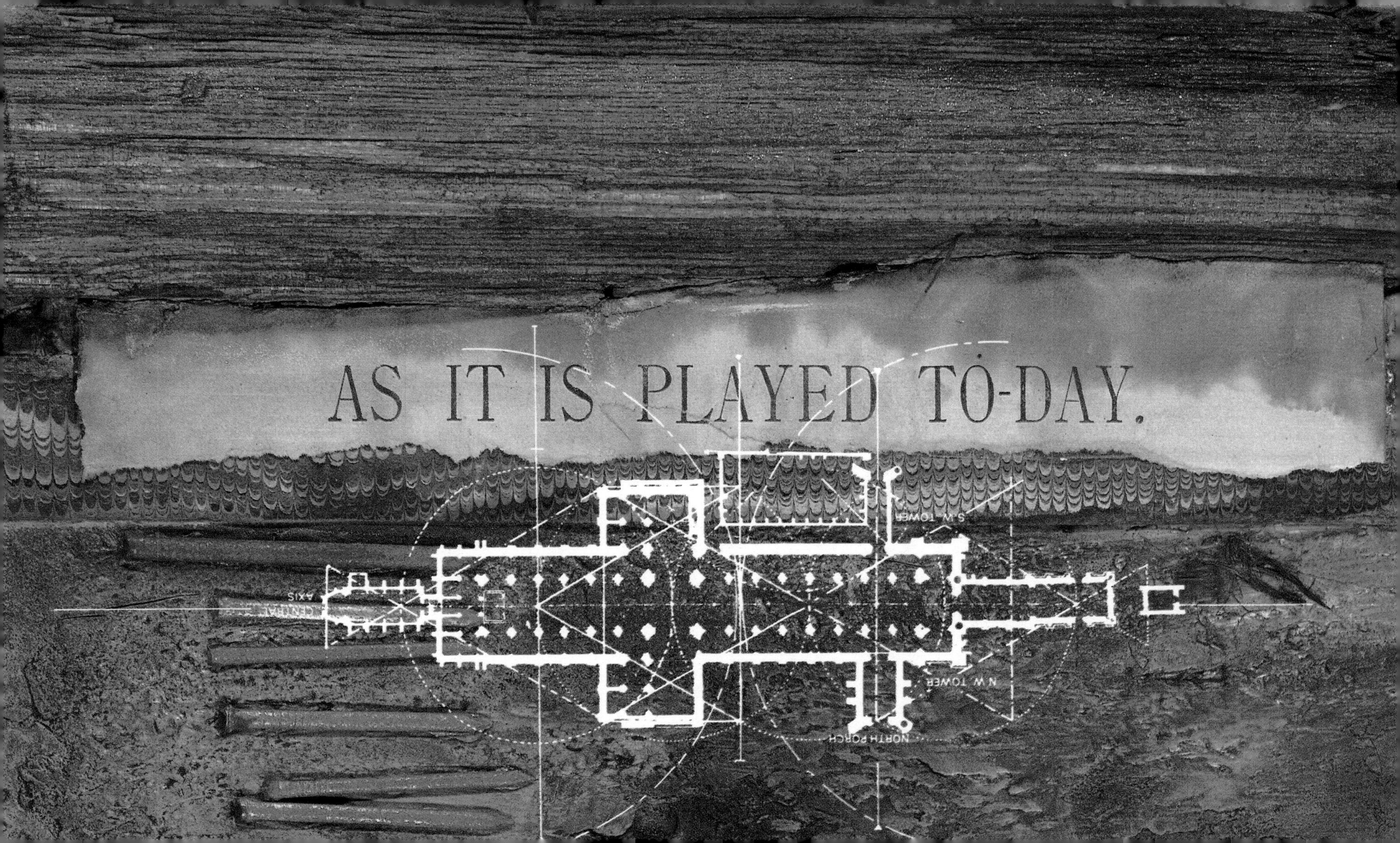
AS IT IS PLAYED TO-DAY.
CENTRAL AXIS
S.W. TOWER
N.W. TOWER
NORTH PORCH

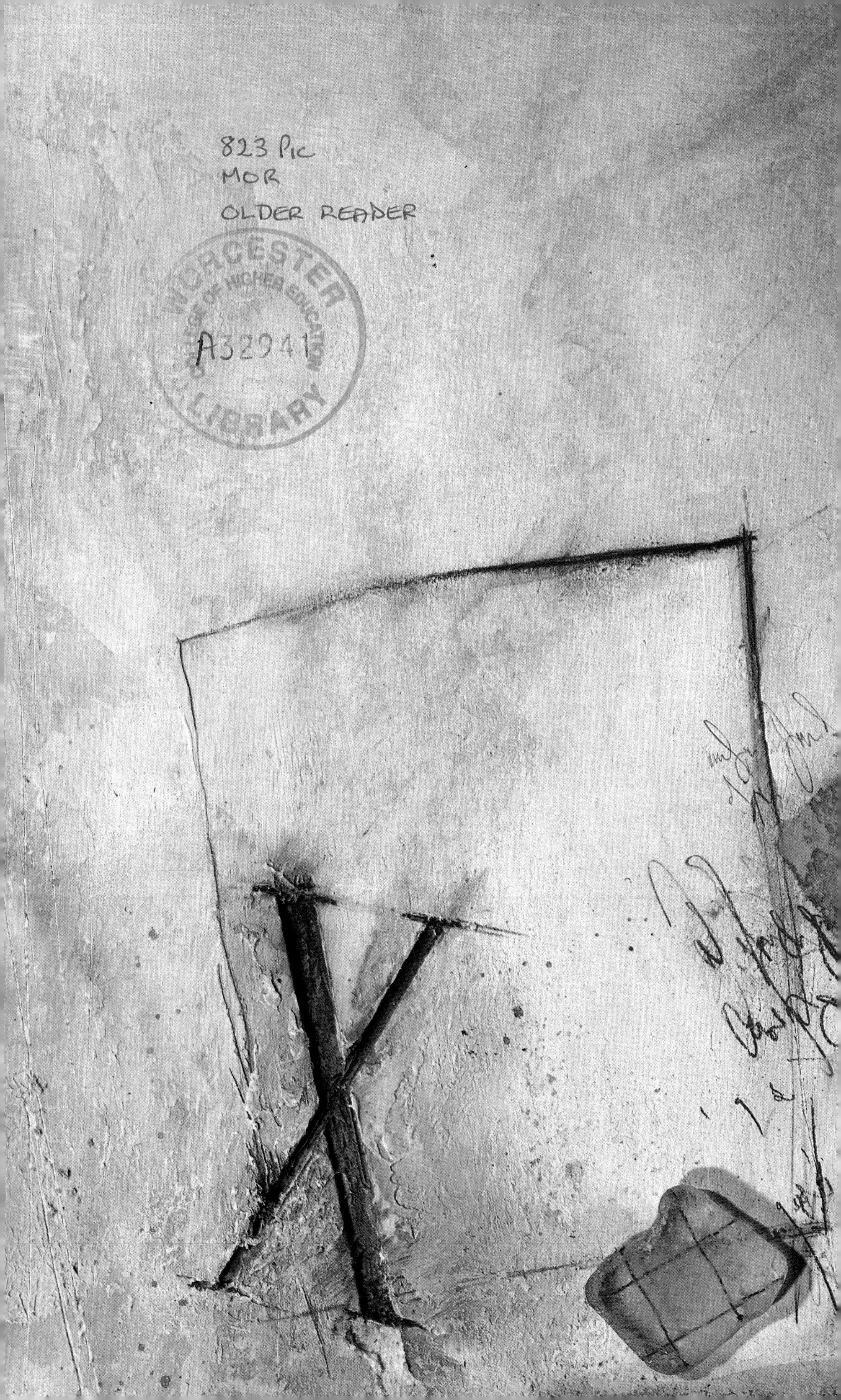

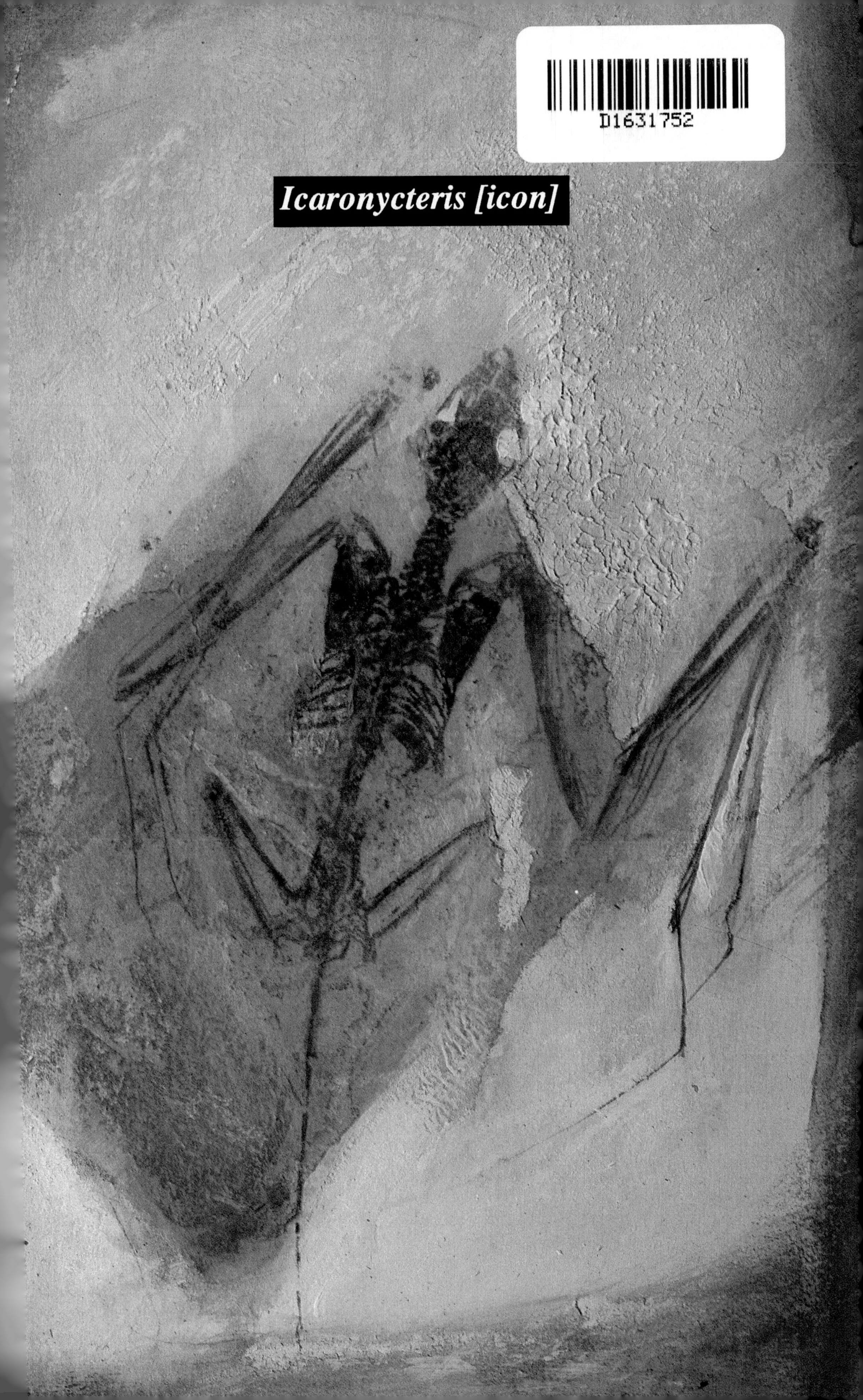
Icaronycteris [icon]

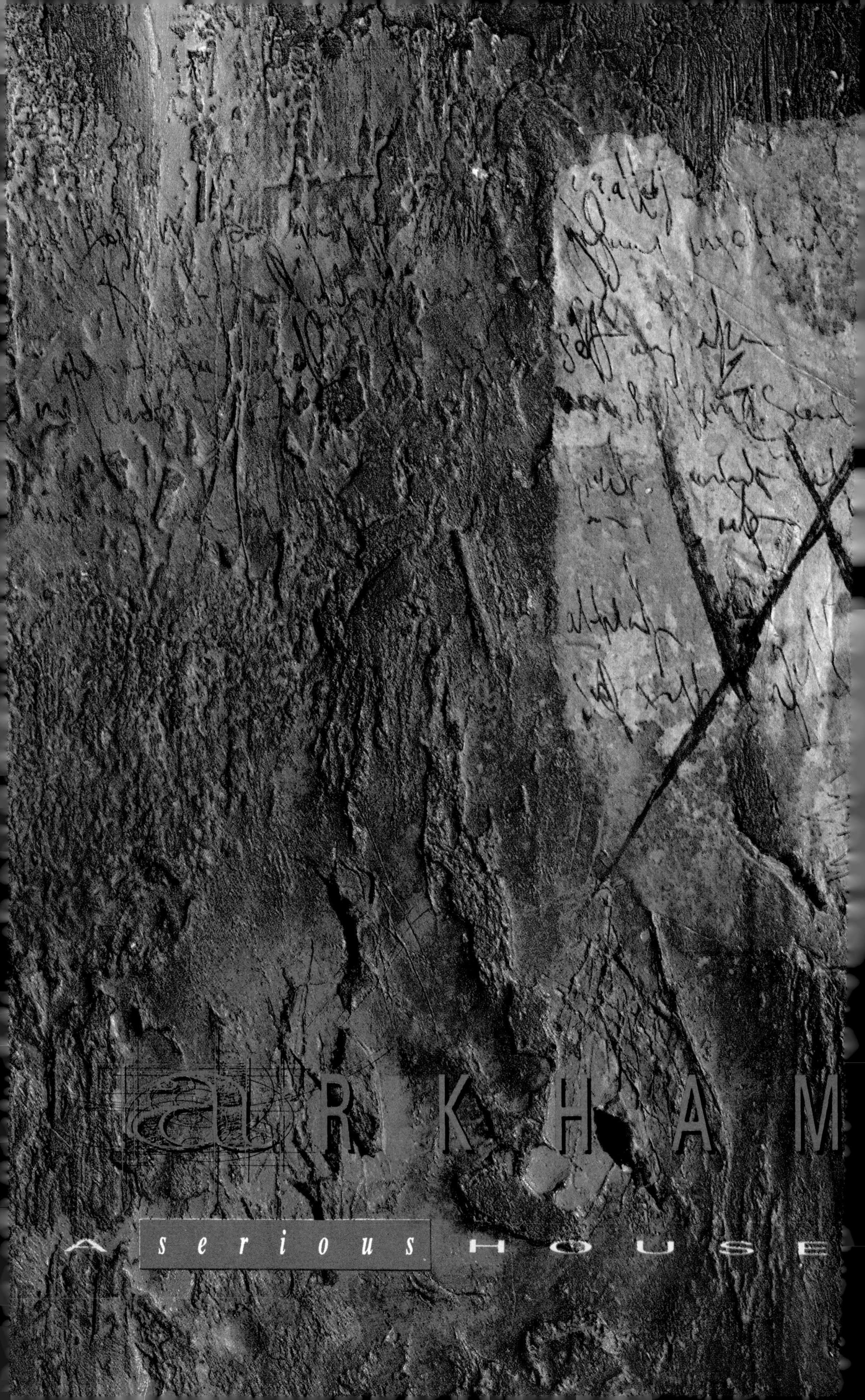
aRKHAM
A serious HOUSE

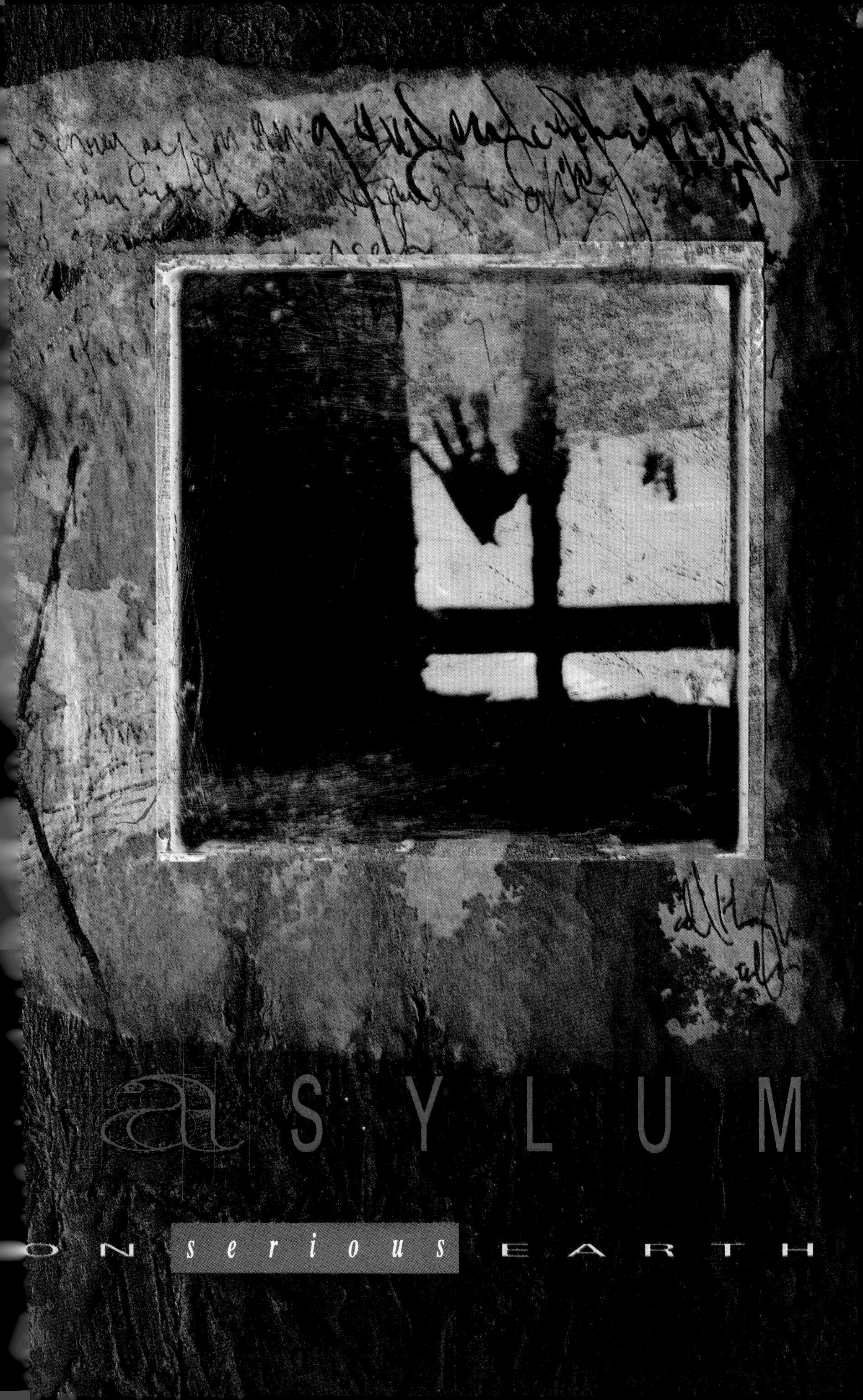
aSYLUM
ON serious EARTH

WRITTEN by

gRANT mORRISON

Batman create

Book design by Dave McKean

JENETTE KAHN *President & Editor-in-Chief* DICK GIORDANO *VP—Editorial*
KAREN BERGER *Editor* ART YOUNG *Asst. Editor* RICHARD BRUNING *Design*
Director TERRI CUNNINGHAM *Managing Editor* BOB ROZAKIS *Production Director*

iLLUSTRATED by

*d*AVE *m*cKEAN

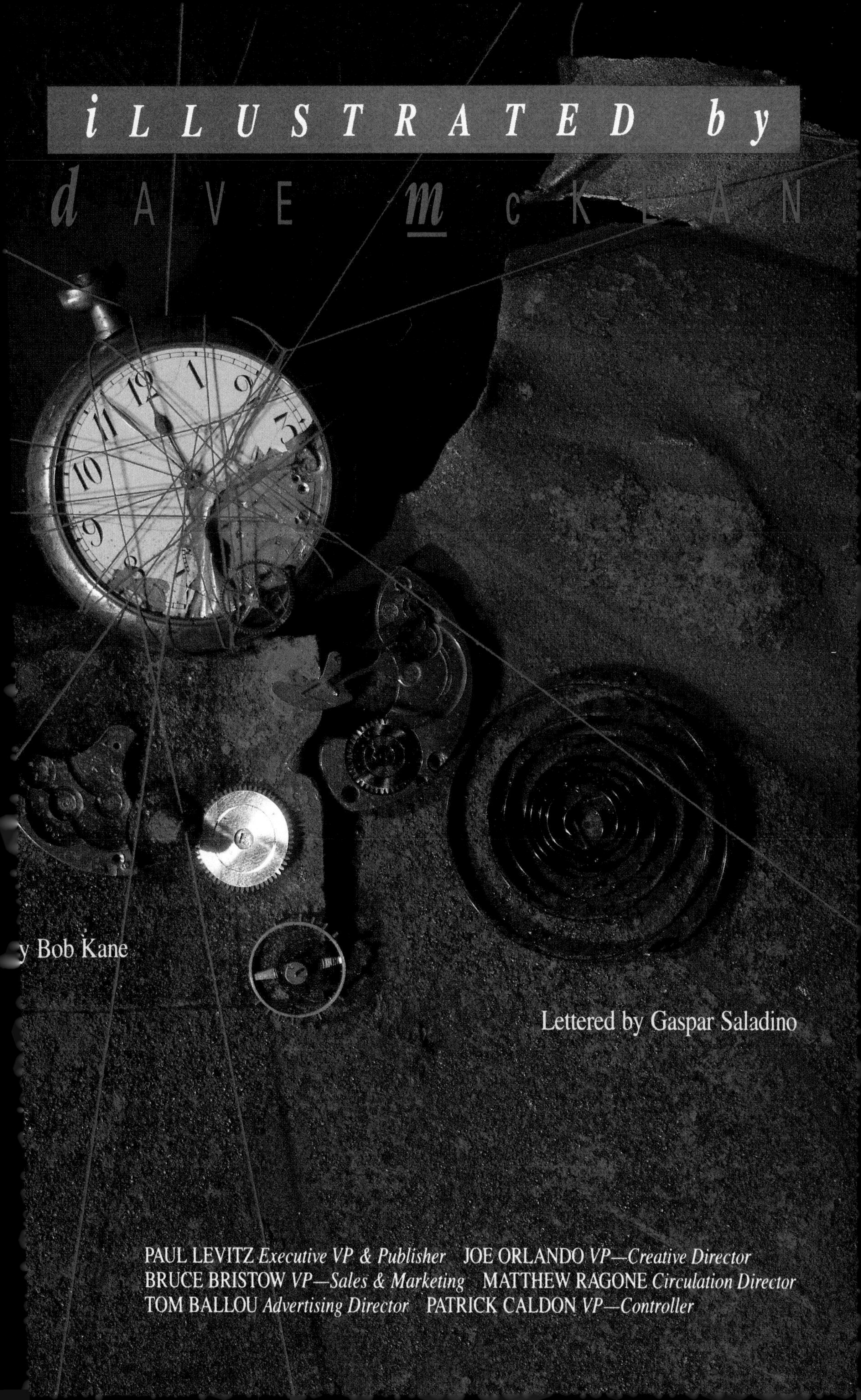

y Bob Kane

Lettered by Gaspar Saladino

PAUL LEVITZ *Executive VP & Publisher* JOE ORLANDO *VP—Creative Director*
BRUCE BRISTOW *VP—Sales & Marketing* MATTHEW RAGONE *Circulation Director*
TOM BALLOU *Advertising Director* PATRICK CALDON *VP—Controller*

*B*UT I DON'T WANT TO GO AMONG MAD PEOPLE,' ALICE REMARKED.

'OH, YOU CAN'T HELP THAT,' SAID THE CAT. 'WE'RE ALL MAD HERE.

I'M MAD, YOU'RE MAD.'

'HOW DO YOU KNOW I'M MAD?' SAID ALICE.

'YOU MUST BE,' SAID THE CAT, 'OR YOU WOULDN'T HAVE COME HERE.'

LEWIS CARROLL

'Alice's Adventures in Wonderland'

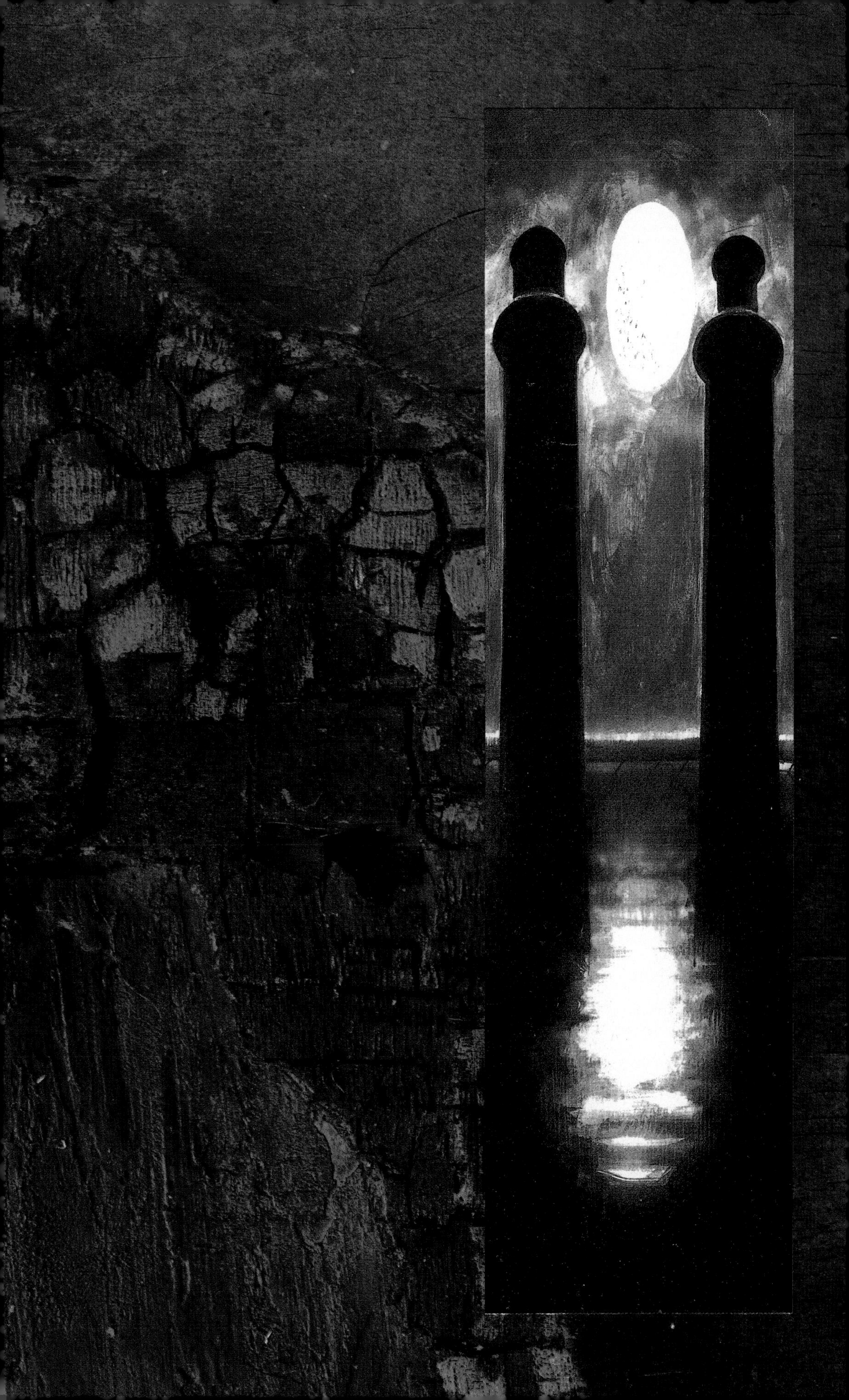

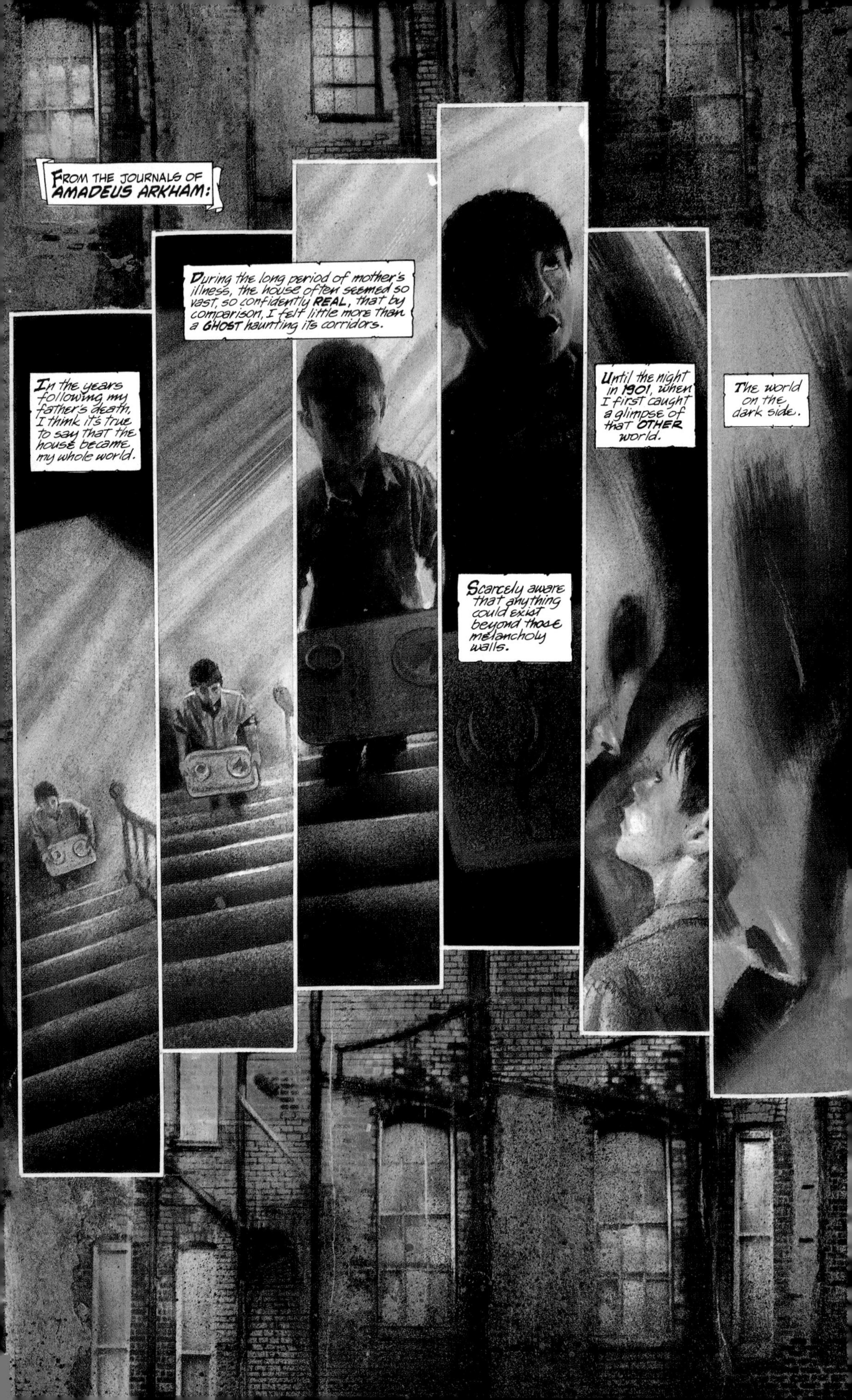
FROM THE JOURNALS OF AMADEUS ARKHAM:
In the years following my father's death, I think it's true to say that the house became my whole world.
During the long period of mother's illness, the house often seemed so vast, so confidently REAL, that by comparison, I felt little more than a GHOST haunting its corridors.
Scarcely aware that anything could exist beyond those melancholy walls.
Until the night in 1901, when I first caught a glimpse of that OTHER world.
The world on the dark side.

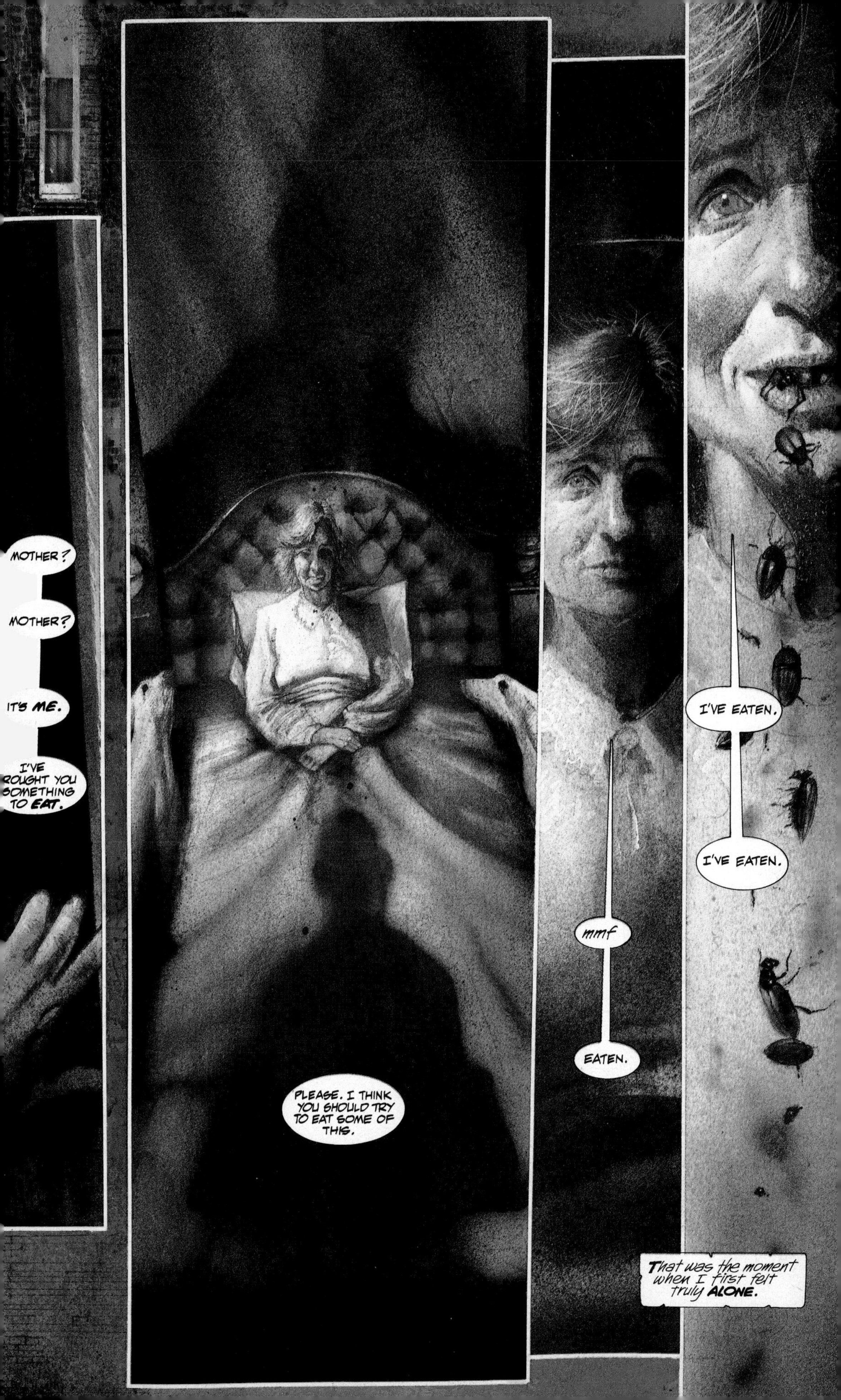

MOTHER?
MOTHER?
IT'S ME.
I'VE BROUGHT YOU SOMETHING TO EAT.
PLEASE. I THINK YOU SHOULD TRY TO EAT SOME OF THIS.
mmf
EATEN.
I'VE EATEN.
I'VE EATEN.
That was the moment when I first felt truly ALONE.

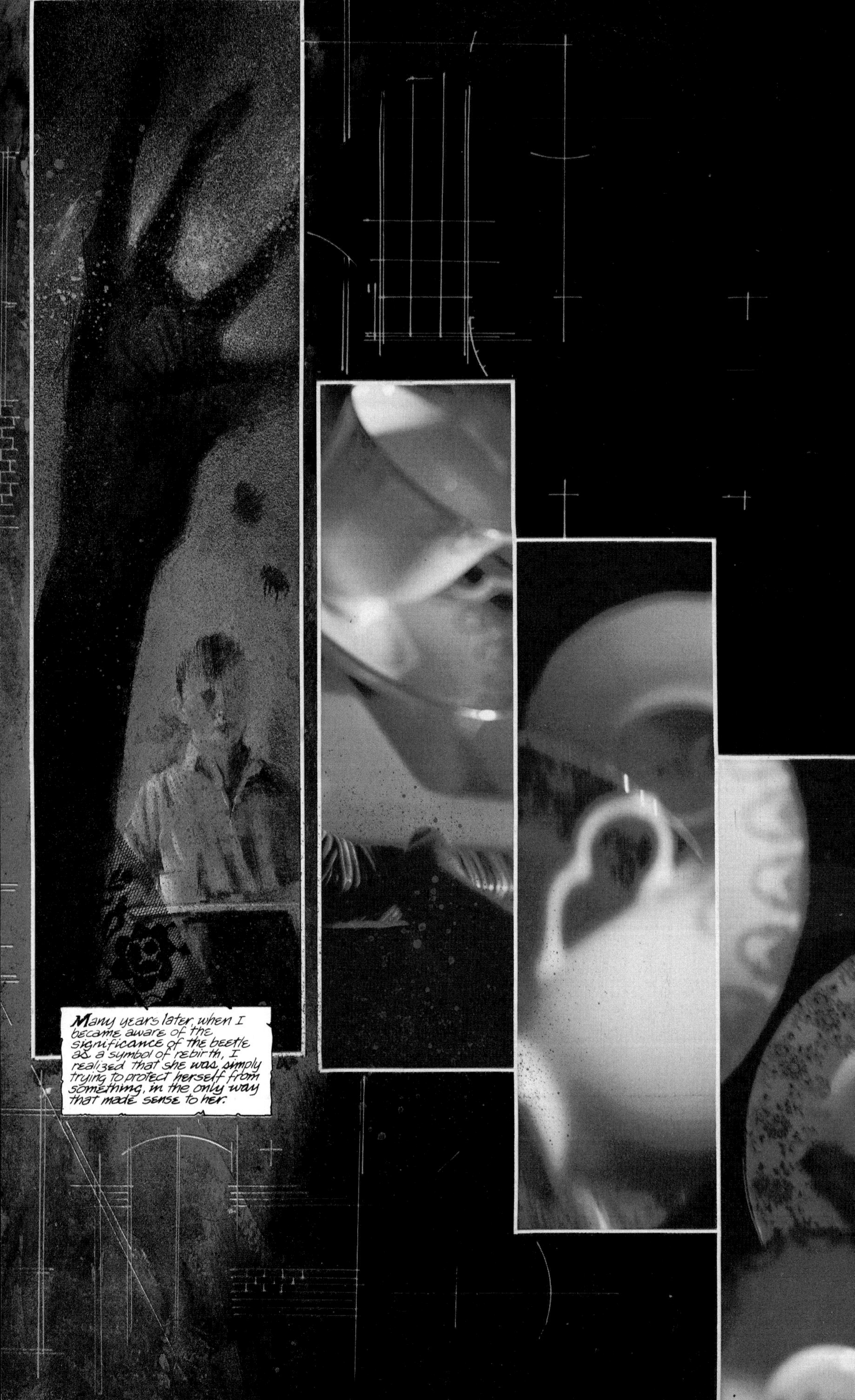
Many years later, when I became aware of the significance of the beetle as a symbol of rebirth, I realized that she was simply trying to protect herself from something, in the only way that made sense to her.

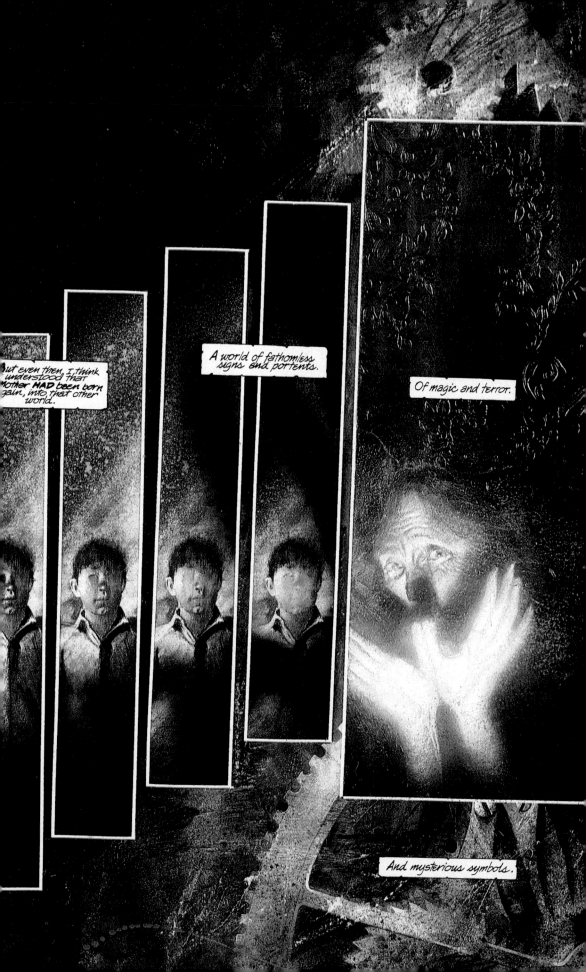

But even then, I think I understood that mother **HAD** been born again, into that other world.

A world of fathomless signs and portents.

Of magic and terror.

And mysterious symbols.

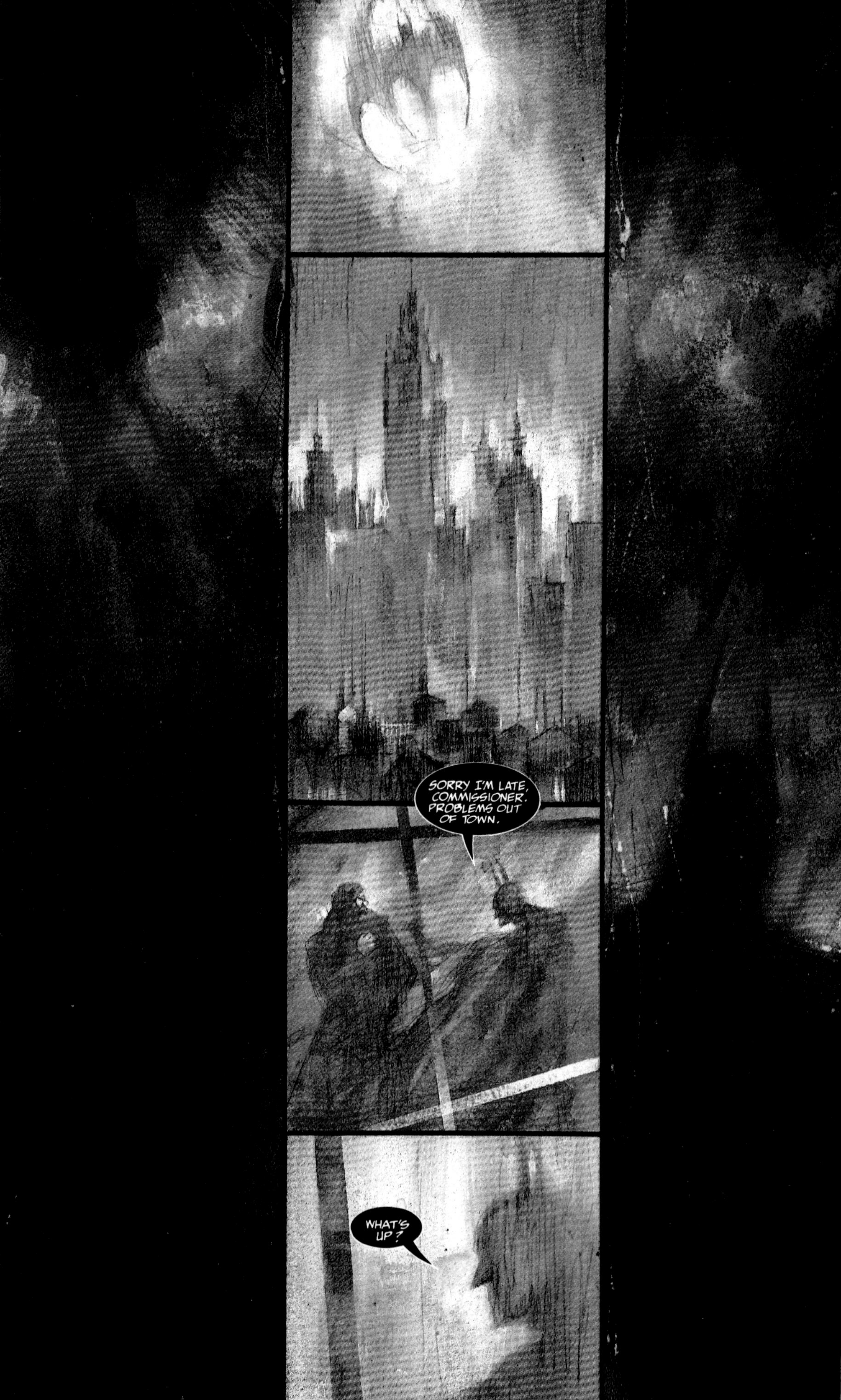
SORRY I'M LATE, COMMISSIONER. PROBLEMS OUT OF TOWN.
WHAT'S UP?

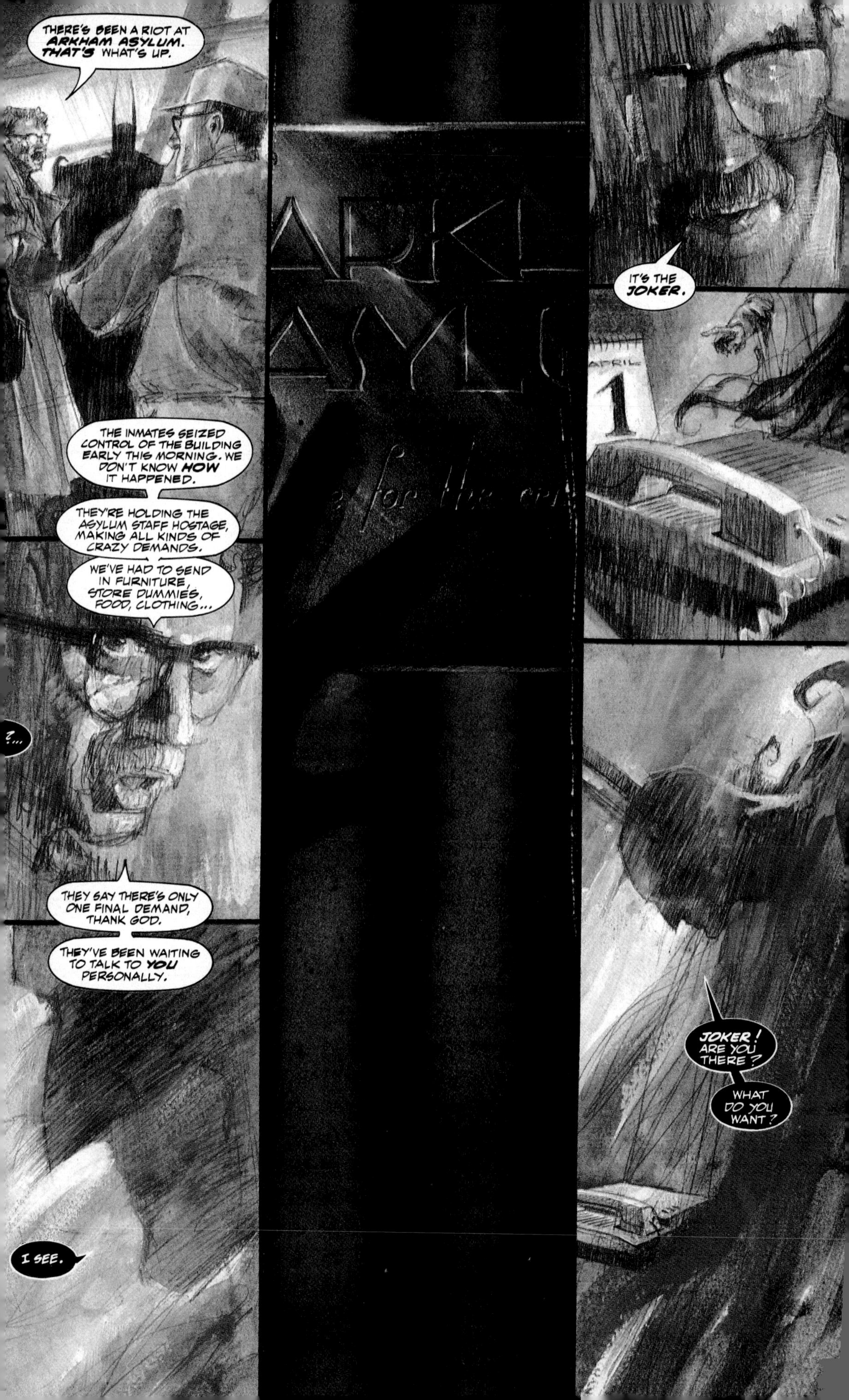
THERE'S BEEN A RIOT AT ARKHAM ASYLUM. THAT'S WHAT'S UP.
THE INMATES SEIZED CONTROL OF THE BUILDING EARLY THIS MORNING. WE DON'T KNOW HOW IT HAPPENED.
THEY'RE HOLDING THE ASYLUM STAFF HOSTAGE, MAKING ALL KINDS OF CRAZY DEMANDS.
WE'VE HAD TO SEND IN FURNITURE, STORE DUMMIES, FOOD, CLOTHING...
?...
THEY SAY THERE'S ONLY ONE FINAL DEMAND, THANK GOD.
THEY'VE BEEN WAITING TO TALK TO YOU PERSONALLY.
I SEE.
IT'S THE JOKER.
APRIL
1
JOKER! ARE YOU THERE?
WHAT DO YOU WANT?

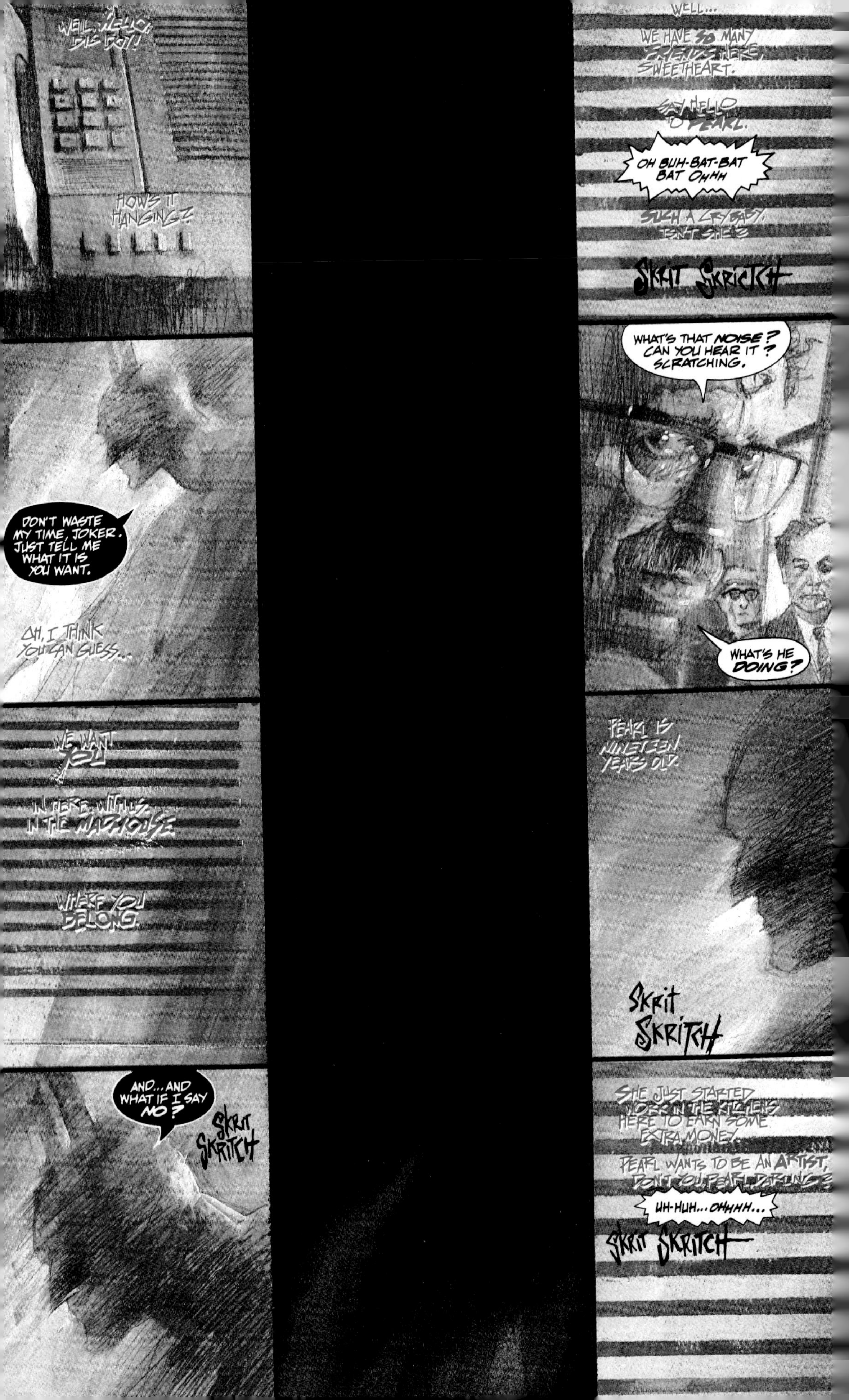
WELL, HELLO, BIG BOY!
HOW'S IT HANGING?
DON'T WASTE MY TIME, JOKER. JUST TELL ME WHAT IT IS YOU WANT.
OH, I THINK YOU CAN GUESS...
WE WANT YOU
IN HERE, WITH US. IN THE MADHOUSE
WHERE YOU BELONG.
AND... AND WHAT IF I SAY NO?
SKRIT SKRITCH
WELL...
WE HAVE SO MANY FRIENDS HERE, SWEETHEART.
SAY HELLO TO PEARL.
OH BUH-BAT-BAT BAT OHHH
SUCH A CRYBABY, ISN'T SHE?
SKRIT SKRITCH
WHAT'S THAT NOISE? CAN YOU HEAR IT? SCRATCHING.
WHAT'S HE DOING?
PEARL IS NINETEEN YEARS OLD.
SKRIT SKRITCH
SHE JUST STARTED WORK IN THE KITCHENS HERE TO EARN SOME EXTRA MONEY.
PEARL WANTS TO BE AN ARTIST, DON'T YOU PEARL DARLING?
UH-HUH... OHHHH...
SKRIT SKRITCH

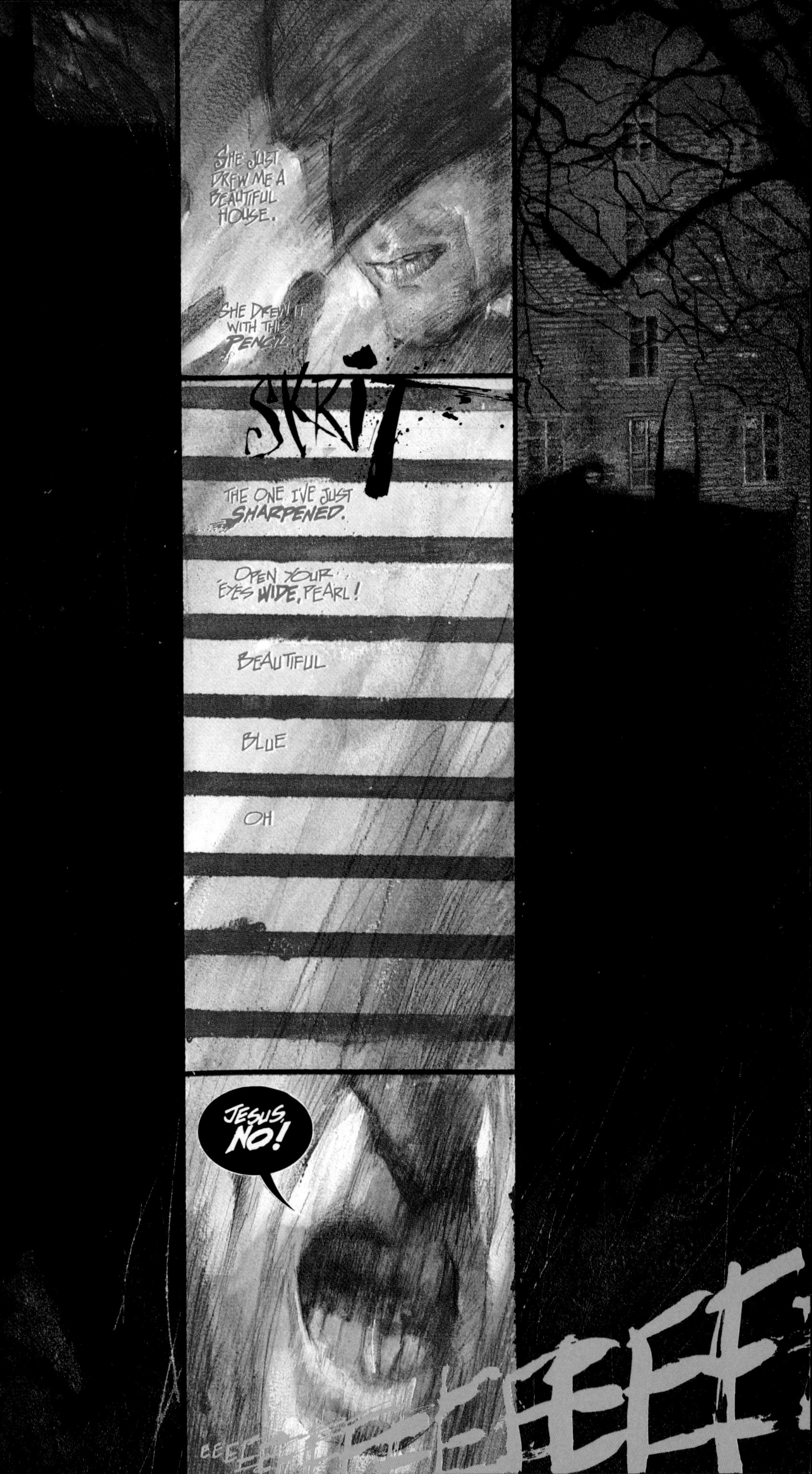
SHE JUST DREW ME A BEAUTIFUL HOUSE.
SHE DREW IT WITH THIS PENCIL
SKRIT
THE ONE I'VE JUST SHARPENED.
OPEN YOUR EYES WIDE, PEARL!
BEAUTIFUL
BLUE
OH
JESUS, NO!
EEEEEEEEEE

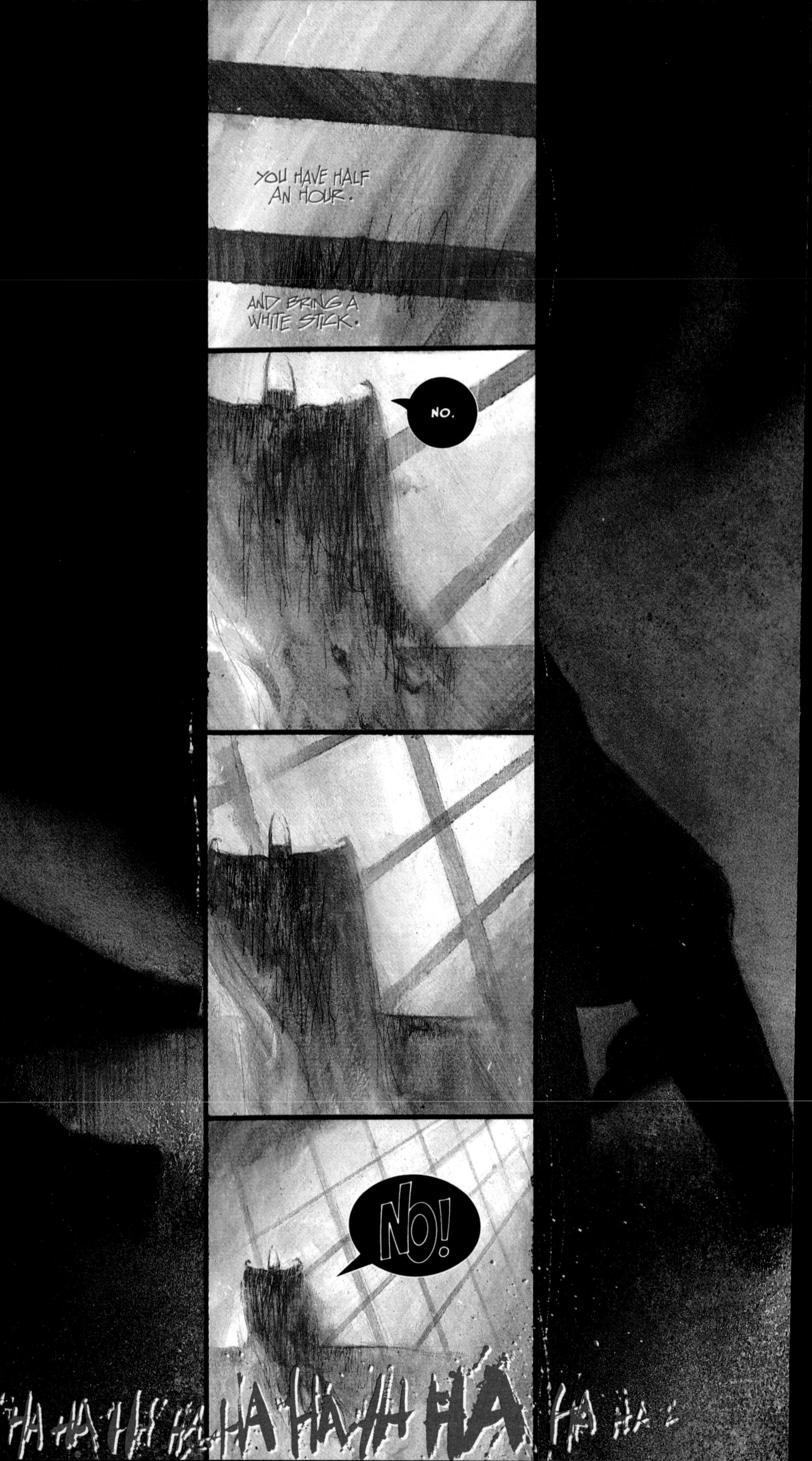
YOU HAVE HALF AN HOUR.
AND BRING A WHITE STICK.
NO.
NO!
HA HA HA HA HA HA HA HA HA HA HA HA HA

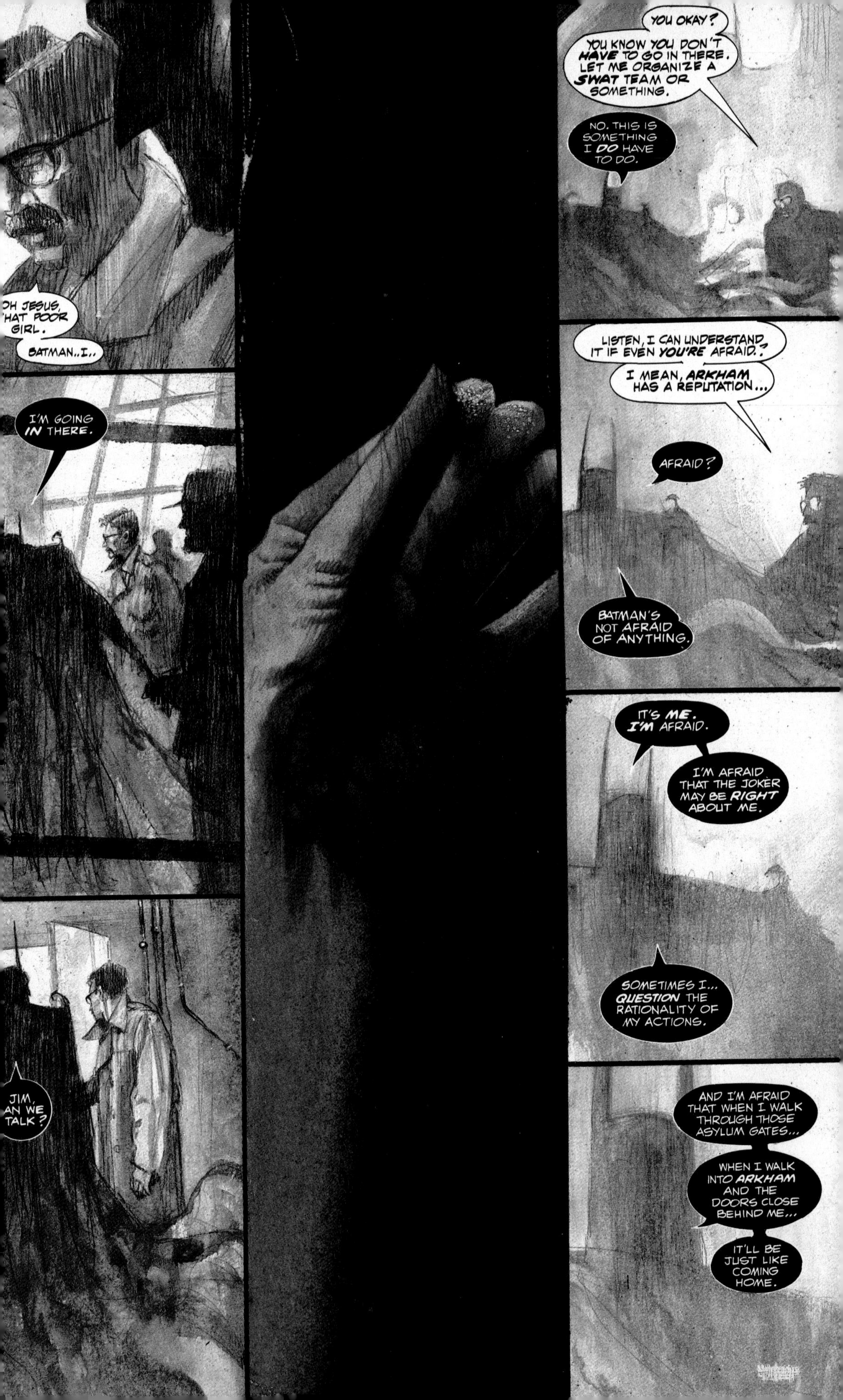
OH JESUS, THAT POOR GIRL.
BATMAN.. I..
I'M GOING IN THERE.
JIM, AN WE TALK?
YOU OKAY?
YOU KNOW YOU DON'T HAVE TO GO IN THERE. LET ME ORGANIZE A SWAT TEAM OR SOMETHING.
NO. THIS IS SOMETHING I DO HAVE TO DO.
LISTEN, I CAN UNDERSTAND IT IF EVEN YOU'RE AFRAID.
I MEAN, ARKHAM HAS A REPUTATION...
AFRAID?
BATMAN'S NOT AFRAID OF ANYTHING.
IT'S ME. I'M AFRAID.
I'M AFRAID THAT THE JOKER MAY BE RIGHT ABOUT ME.
SOMETIMES I... QUESTION THE RATIONALITY OF MY ACTIONS.
AND I'M AFRAID THAT WHEN I WALK THROUGH THOSE ASYLUM GATES...
WHEN I WALK INTO ARKHAM AND THE DOORS CLOSE BEHIND ME...
IT'LL BE JUST LIKE COMING HOME.

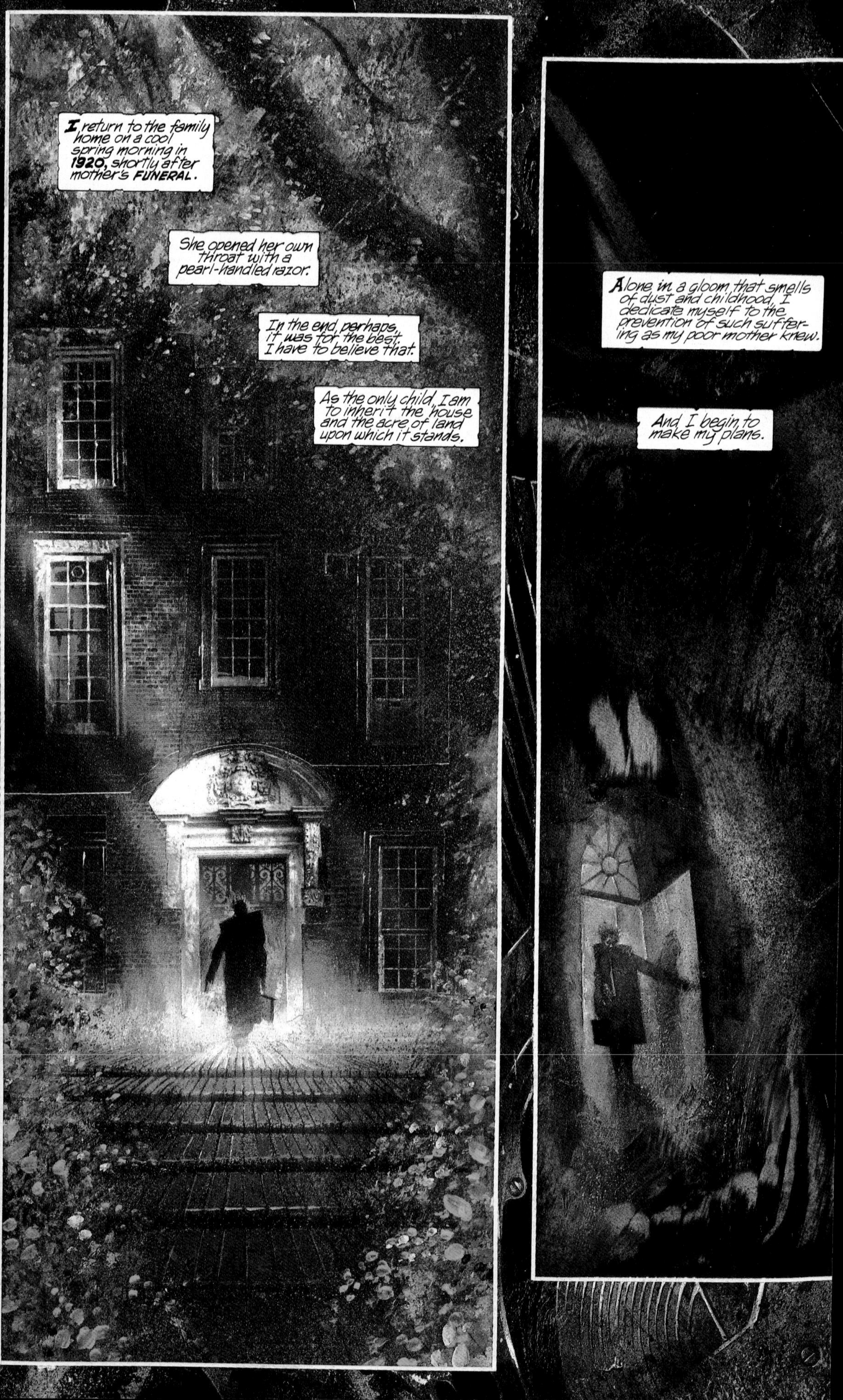
I return to the family home on a cool spring morning in 1920, shortly after mother's FUNERAL.
She opened her own throat with a pearl-handled razor.
In the end, perhaps, it was for the best. I have to believe that.
As the only child, I am to inherit the house and the acre of land upon which it stands.
Alone in a gloom that smells of dust and childhood, I dedicate myself to the prevention of such suffering as my poor mother knew.
And I begin to make my plans.

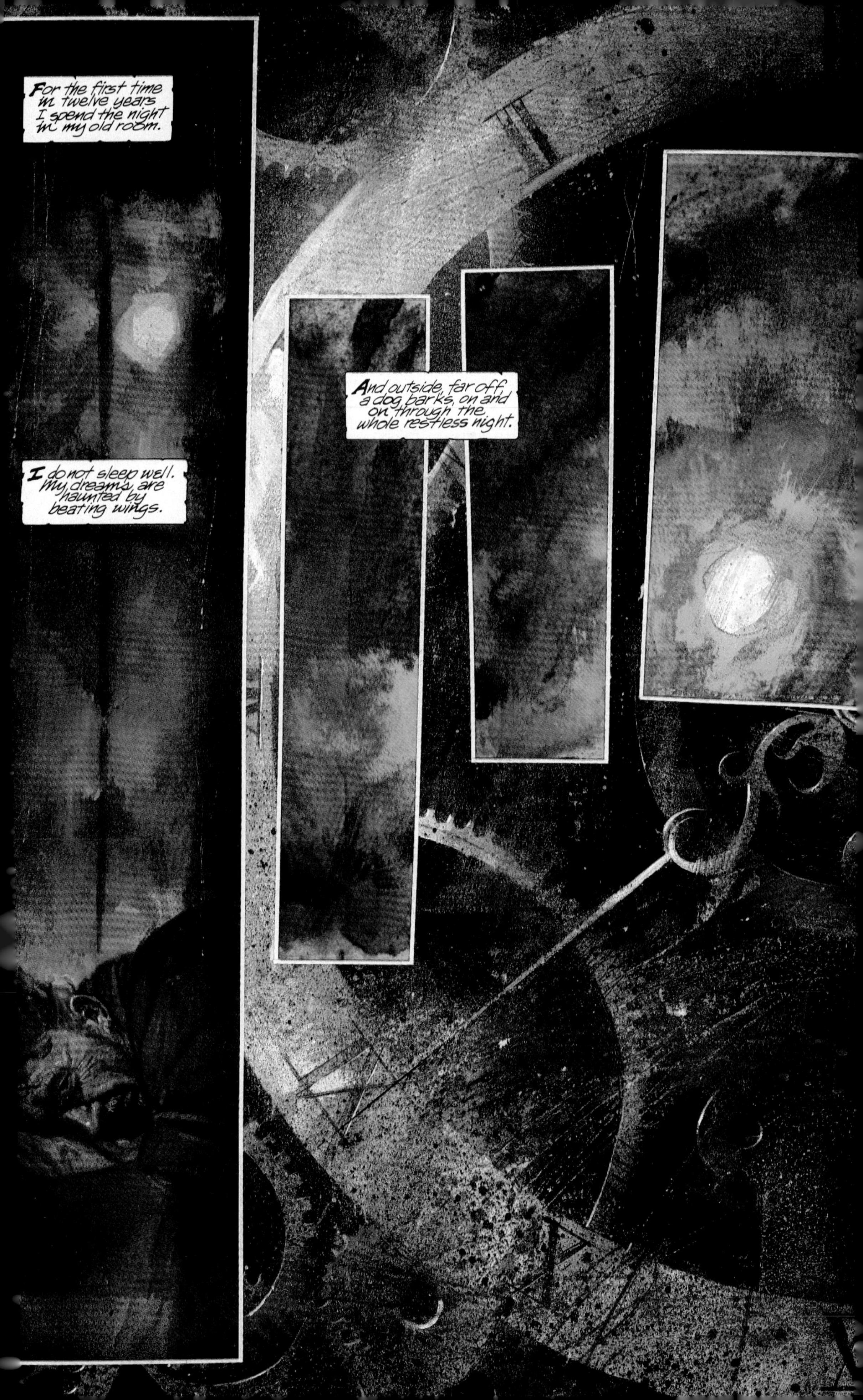
For the first time in twelve years I spend the night in my old room.
I do not sleep well. My dreams are haunted by beating wings.
And outside, far off, a dog barks, on and on through the whole restless night.

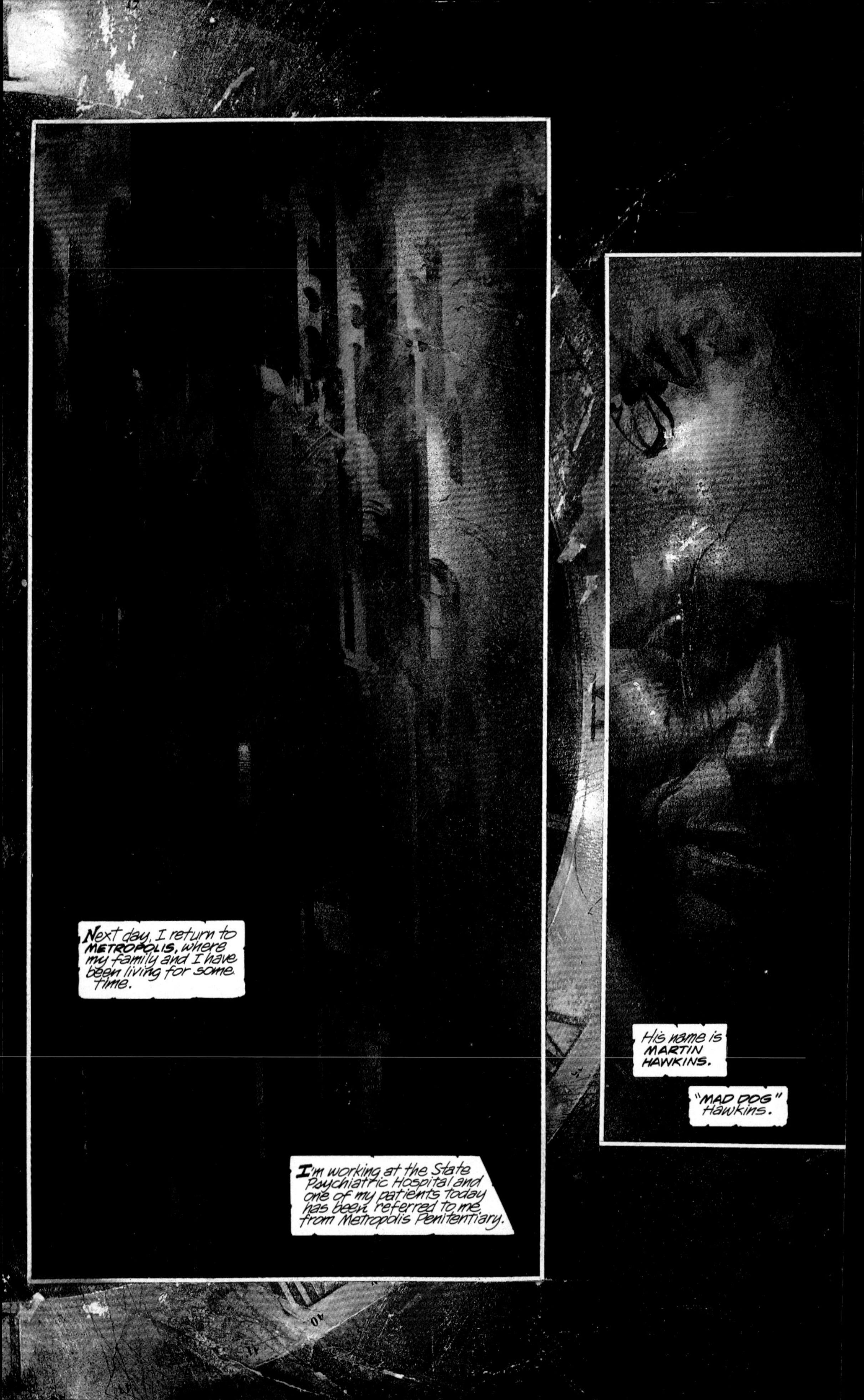
Next day, I return to METROPOLIS, where my family and I have been living for some time.
I'm working at the State Psychiatric Hospital and one of my patients today has been referred to me from Metropolis Penitentiary.
His name is MARTIN HAWKINS.
"MAD DOG" Hawkins.

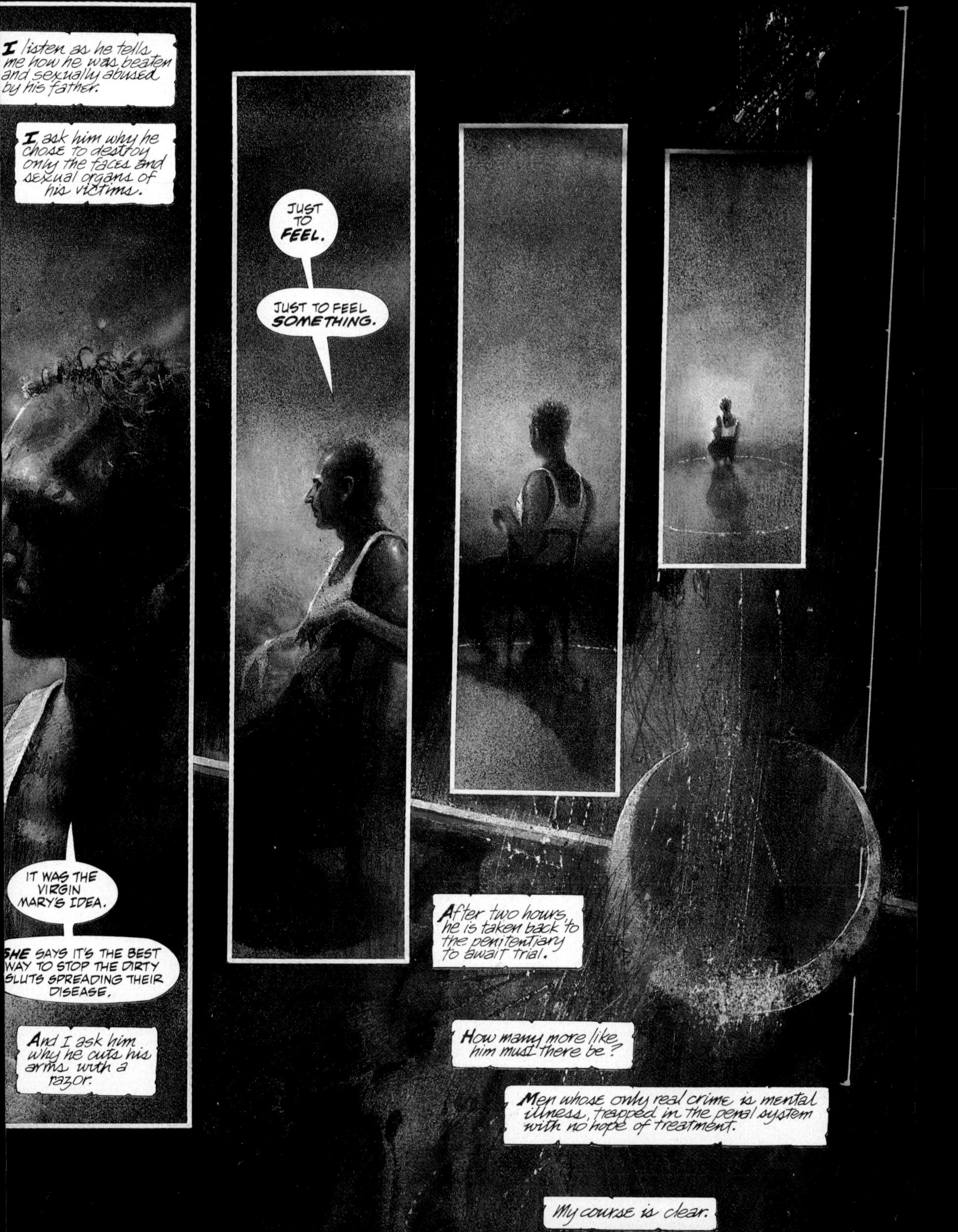
I listen as he tells me how he was beaten and sexually abused by his father.
I ask him why he chose to destroy only the faces and sexual organs of his victims.
IT WAS THE VIRGIN MARY'S IDEA.
SHE SAYS IT'S THE BEST WAY TO STOP THE DIRTY SLUTS SPREADING THEIR DISEASE.
And I ask him why he cuts his arms with a razor.
JUST TO FEEL.
JUST TO FEEL SOMETHING.
After two hours, he is taken back to the penitentiary to await trial.
How many more like him must there be?
Men whose only real crime is mental illness, trapped in the penal system with no hope of treatment.
My course is clear.

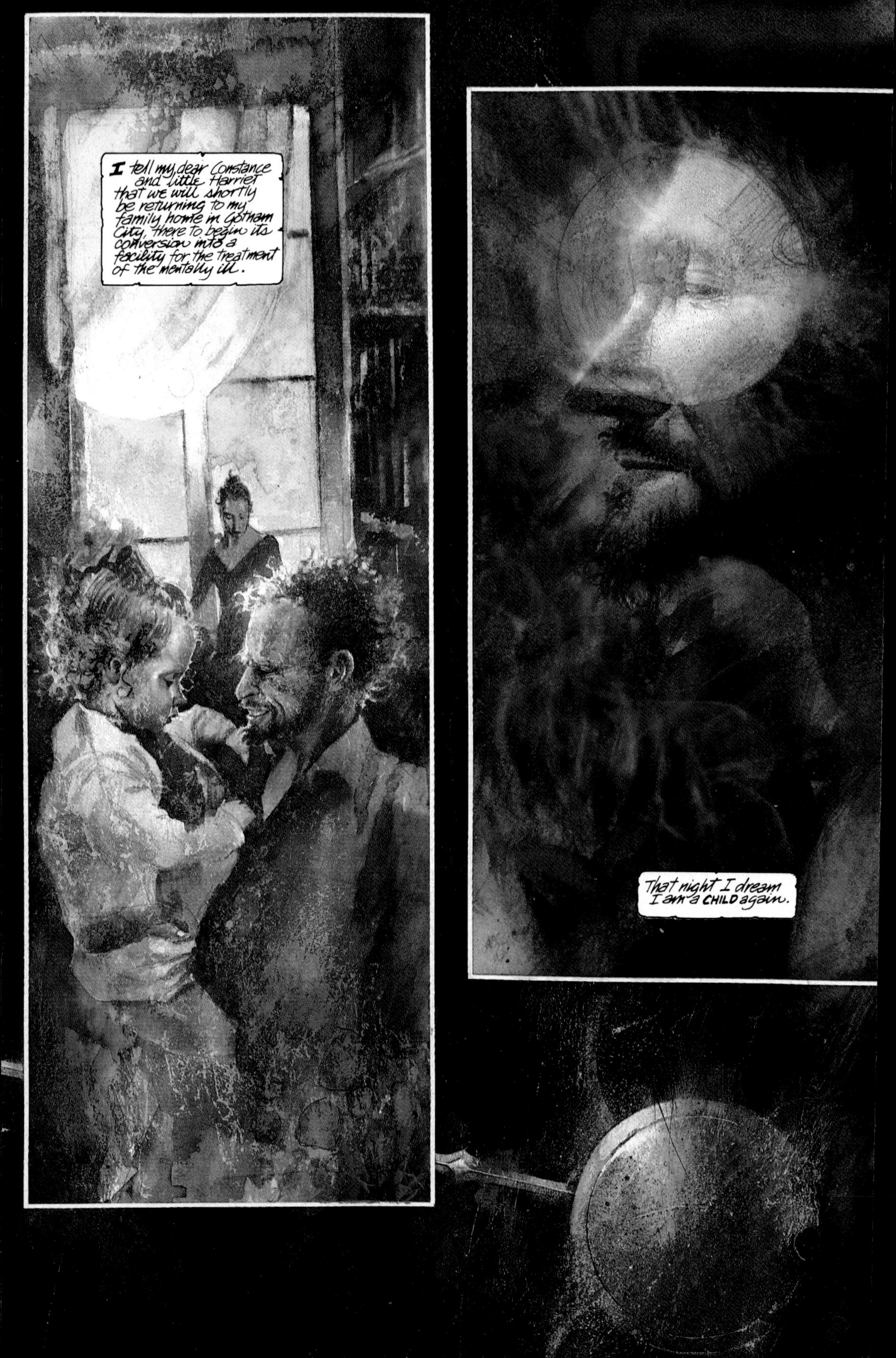
I tell my dear Constance and little Harriet that we will shortly be returning to my family home in Gotham City, there to begin its conversion into a facility for the treatment of the mentally ill.
That night I dream I am a CHILD again.

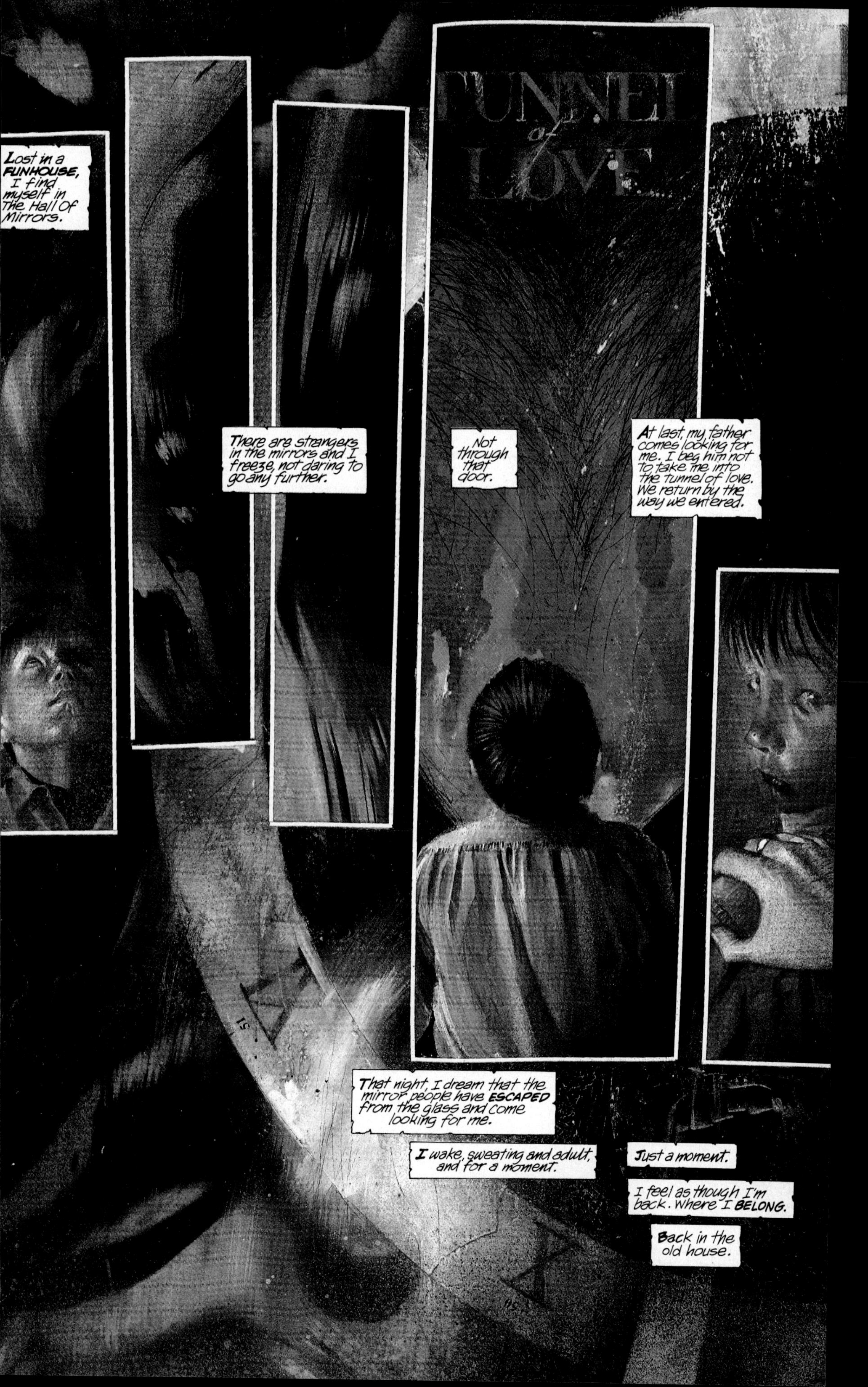

Lost in a FUNHOUSE, I find myself in The Hall Of Mirrors.
There are strangers in the mirrors and I freeze, not daring to go any further.
TUNNEL of LOVE
Not through that door.
At last, my father comes looking for me. I beg him not to take me into the tunnel of love. We return by the way we entered.
That night, I dream that the mirror people have ESCAPED from the glass and come looking for me.
I wake, sweating and adult, and for a moment.
Just a moment.
I feel as though I'm back. Where I BELONG.
Back in the old house.

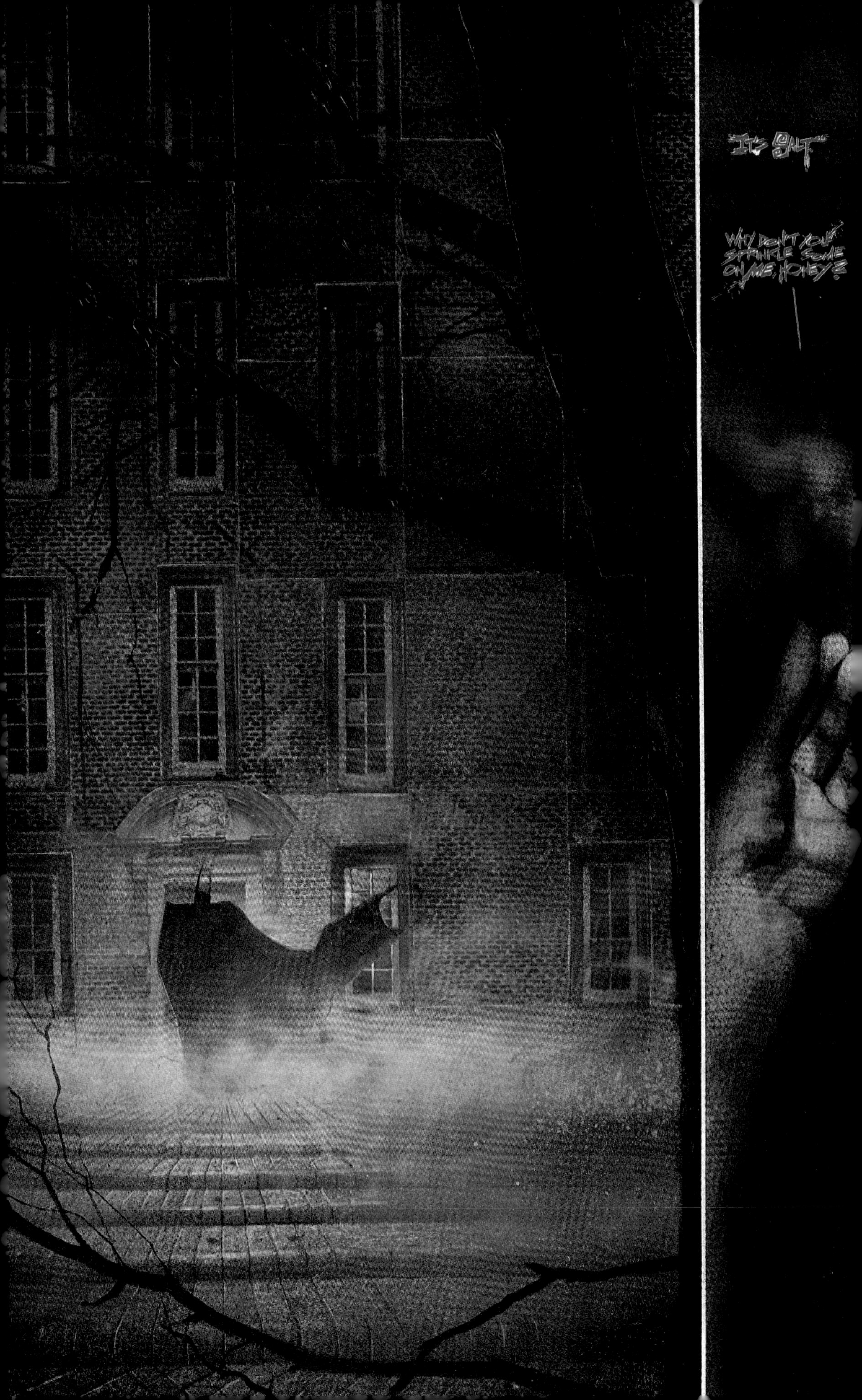
IT'S SALT.
WHY DON'T YOU SPRINKLE SOME ON ME, HONEY?

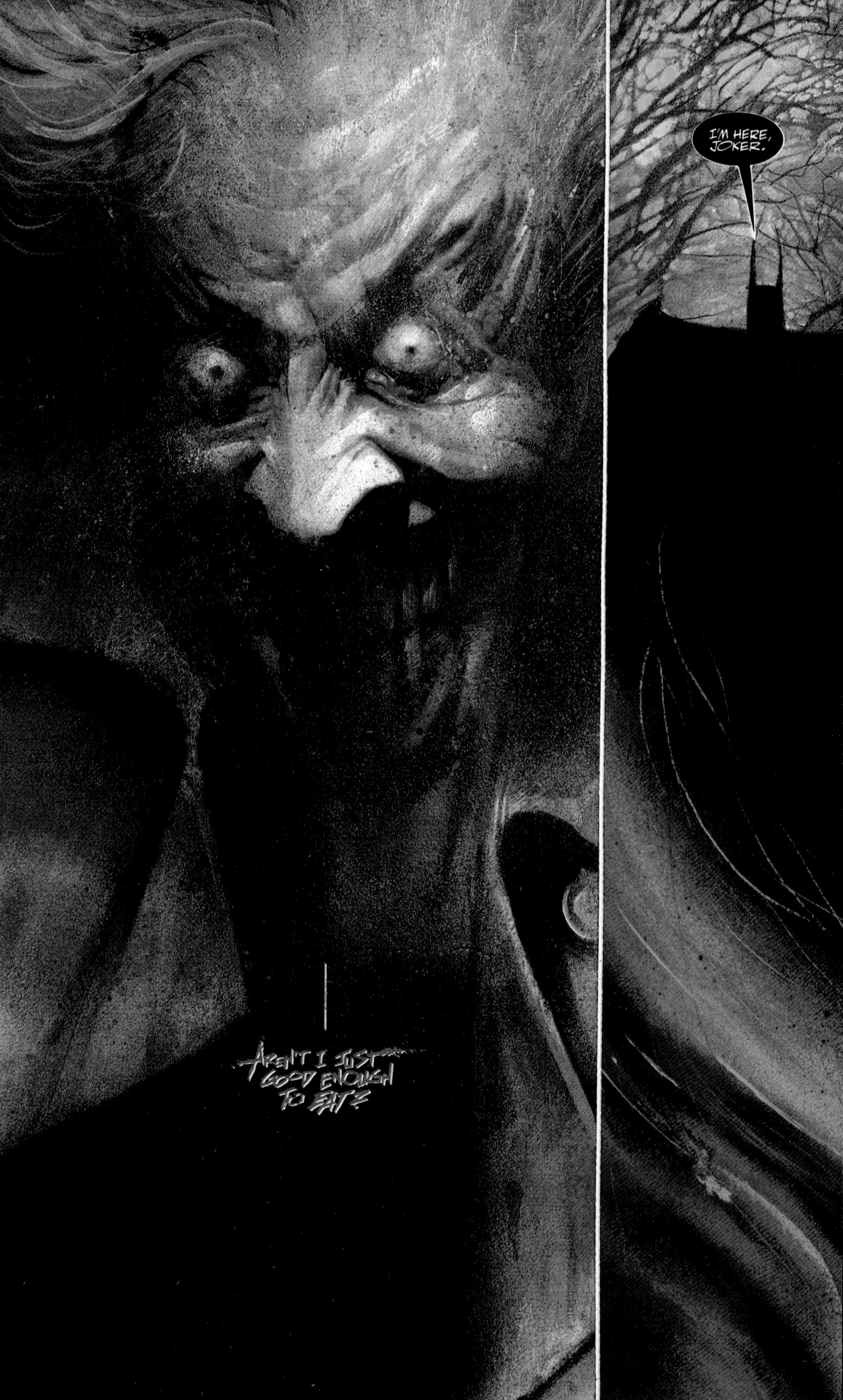
AREN'T I JUST GOOD ENOUGH TO EAT?
I'M HERE, JOKER.

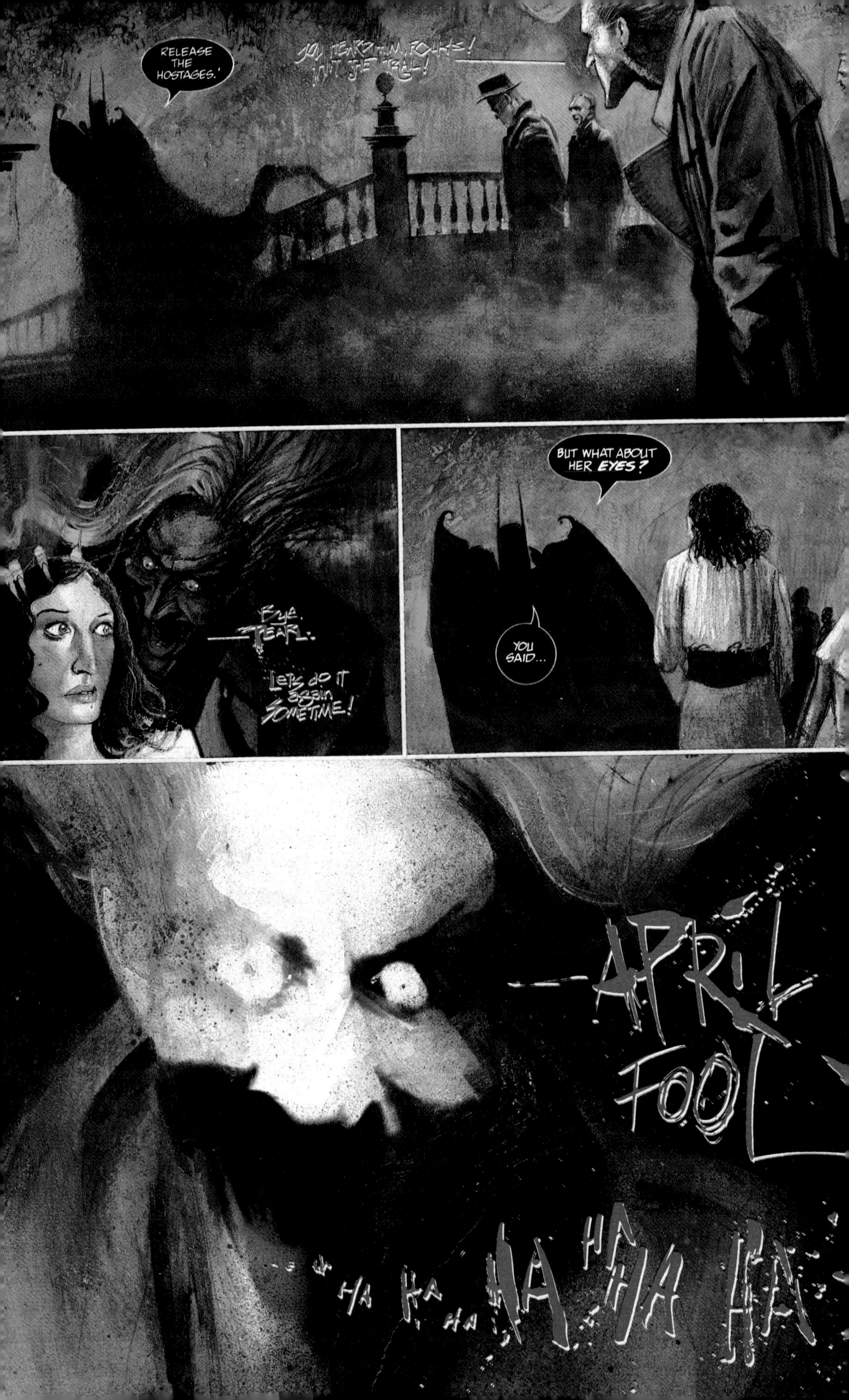
RELEASE THE HOSTAGES.'
YOU HEARD HIM, FOLKS! HIT THE TRAIL!
Bye, PEARL.
Let's do it again SOMETIME!
BUT WHAT ABOUT HER EYES?
YOU SAID...
APRIL FOOL
HA HA HA HA HA HA HA HA

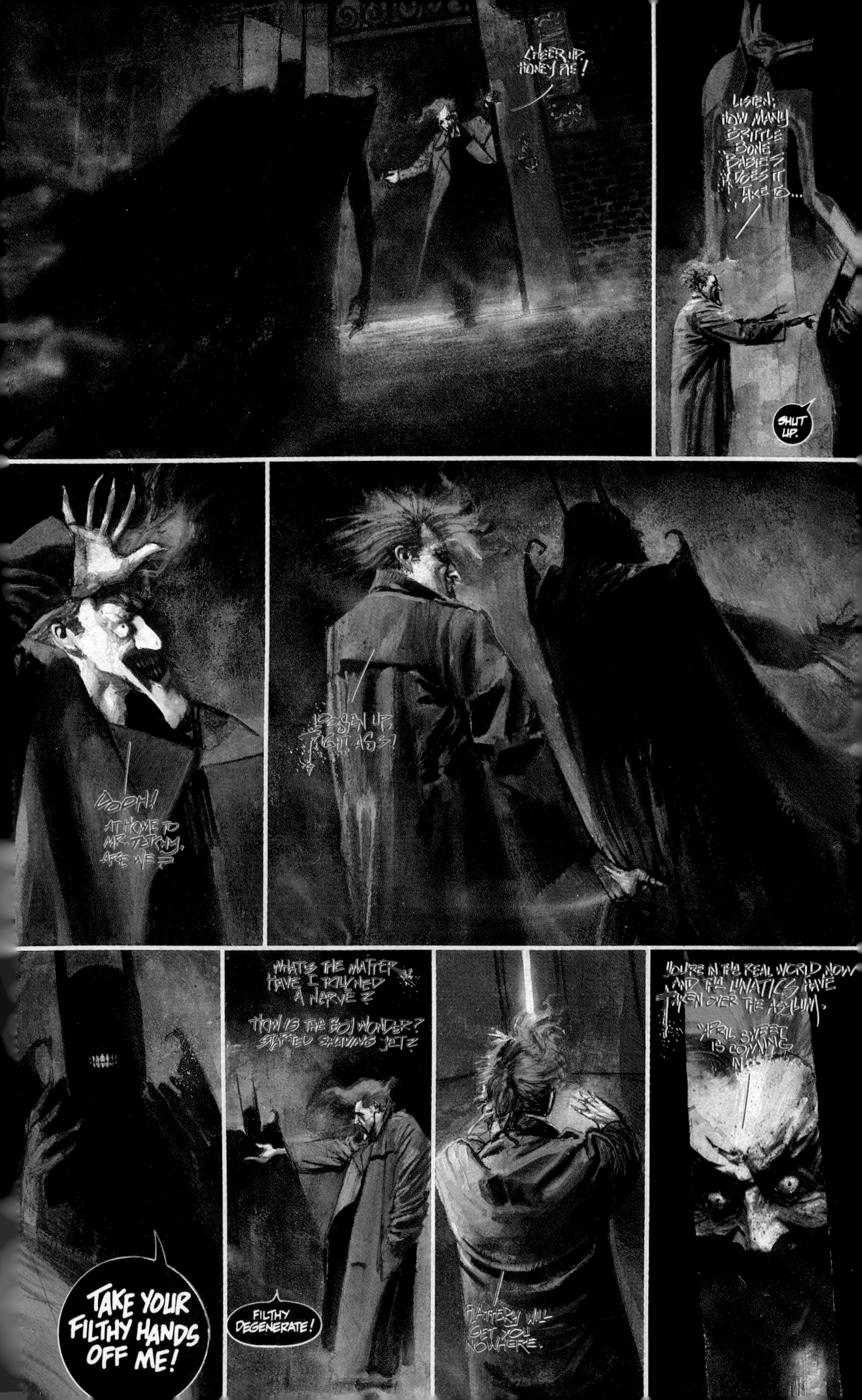
CHEER UP, HONEY PIE!
LISTEN; HOW MANY BRITTLE BONE BABIES DOES IT TAKE TO...
SHUT UP.
OOOH! AT HOME TO MR. TETCHY, ARE WE?
LOOSEN UP, TIGHT ASS!
TAKE YOUR FILTHY HANDS OFF ME!
WHAT'S THE MATTER HAVE I TOUCHED A NERVE?
HOW IS THE BOY WONDER? STARTED SHAVING YET?
FILTHY DEGENERATE!
FLATTERY WILL GET YOU NOWHERE.
YOU'RE IN THE REAL WORLD NOW AND THE LUNATICS HAVE TAKEN OVER THE ASYLUM.
"APRIL SWEET IS COMING IN...

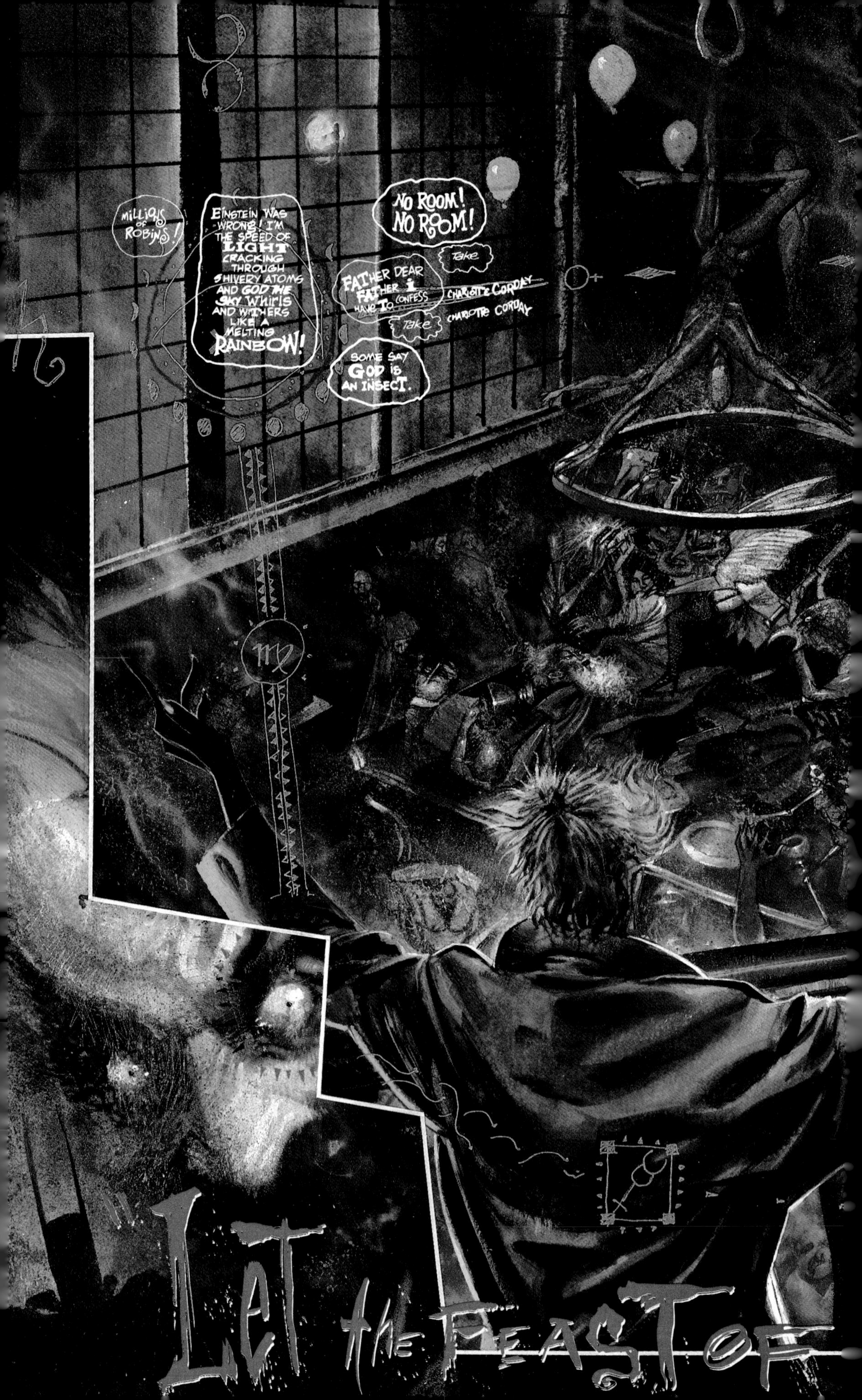
MILLIONS OF ROBINS!
EINSTEIN WAS WRONG! I'M THE SPEED OF LIGHT CRACKING THROUGH SHIVERY ATOMS AND GOD THE SKY WHIRLS AND WITHERS LIKE A MELTING RAINBOW!
NO ROOM! NO ROOM!
Take
FATHER DEAR FATHER I HAVE TO CONFESS
CHARLOTTE CORDAY
Take
CHARLOTTE CORDAY
SOME SAY GOD IS AN INSECT.
LET THE FEAST OF

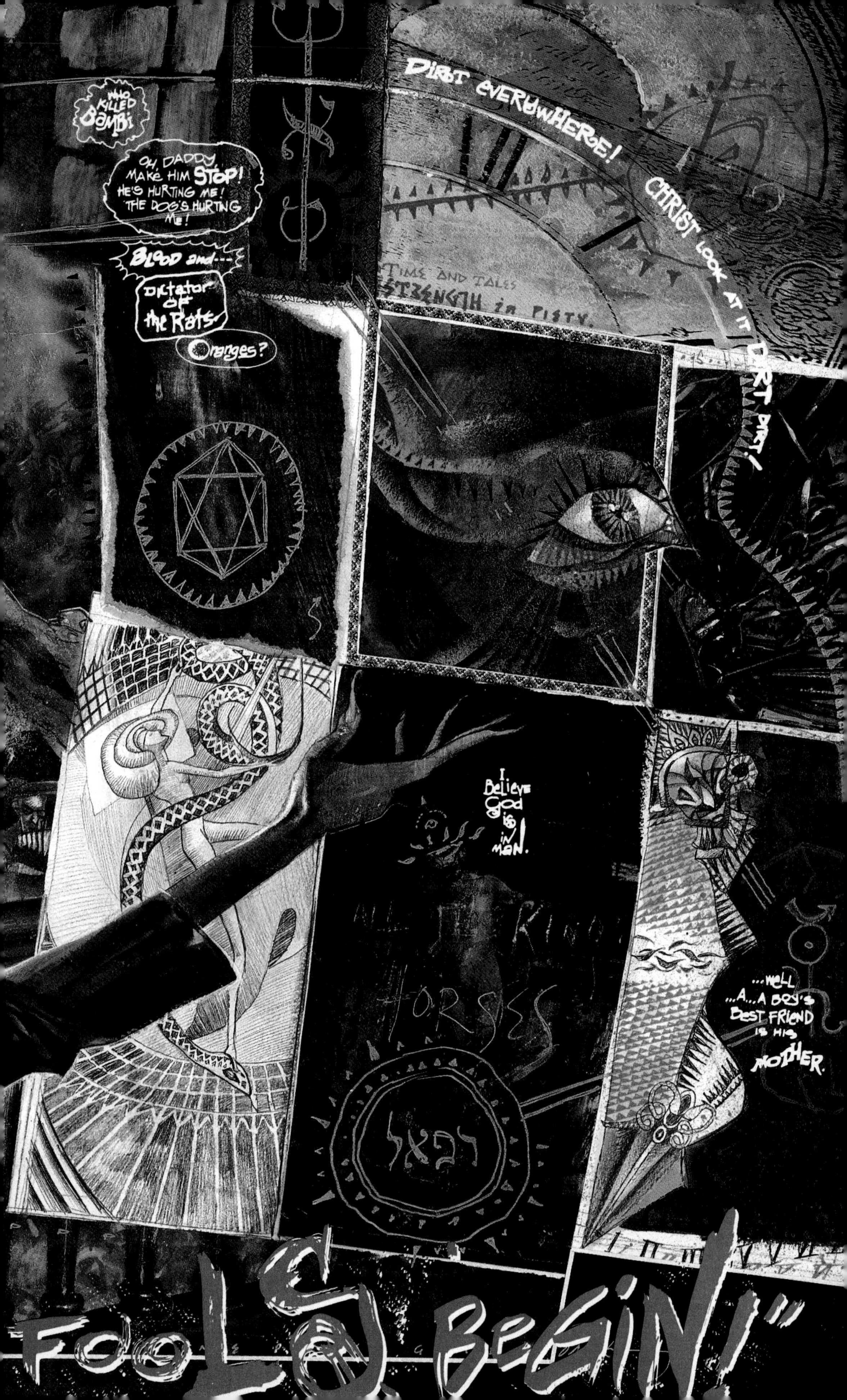
WHO KILLED BAMBI
OH, DADDY, MAKE HIM STOP! HE'S HURTING ME! THE DOG'S HURTING ME!
BLOOD AND---
DICTATOR OF THE RATS.
ORANGES?
DIRT EVERYWHERE!
CHRIST LOOK AT IT DIRT DIRT DIRT!
TIME AND TALES
STRENGTH IN PIETY.
I BELIEVE GOD IS IN MAN.
HORSES
...WELL ...A...A BOY'S BEST FRIEND IS HIS MOTHER.
FOOLS BEGIN!"

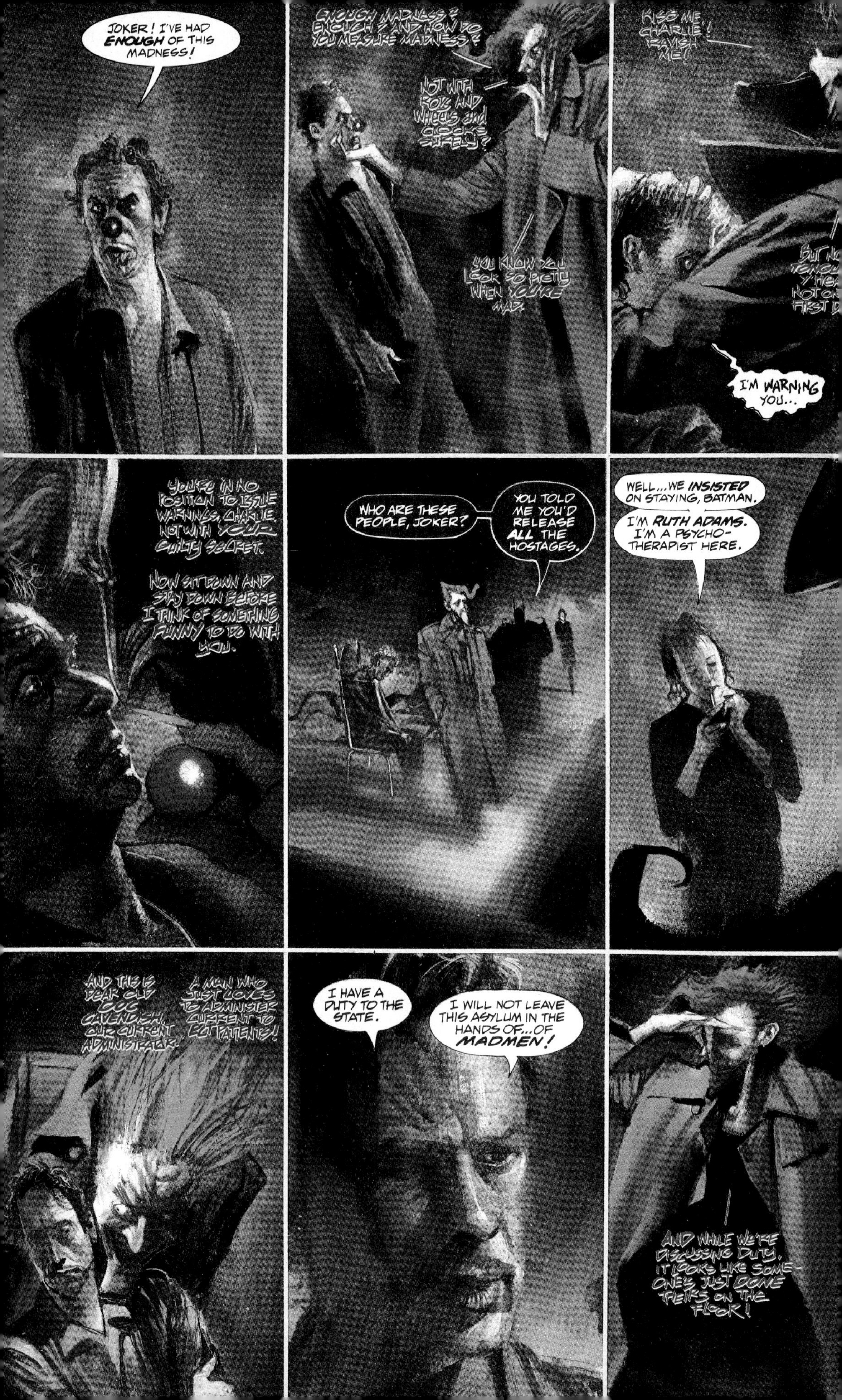

JOKER! I'VE HAD ENOUGH OF THIS MADNESS!
ENOUGH MADNESS? ENOUGH? AND HOW DO YOU MEASURE MADNESS?
NOT WITH RODS AND WHEELS AND CLOCKS SURELY?
YOU KNOW YOU LOOK SO PRETTY WHEN YOU'RE MAD.
KISS ME, CHARLIE! RAVISH ME!
I'M WARNING YOU...
YOU'RE IN NO POSITION TO ISSUE WARNINGS, CHARLIE. NOT WITH YOUR GUILTY SECRET.
NOW SIT DOWN AND STAY DOWN BEFORE I THINK OF SOMETHING FUNNY TO DO WITH YOU.
WHO ARE THESE PEOPLE, JOKER?
YOU TOLD ME YOU'D RELEASE ALL THE HOSTAGES.
WELL... WE INSISTED ON STAYING, BATMAN.
I'M RUTH ADAMS. I'M A PSYCHO-THERAPIST HERE.
AND THIS IS DEAR OLD DOC CAVENDISH, OUR CURRENT ADMINISTRATOR.
A MAN WHO JUST LOVES TO ADMINISTER CURRENT TO ECT PATIENTS!
I HAVE A DUTY TO THE STATE.
I WILL NOT LEAVE THIS ASYLUM IN THE HANDS OF... OF MADMEN!
AND WHILE WE'RE DISCUSSING DUTY, IT LOOKS LIKE SOME-ONE'S JUST DONE THEIRS ON THE FLOOR!

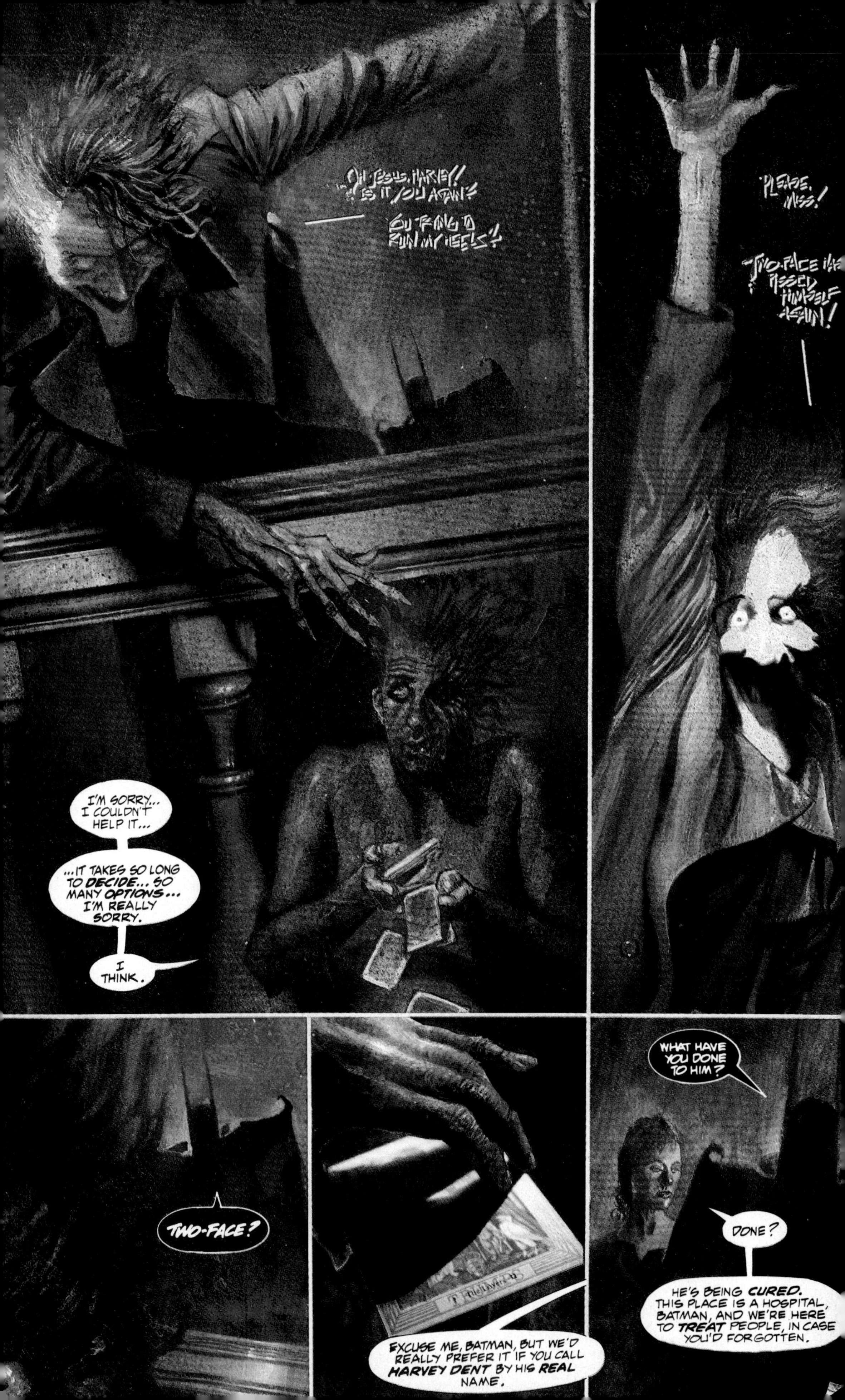
...OH JESUS, HARVEY!
IS IT YOU AGAIN?
YOU TRYING TO RUIN MY HEELS?
PLEASE, MISS!
TWO-FACE HAS PISSED HIMSELF AGAIN!
I'M SORRY... I COULDN'T HELP IT...
...IT TAKES SO LONG TO DECIDE... SO MANY OPTIONS... I'M REALLY SORRY.
I THINK.
TWO-FACE?
EXCUSE ME, BATMAN, BUT WE'D REALLY PREFER IT IF YOU CALL HARVEY DENT BY HIS REAL NAME.
WHAT HAVE YOU DONE TO HIM?
DONE?
HE'S BEING CURED. THIS PLACE IS A HOSPITAL, BATMAN, AND WE'RE HERE TO TREAT PEOPLE, IN CASE YOU'D FORGOTTEN.

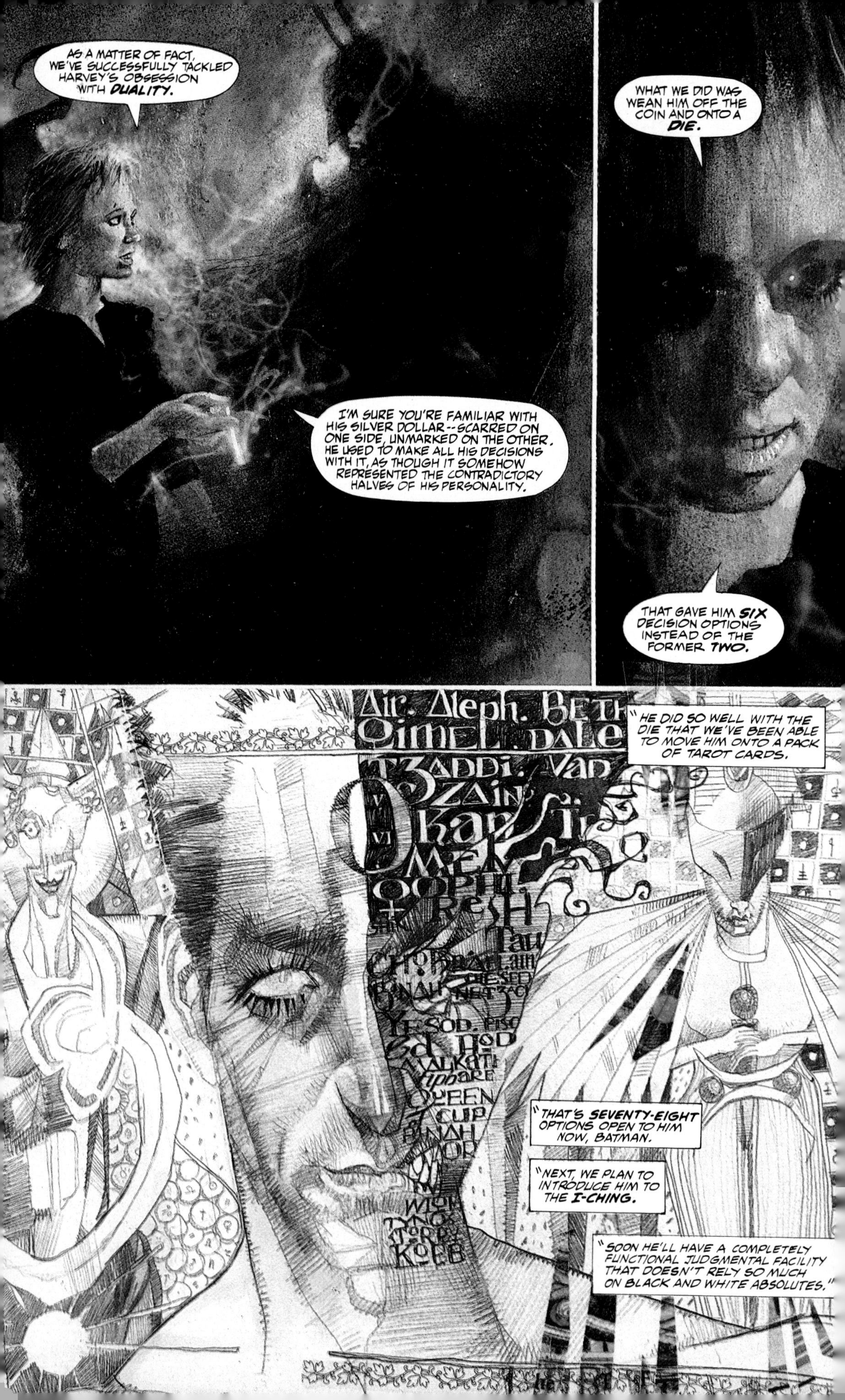
AS A MATTER OF FACT, WE'VE SUCCESSFULLY TACKLED HARVEY'S OBSESSION WITH DUALITY.
I'M SURE YOU'RE FAMILIAR WITH HIS SILVER DOLLAR--SCARRED ON ONE SIDE, UNMARKED ON THE OTHER. HE USED TO MAKE ALL HIS DECISIONS WITH IT, AS THOUGH IT SOMEHOW REPRESENTED THE CONTRADICTORY HALVES OF HIS PERSONALITY.
WHAT WE DID WAS WEAN HIM OFF THE COIN AND ONTO A DIE.
THAT GAVE HIM SIX DECISION OPTIONS INSTEAD OF THE FORMER TWO.
"HE DID SO WELL WITH THE DIE THAT WE'VE BEEN ABLE TO MOVE HIM ONTO A PACK OF TAROT CARDS.
"THAT'S SEVENTY-EIGHT OPTIONS OPEN TO HIM NOW, BATMAN.
"NEXT, WE PLAN TO INTRODUCE HIM TO THE I-CHING.
"SOON HE'LL HAVE A COMPLETELY FUNCTIONAL JUDGMENTAL FACILITY THAT DOESN'T RELY SO MUCH ON BLACK AND WHITE ABSOLUTES."

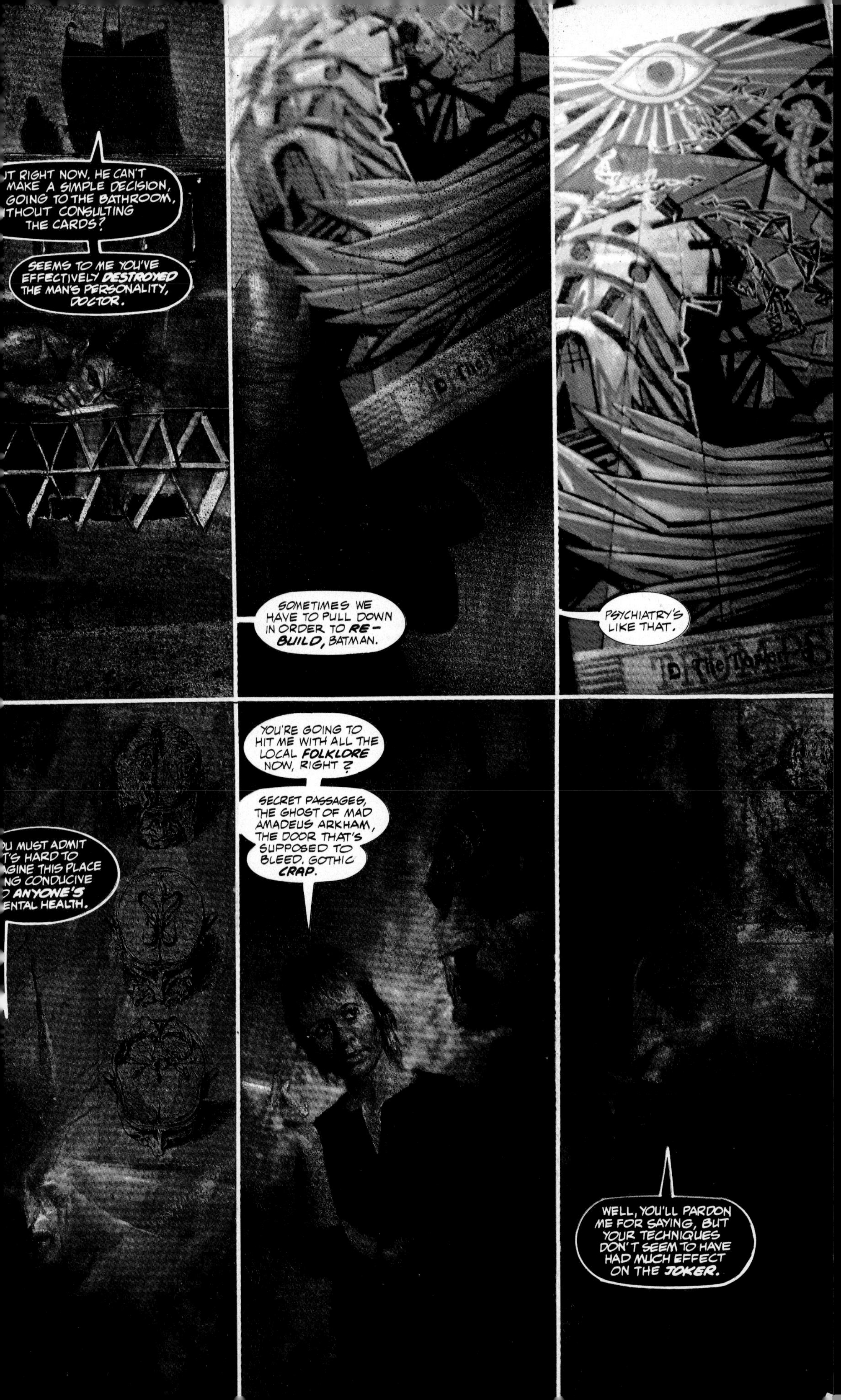

UT RIGHT NOW, HE CAN'T MAKE A SIMPLE DECISION, GOING TO THE BATHROOM, THOUT CONSULTING THE CARDS?
SEEMS TO ME YOU'VE EFFECTIVELY DESTROYED THE MAN'S PERSONALITY, DOCTOR.
SOMETIMES WE HAVE TO PULL DOWN IN ORDER TO RE-BUILD, BATMAN.
PSYCHIATRY'S LIKE THAT.
TRUMPS
The Tower
OU MUST ADMIT T'S HARD TO AGINE THIS PLACE NG CONDUCIVE O ANYONE'S ENTAL HEALTH.
YOU'RE GOING TO HIT ME WITH ALL THE LOCAL FOLKLORE NOW, RIGHT?
SECRET PASSAGES, THE GHOST OF MAD AMADEUS ARKHAM, THE DOOR THAT'S SUPPOSED TO BLEED. GOTHIC CRAP.
WELL, YOU'LL PARDON ME FOR SAYING, BUT YOUR TECHNIQUES DON'T SEEM TO HAVE HAD MUCH EFFECT ON THE JOKER.

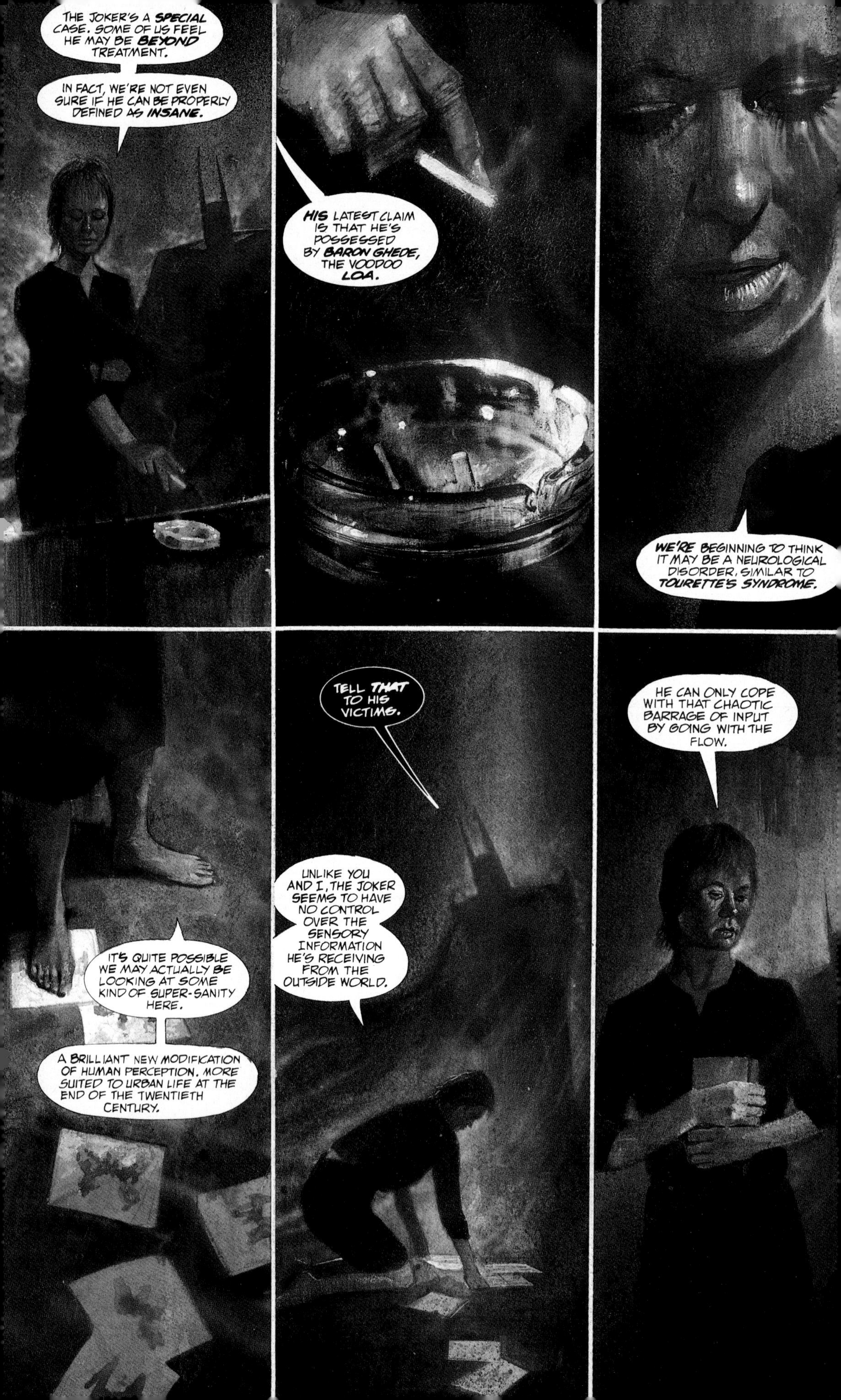
THE JOKER'S A SPECIAL CASE. SOME OF US FEEL HE MAY BE BEYOND TREATMENT.
IN FACT, WE'RE NOT EVEN SURE IF HE CAN BE PROPERLY DEFINED AS INSANE.
HIS LATEST CLAIM IS THAT HE'S POSSESSED BY BARON GHEDE, THE VOODOO LOA.
WE'RE BEGINNING TO THINK IT MAY BE A NEUROLOGICAL DISORDER, SIMILAR TO TOURETTE'S SYNDROME.
IT'S QUITE POSSIBLE WE MAY ACTUALLY BE LOOKING AT SOME KIND OF SUPER-SANITY HERE.
A BRILLIANT NEW MODIFICATION OF HUMAN PERCEPTION. MORE SUITED TO URBAN LIFE AT THE END OF THE TWENTIETH CENTURY.
TELL THAT TO HIS VICTIMS.
UNLIKE YOU AND I, THE JOKER SEEMS TO HAVE NO CONTROL OVER THE SENSORY INFORMATION HE'S RECEIVING FROM THE OUTSIDE WORLD.
HE CAN ONLY COPE WITH THAT CHAOTIC BARRAGE OF INPUT BY GOING WITH THE FLOW.

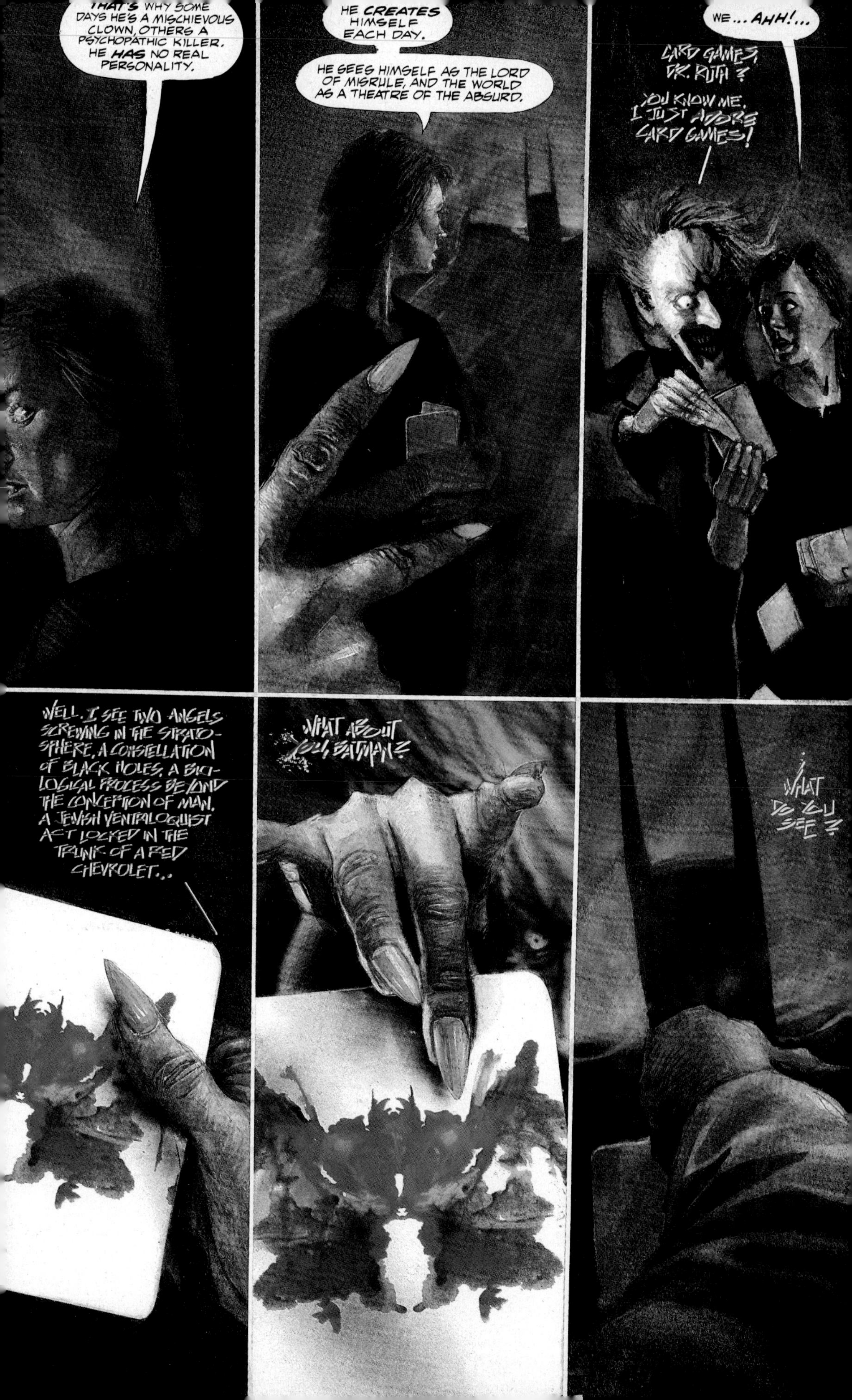
THAT'S WHY SOME DAYS HE'S A MISCHIEVOUS CLOWN, OTHERS A PSYCHOPATHIC KILLER. HE HAS NO REAL PERSONALITY.
HE CREATES HIMSELF EACH DAY.
HE SEES HIMSELF AS THE LORD OF MISRULE, AND THE WORLD AS A THEATRE OF THE ABSURD.
WE... AHH!...
CARD GAMES, DR. RUTH ?
YOU KNOW ME. I JUST ADORE CARD GAMES!
WELL. I SEE TWO ANGELS SCREWING IN THE STRATO-SPHERE, A CONSTELLATION OF BLACK HOLES, A BIO-LOGICAL PROCESS BEYOND THE CONCEPTION OF MAN. A JEWISH VENTRALOQUIST ACT LOCKED IN THE TRUNK OF A RED CHEVROLET...
WHAT ABOUT YOU, BATMAN ?
WHAT DO YOU SEE ?

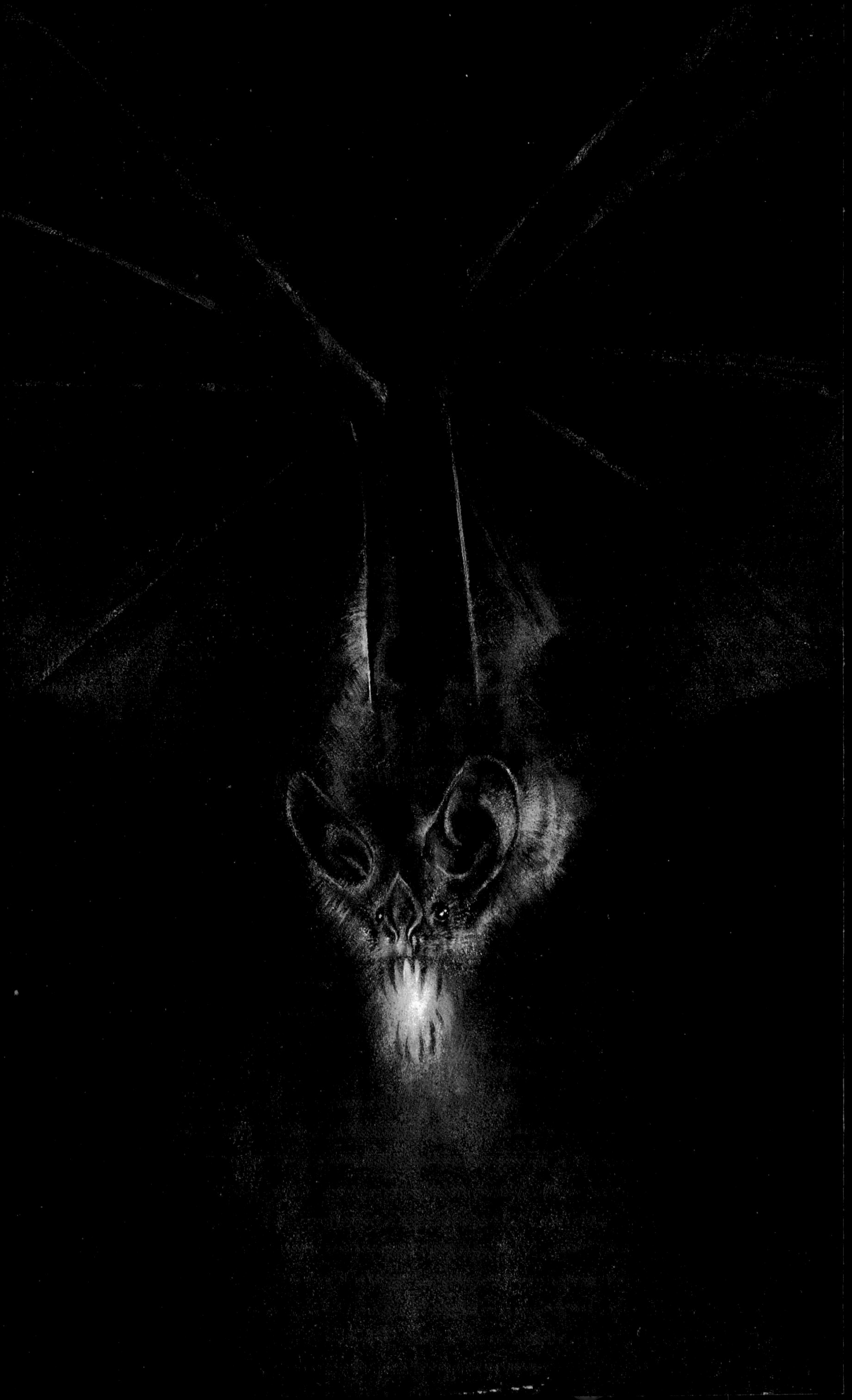

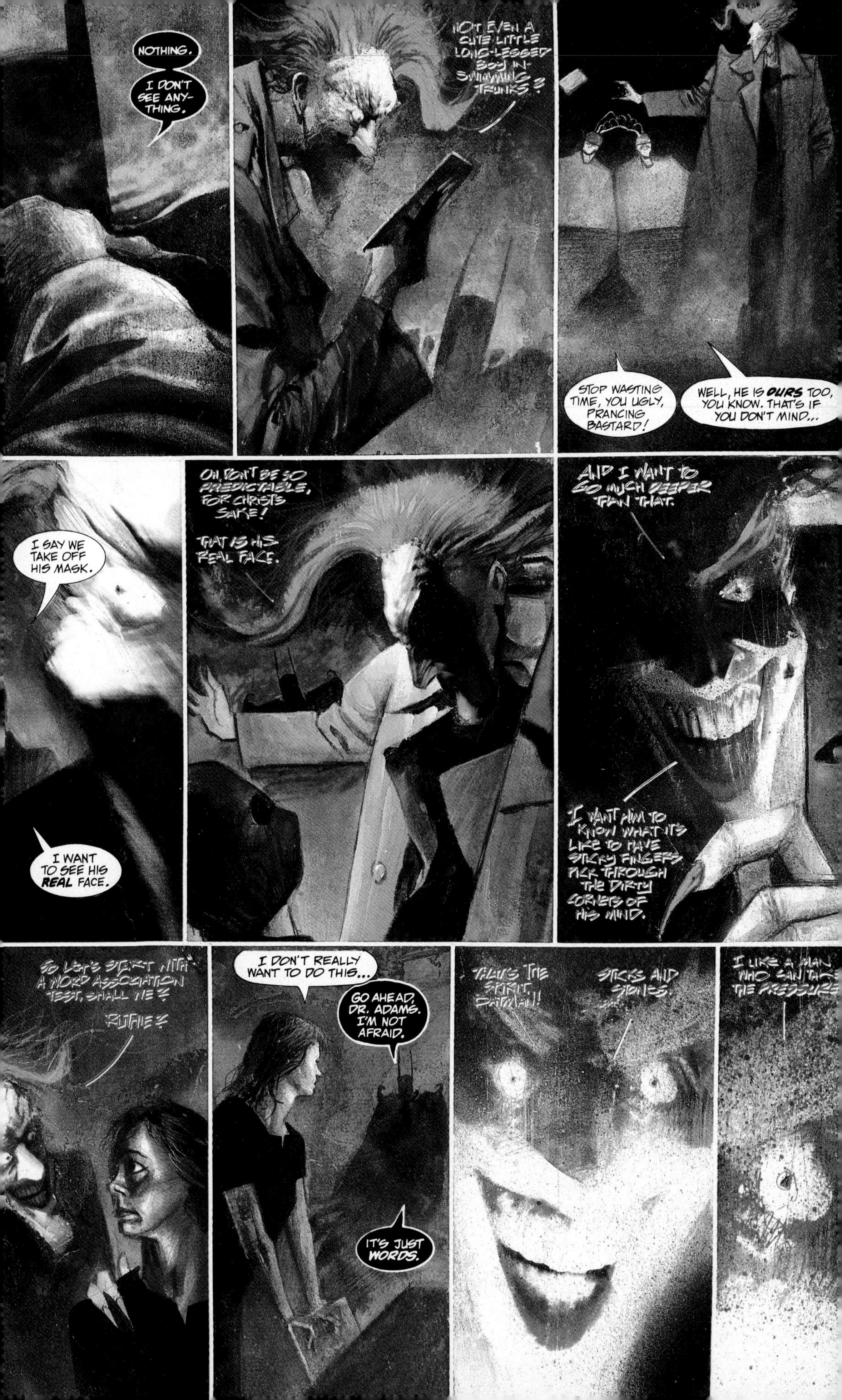
NOTHING.
I DON'T SEE ANY-THING.
NOT EVEN A CUTE LITTLE LONG-LEGGED BOY IN SWIMMING TRUNKS?
STOP WASTING TIME, YOU UGLY, PRANCING BASTARD!
WELL, HE IS **OURS** TOO, YOU KNOW. THAT'S IF YOU DON'T MIND...
I SAY WE TAKE OFF HIS MASK.
I WANT TO SEE HIS **REAL** FACE.
OH, DON'T BE SO PREDICTABLE, FOR CHRIST'S SAKE!
THAT IS HIS REAL FACE.
AND I WANT TO GO MUCH DEEPER THAN THAT.
I WANT HIM TO KNOW WHAT IT'S LIKE TO HAVE STICKY FINGERS PICK THROUGH THE DIRTY CORNERS OF HIS MIND.
SO LET'S START WITH A WORD ASSOCIATION TEST, SHALL WE?
RUTHIE?
I DON'T REALLY WANT TO DO THIS...
GO AHEAD, DR. ADAMS. I'M NOT AFRAID.
IT'S JUST **WORDS.**
THAT'S THE SPIRIT, BATMAN!
STICKS AND STONES.
I LIKE A MAN WHO CAN TAK
THE PRESSURE

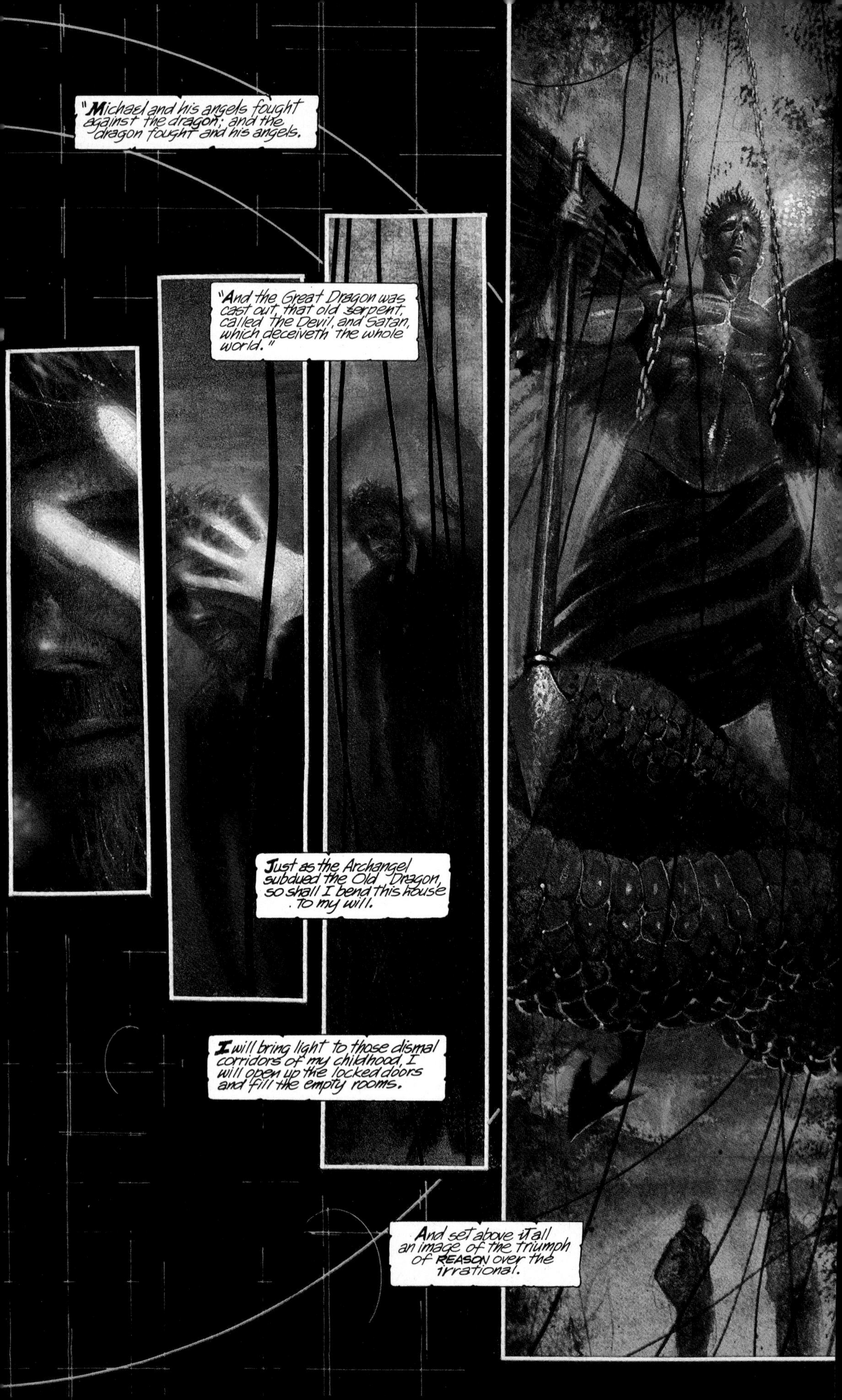
"Michael and his angels fought against the dragon; and the dragon fought and his angels.
"And the Great Dragon was cast out, that old serpent, called the Devil, and Satan, which deceiveth the whole world."
Just as the Archangel subdued the Old Dragon, so shall I bend this house to my will.
I will bring light to those dismal corridors of my childhood, I will open up the locked doors and fill the empty rooms.
And set above it all an image of the triumph of REASON over the irrational.

Harriet is plagued by NIGHTMARES.

I blame the LEWIS CARROLL, but she will insist on reading and rereading the books.

Perhaps things will settle when the work on the house is finished.

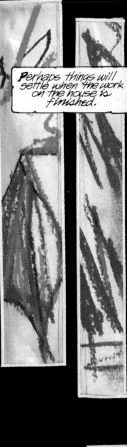

Perhaps.

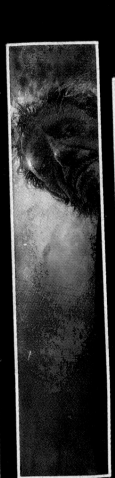

One of the workmen must have dropped it.

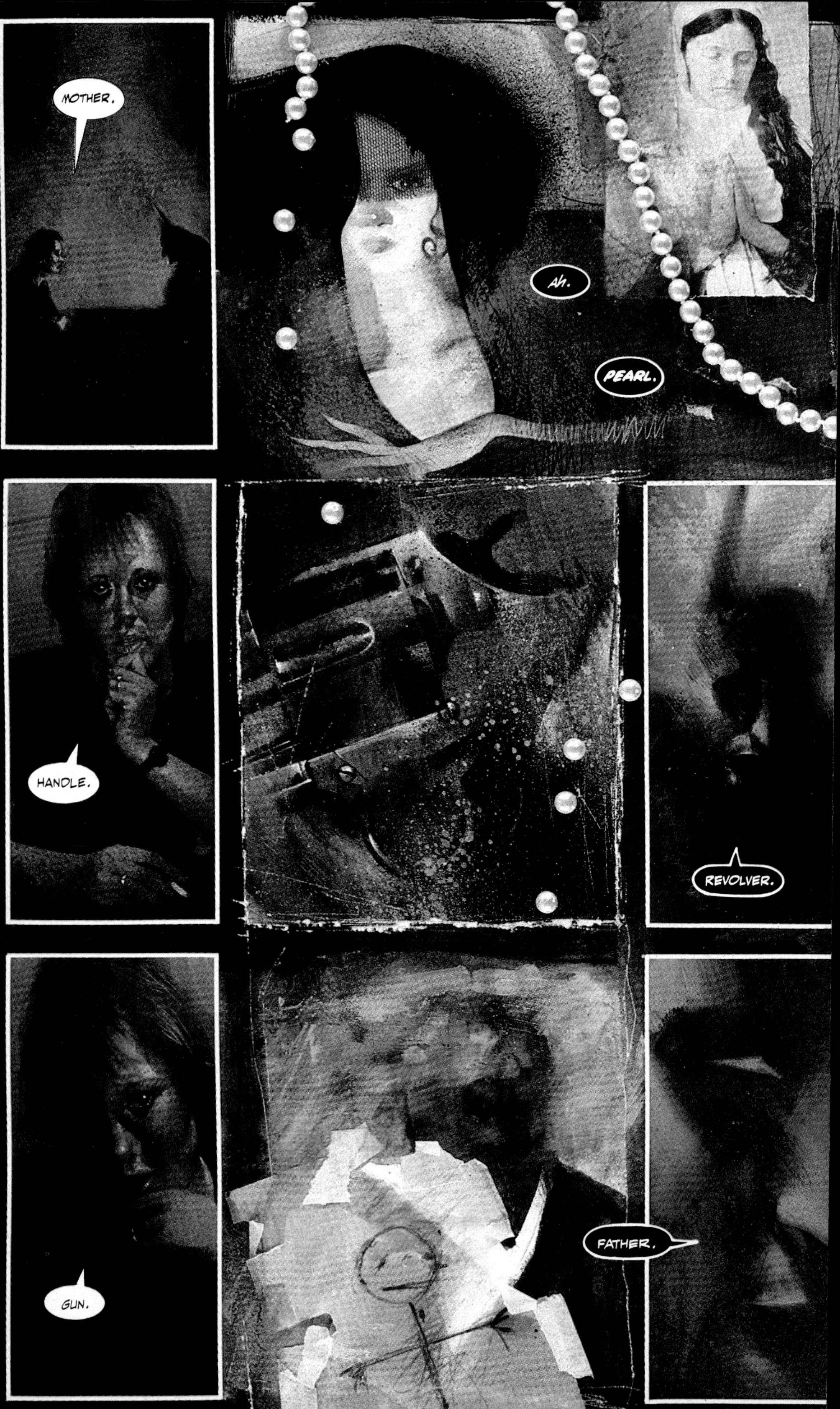
MOTHER.
Ah.
PEARL.
HANDLE.
REVOLVER.
GUN.
FATHER.

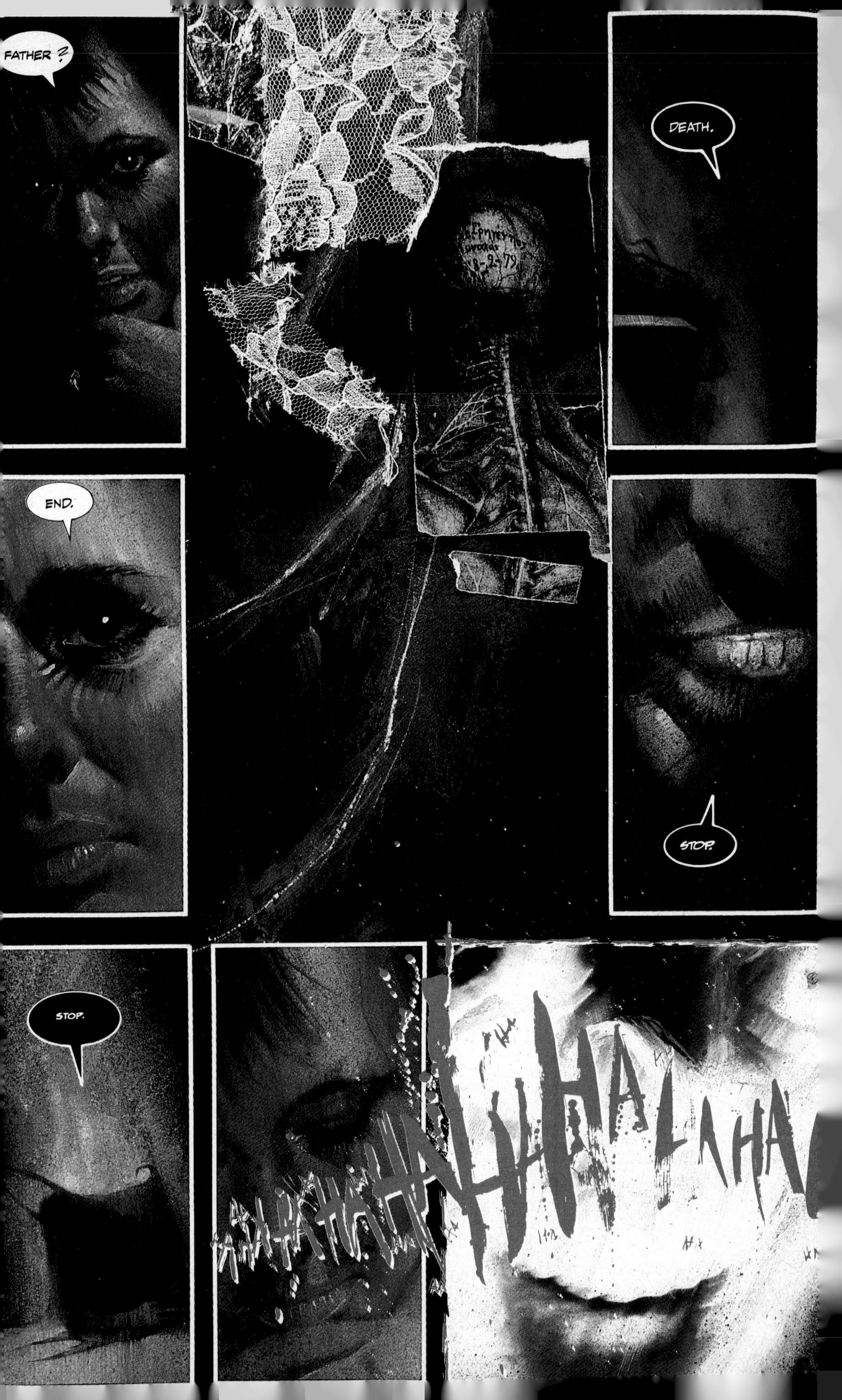
FATHER ?
DEATH.
END.
STOP.
STOP.

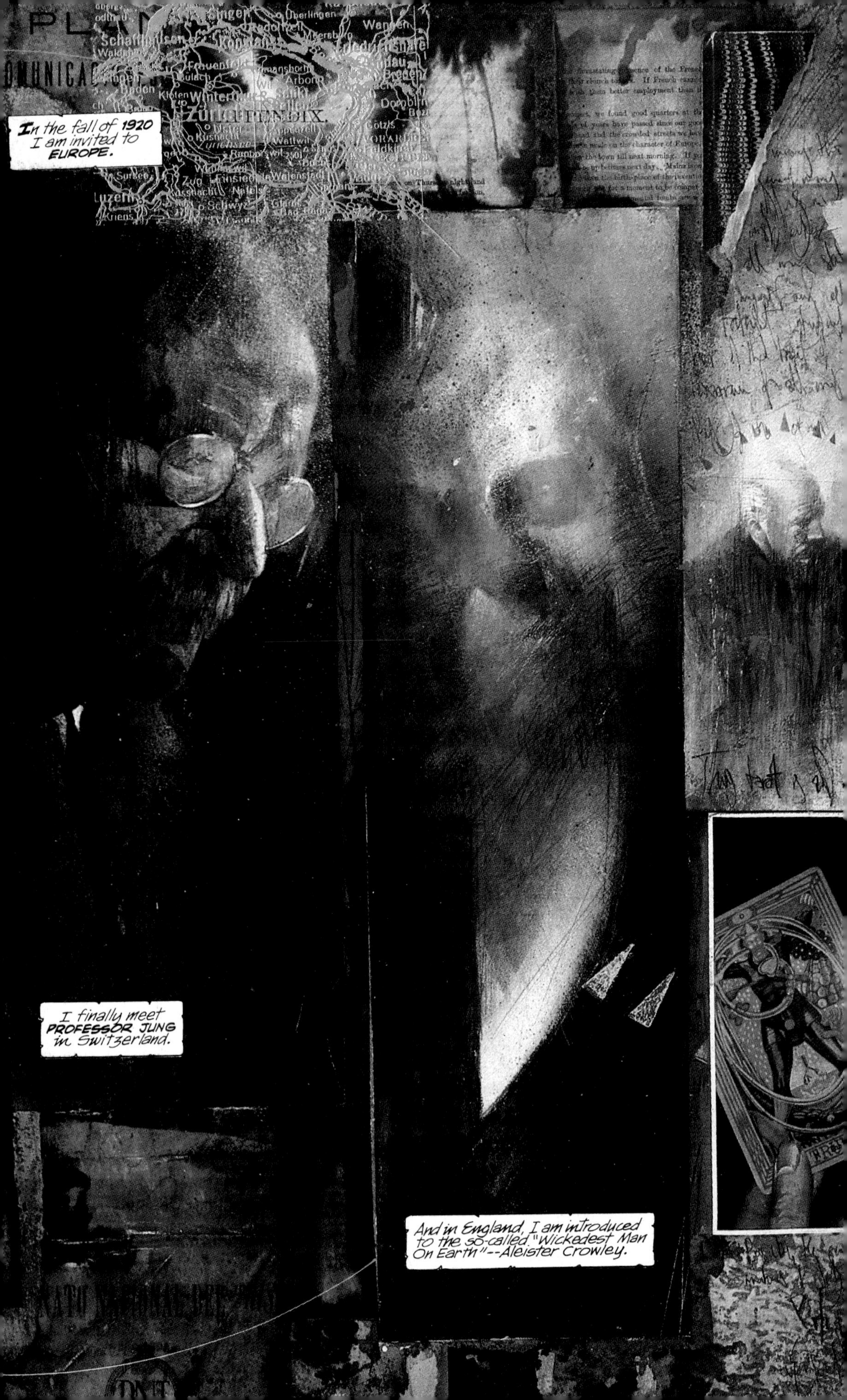
In the fall of 1920 I am invited to EUROPE.
I finally meet PROFESSOR JUNG in Switzerland.
And in England, I am introduced to the so-called "Wickedest Man On Earth"--Aleister Crowley.

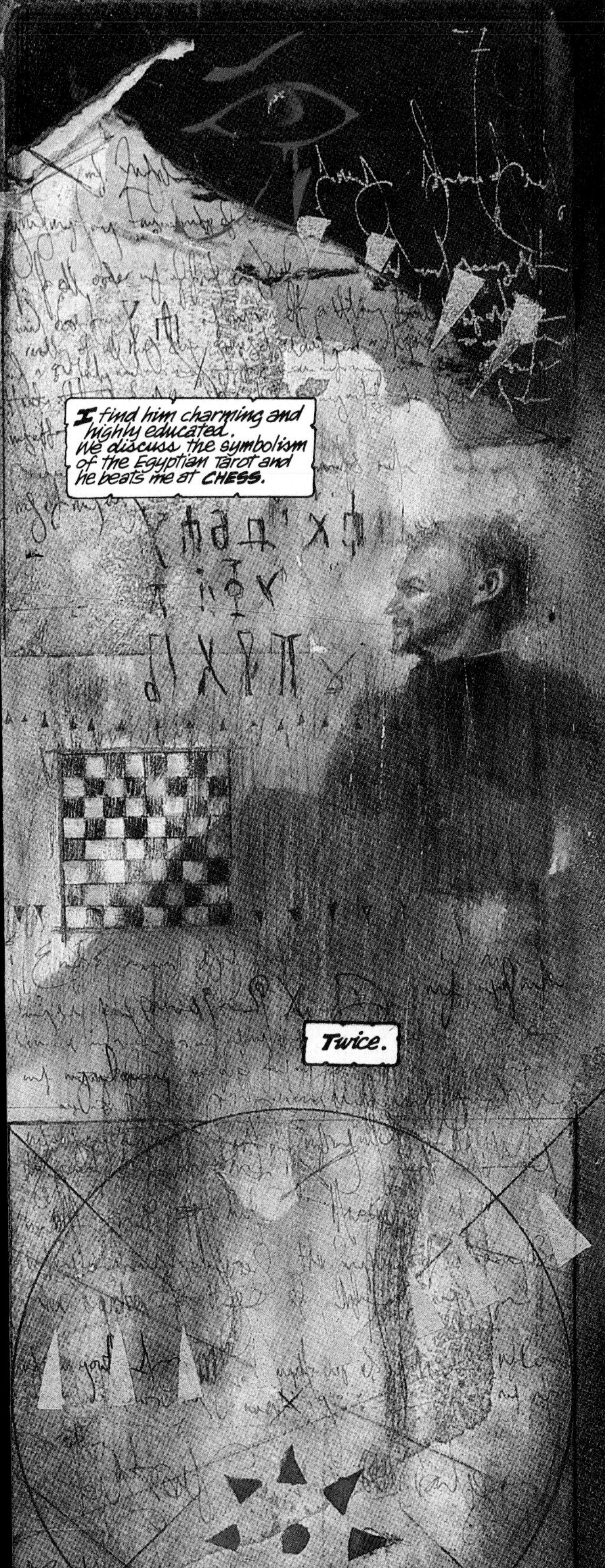
I find him charming and highly educated. We discuss the symbolism of the Egyptian Tarot and he beats me at CHESS.
Twice.
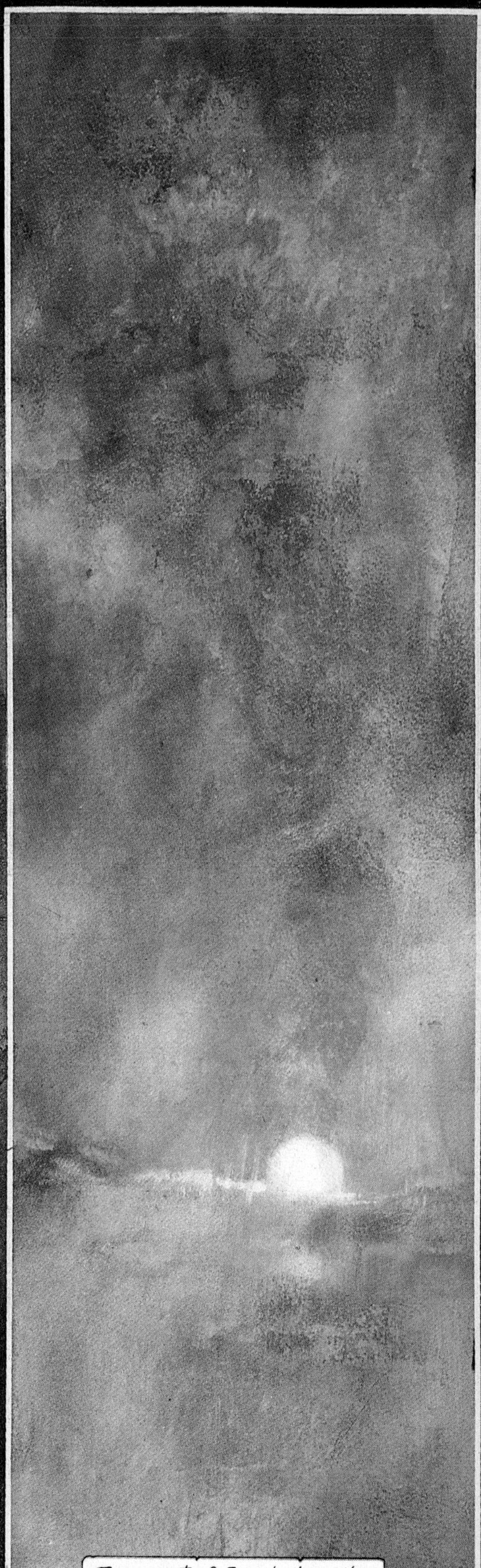
I run out of French cigarettes in the Mid-Atlantic.

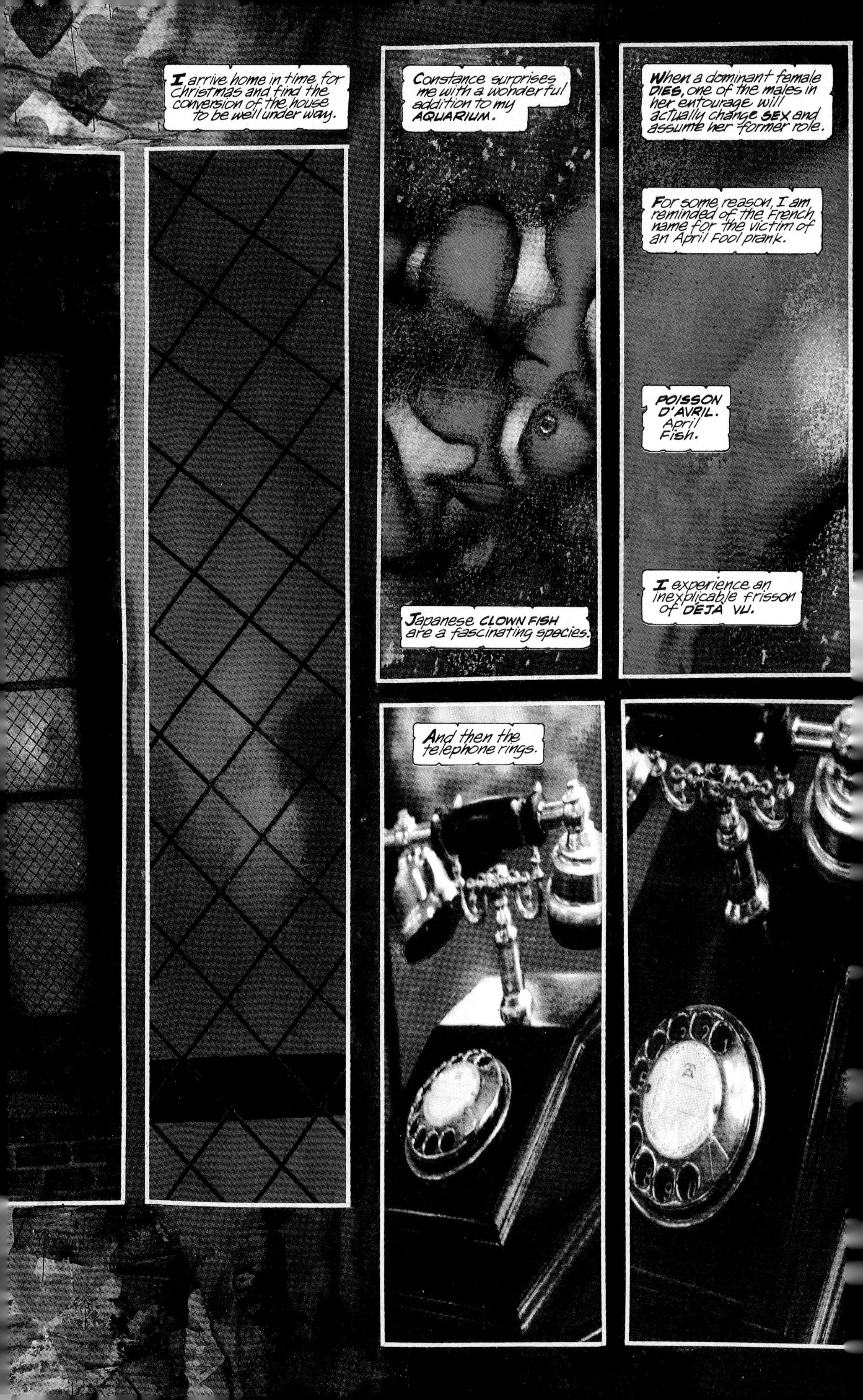

I arrive home in time for Christmas and find the conversion of the house to be well under way.
Constance surprises me with a wonderful addition to my AQUARIUM.
Japanese CLOWN FISH are a fascinating species.
When a dominant female DIES, one of the males in her entourage will actually change SEX and assume her former role.
For some reason, I am reminded of the French name for the victim of an April Fool prank.
POISSON D'AVRIL. April Fish.
I experience an inexplicable frisson of DEJÀ VU.
And then the telephone rings.

It transpires that Martin Hawkins has escaped from the Penitentiary and the Police would like my considered opinion as to his state of mind.

I tell them he may be highly dangerous and I leave them to it.

It's not my problem.

Not tonight.

IS SOMETHING WRONG?

NO. IT'S *NOTHING*.

NOTHING AT ALL.

Harriet is enchanted by the Cuckoo Clock I have brought her from Switzerland.

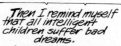

Then I remind myself that all intelligent children suffer bad dreams.

And she is so very intelligent.

And perfectly beautiful.

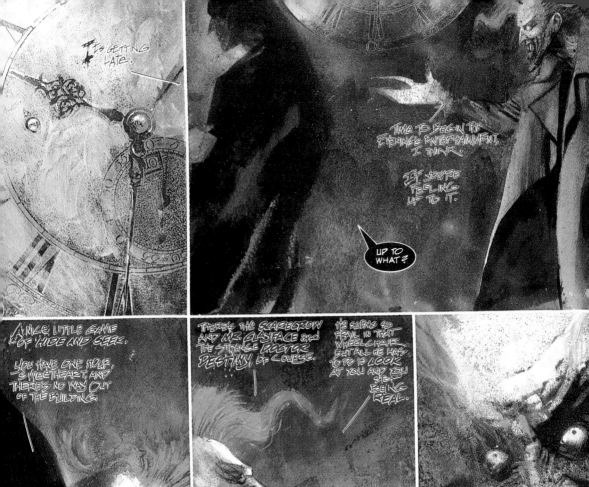

IT'S GETTING LATE.

TIME TO BEGIN THE EVENING'S ENTERTAINMENT, I THINK.

IF YOU'RE FEELING UP TO IT.

UP TO WHAT?

A NICE LITTLE GAME OF HIDE AND SEEK.

YOU HAVE ONE HOUR, SWEETHEART, AND THERE'S NO WAY OUT OF THE BUILDING.

ONE HOUR! BEFORE ALL YOUR FRIENDS COME LOOKING FOR YOU.

THERE'S THE SCARECROW AND MR. CLAYFACE AND THE STRANGE DOCTOR DESTINY, OF COURSE.

HE SEEMS SO FRAIL IN THAT WHEELCHAIR BUT ALL HE HAS TO DO IS LOOK AT YOU AND YOU STOP BEING REAL.

HE DOES SO WANT TO LOOK AT YOU, DARLING.

OH, AND DON'T LET'S FORGET CROC. HE CAME UP OUT OF THAT DAMP, DARK CELLAR THIS MORNING, DRAGGING HIS CHAINS BEHIND HIM.

THEY ALL WANT TO SEE YOU, SO WHY DON'T YOU JUST RUN ALONG NOW.

I DON'T TAKE ORDERS FROM YOU.

WELL...

THIS GUY GOES INTO THE HOSPITAL, OKAY?...HIS WIFE'S JUST HAD A BABY AND HE CAN'T WAIT TO SEE THEM BOTH.

SO HE MEETS THE DOC AND HE SAYS, "OH, I'VE BEEN SO WORRIED, HOW ARE THEY?"

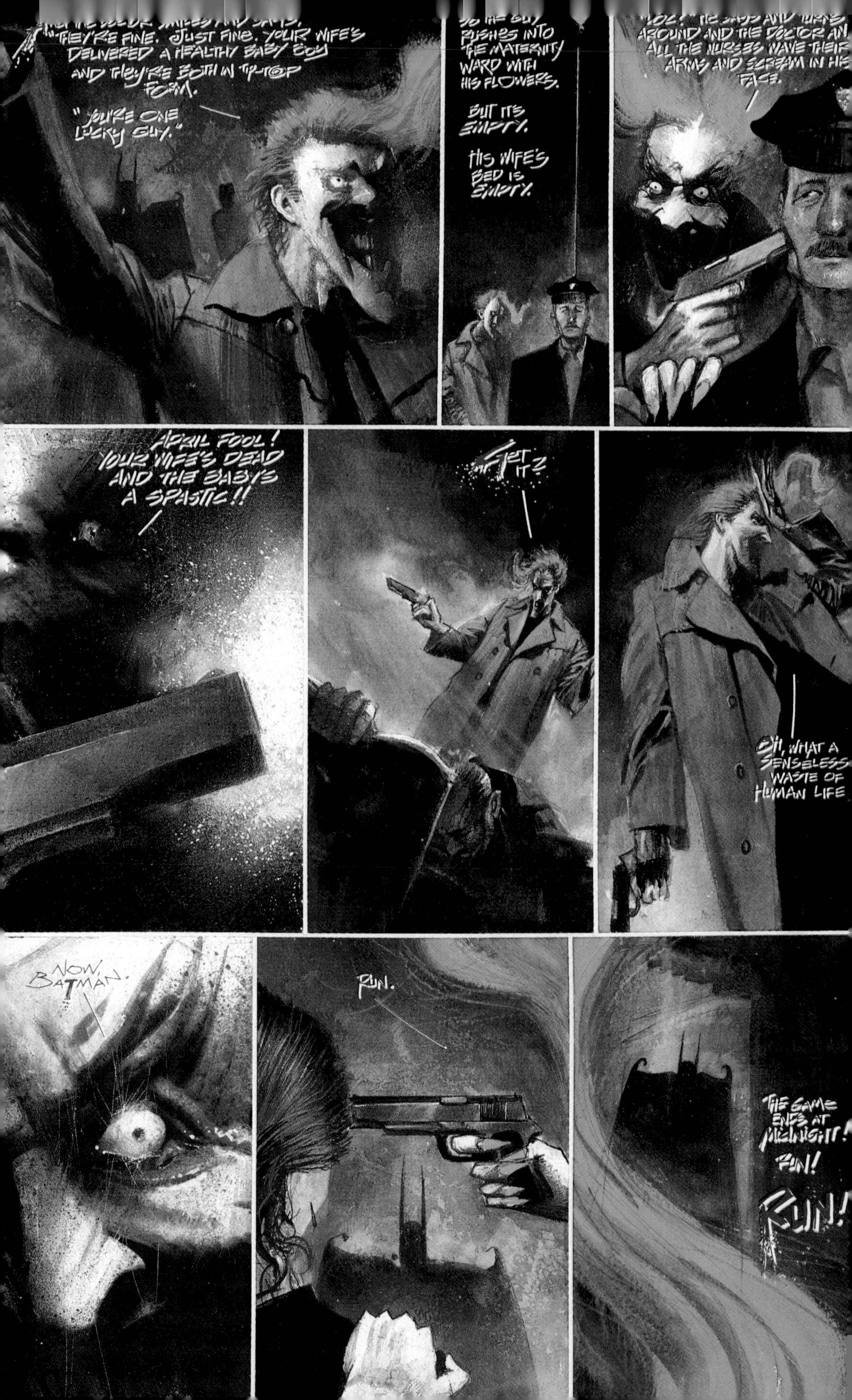
"THEY'RE FINE. JUST FINE. YOUR WIFE'S DELIVERED A HEALTHY BABY BOY AND THEY'RE BOTH IN TIP-TOP FORM.
"YOU'RE ONE LUCKY GUY."
RUSHES INTO THE MATERNITY WARD WITH HIS FLOWERS.
BUT IT'S EMPTY.
HIS WIFE'S BED IS EMPTY.
AROUND AND THE DOCTOR AN ALL THE NURSES WAVE THEIR ARMS AND SCREAM IN HIS FACE.
APRIL FOOL! YOUR WIFE'S DEAD AND THE BABY'S A SPASTIC!!
GET IT?
OH, WHAT A SENSELESS WASTE OF HUMAN LIFE
NOW, BATMAN.
RUN.
THE GAME ENDS AT MIDNIGHT!
RUN!
RUN!

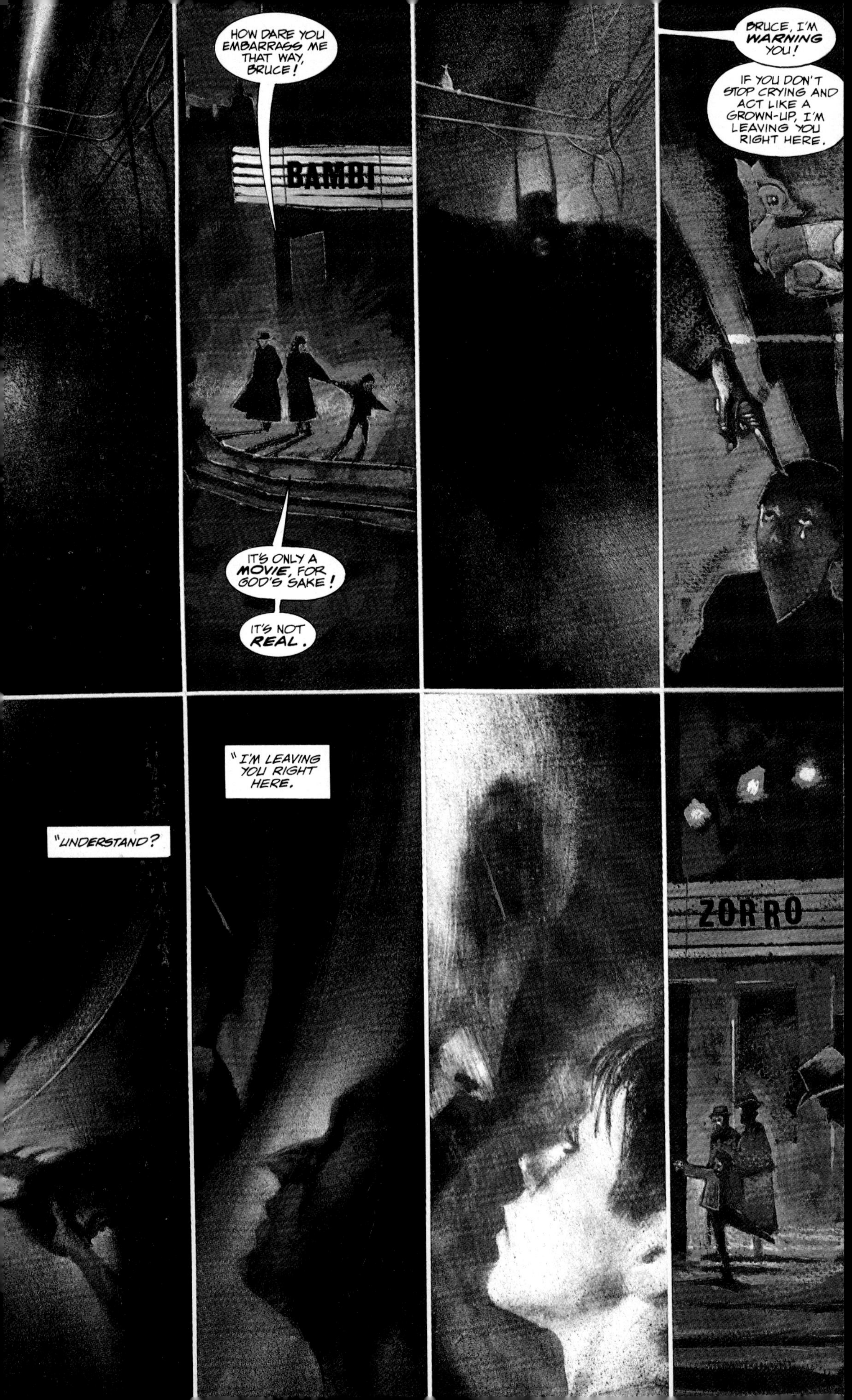

HOW DARE YOU EMBARRASS ME THAT WAY, BRUCE!
BAMBI
IT'S ONLY A MOVIE, FOR GOD'S SAKE!
IT'S NOT REAL.
BRUCE, I'M WARNING YOU!
IF YOU DON'T STOP CRYING AND ACT LIKE A GROWN-UP, I'M LEAVING YOU RIGHT HERE.
"UNDERSTAND?
"I'M LEAVING YOU RIGHT HERE.
ZORRO

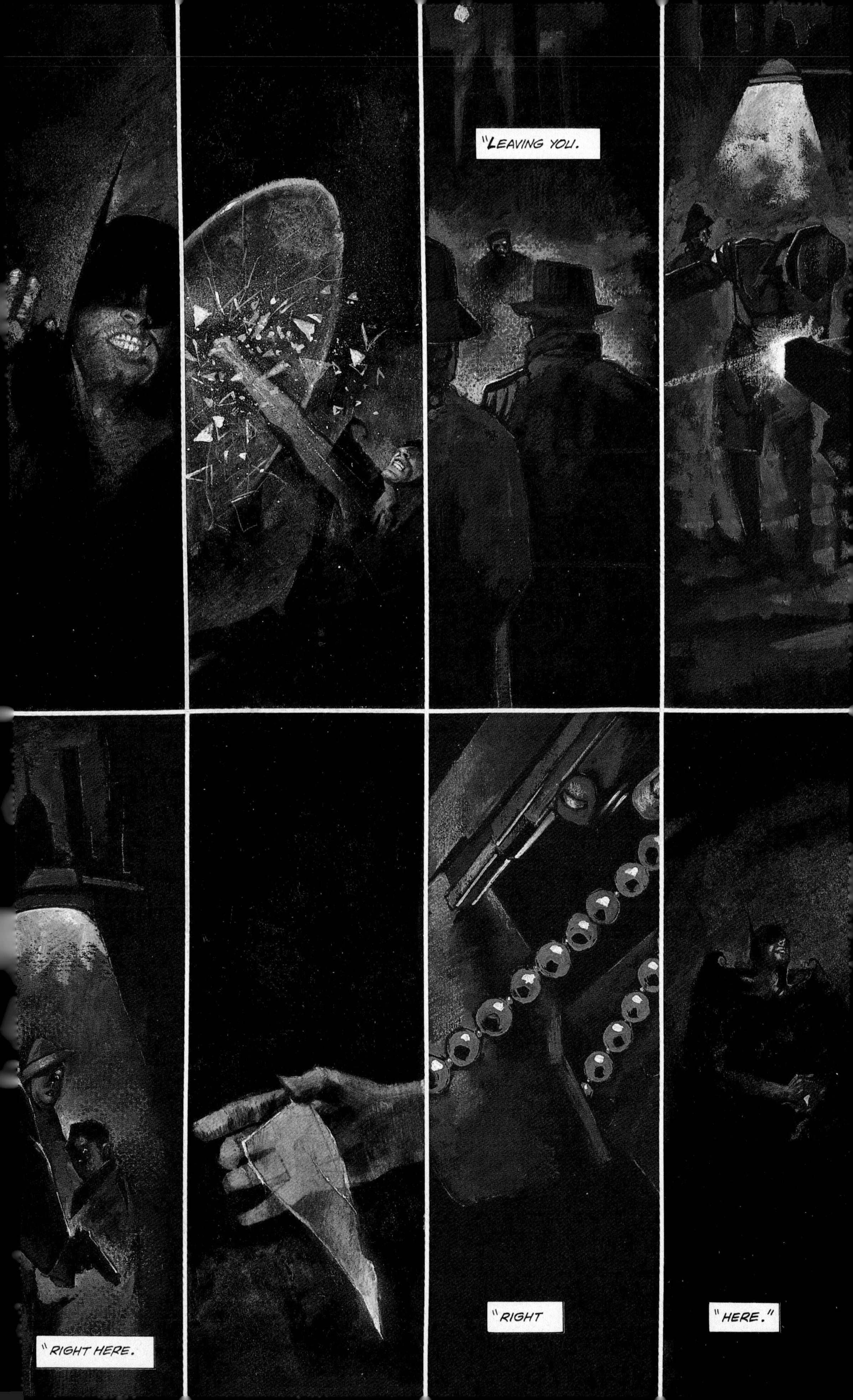
"LEAVING YOU.
"RIGHT HERE.
"RIGHT
"HERE."

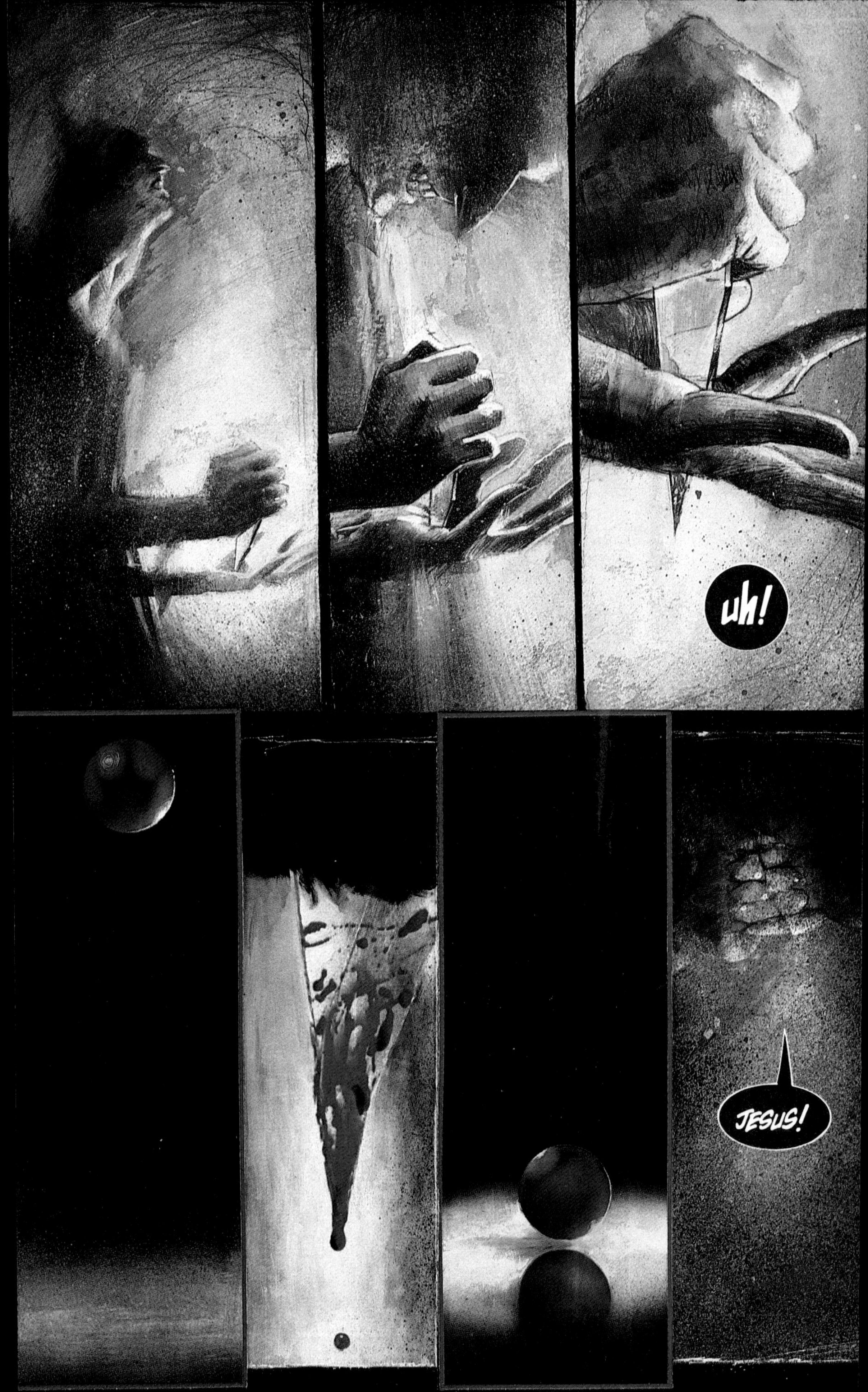
uh!
JESUS!

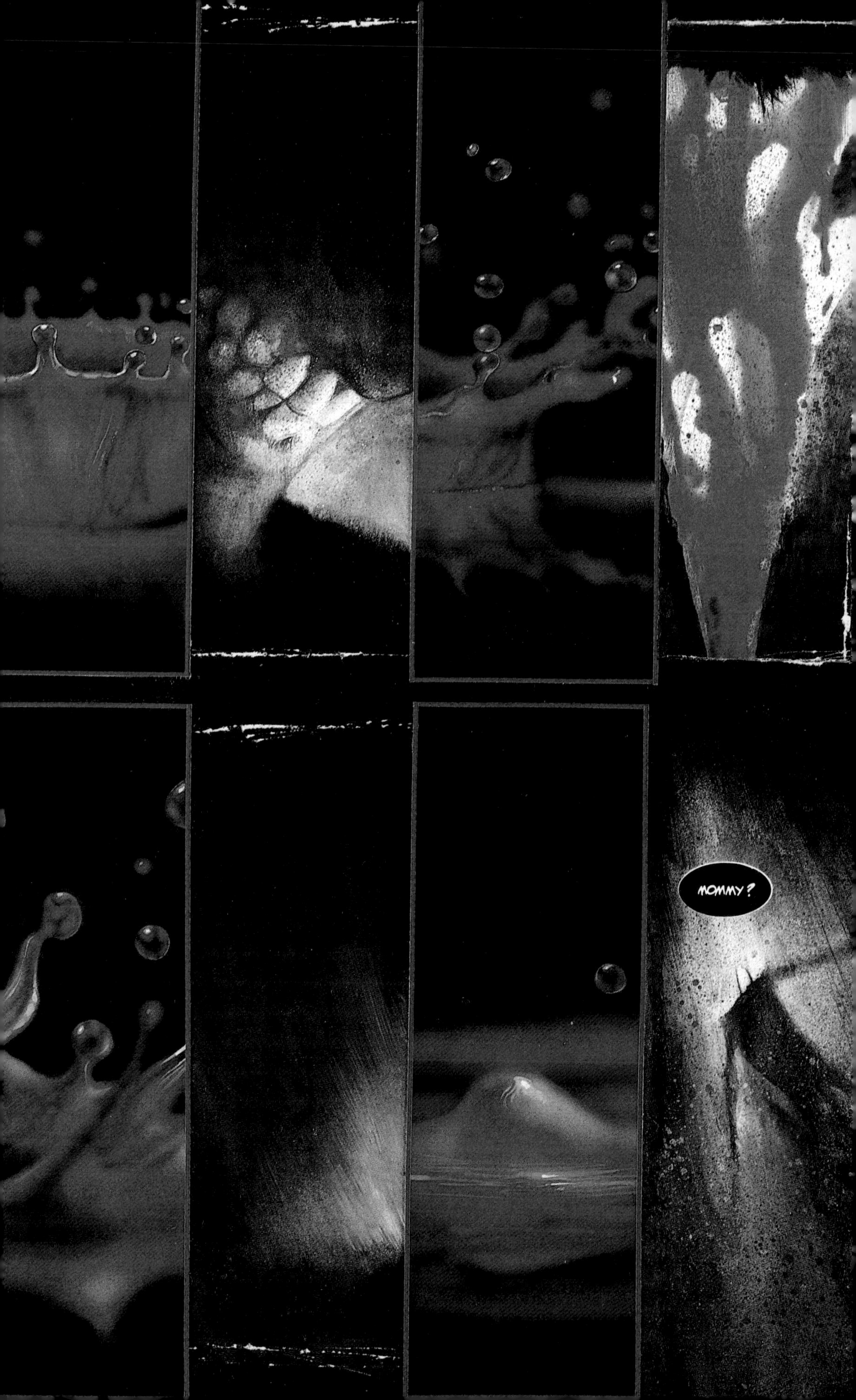
MOMMY?

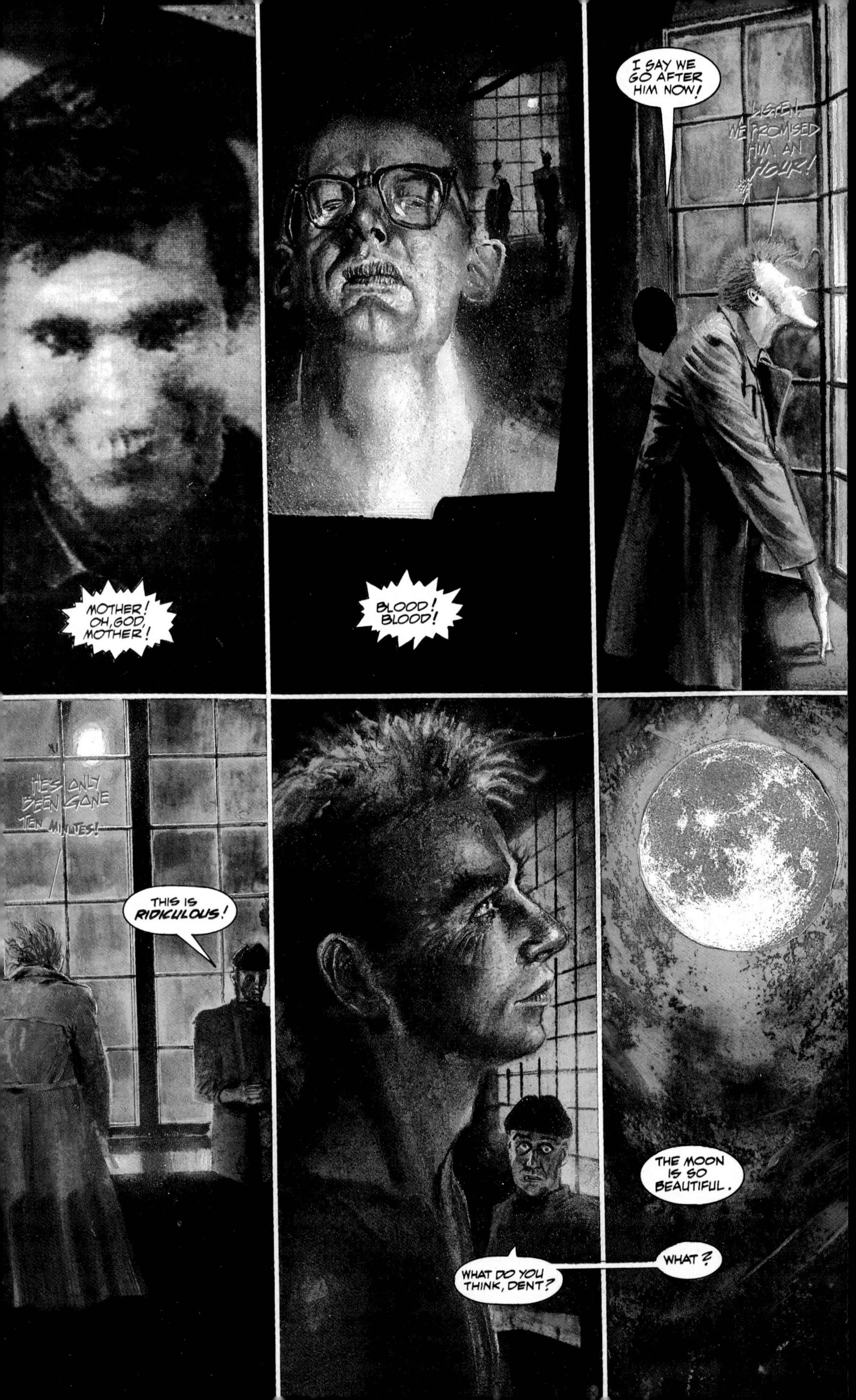
MOTHER! OH, GOD, MOTHER!
BLOOD! BLOOD!
I SAY WE GO AFTER HIM NOW!
LISTEN, WE PROMISED HIM AN HOUR!
HE'S ONLY BEEN GONE TEN MINUTES!
THIS IS RIDICULOUS!
WHAT DO YOU THINK, DENT?
WHAT?
THE MOON IS SO BEAUTIFUL.

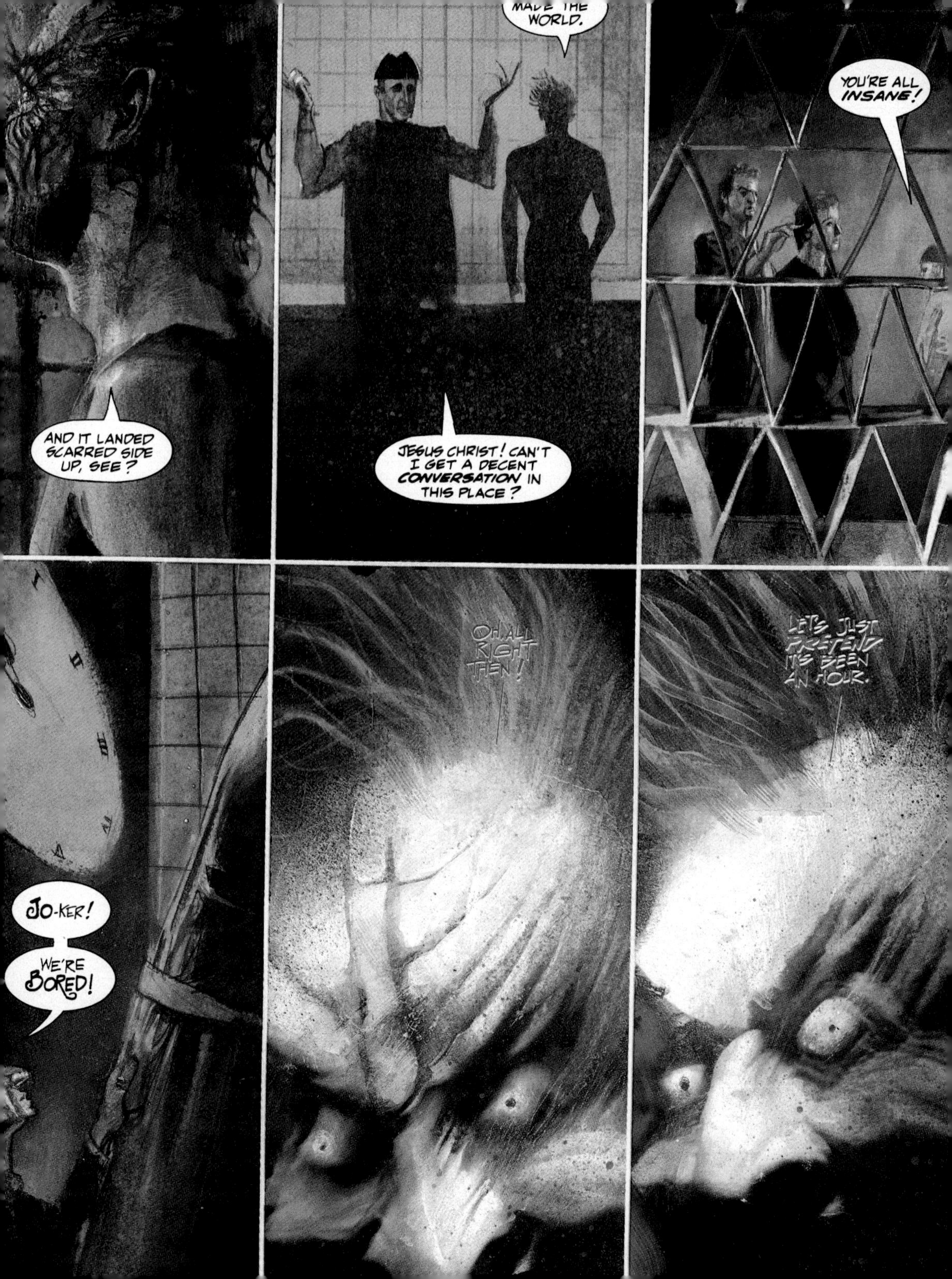

AND IT LANDED SCARRED SIDE UP, SEE?
MADE THE WORLD.
JESUS CHRIST! CAN'T I GET A DECENT CONVERSATION IN THIS PLACE?
YOU'RE ALL INSANE!
JO-KER!
WE'RE BORED!
OH ALL RIGHT THEN!
LET'S JUST PRETEND IT'S BEEN AN HOUR.

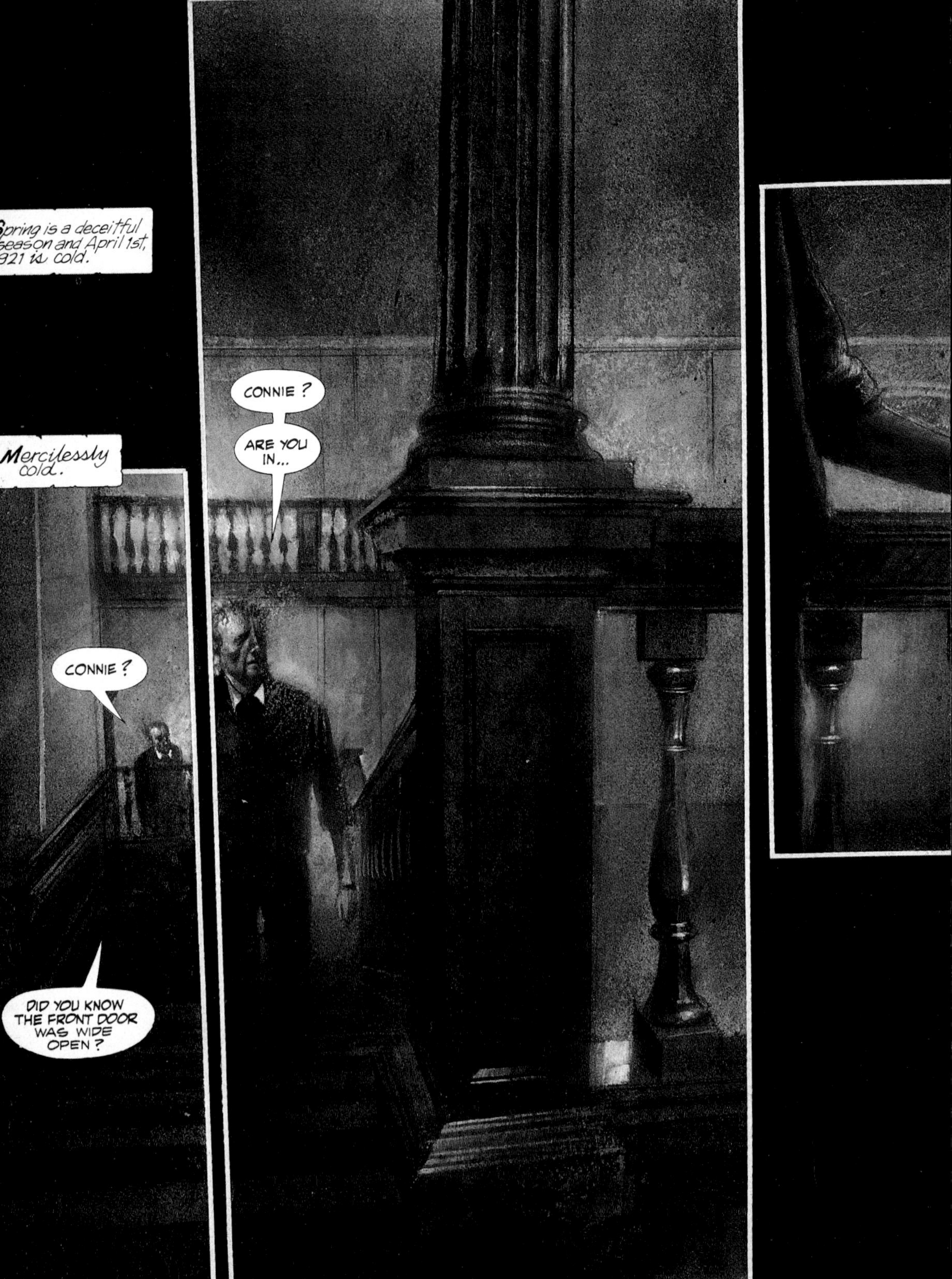

Spring is a deceitful season and April 1st, 1921 is cold.
Mercilessly cold.
CONNIE ?
DID YOU KNOW THE FRONT DOOR WAS WIDE OPEN ?
CONNIE ?
ARE YOU IN...

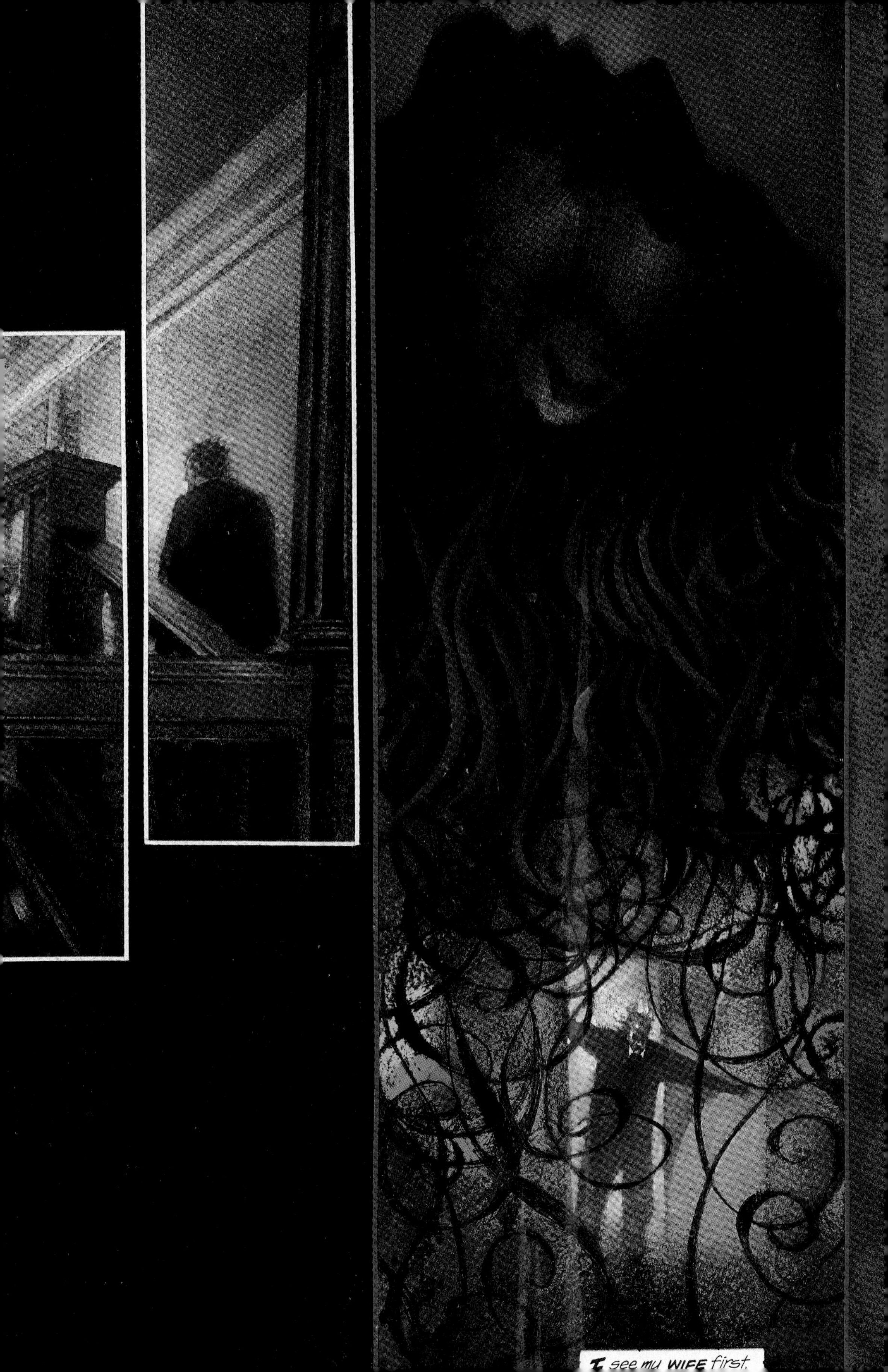
I see my **WIFE** first.

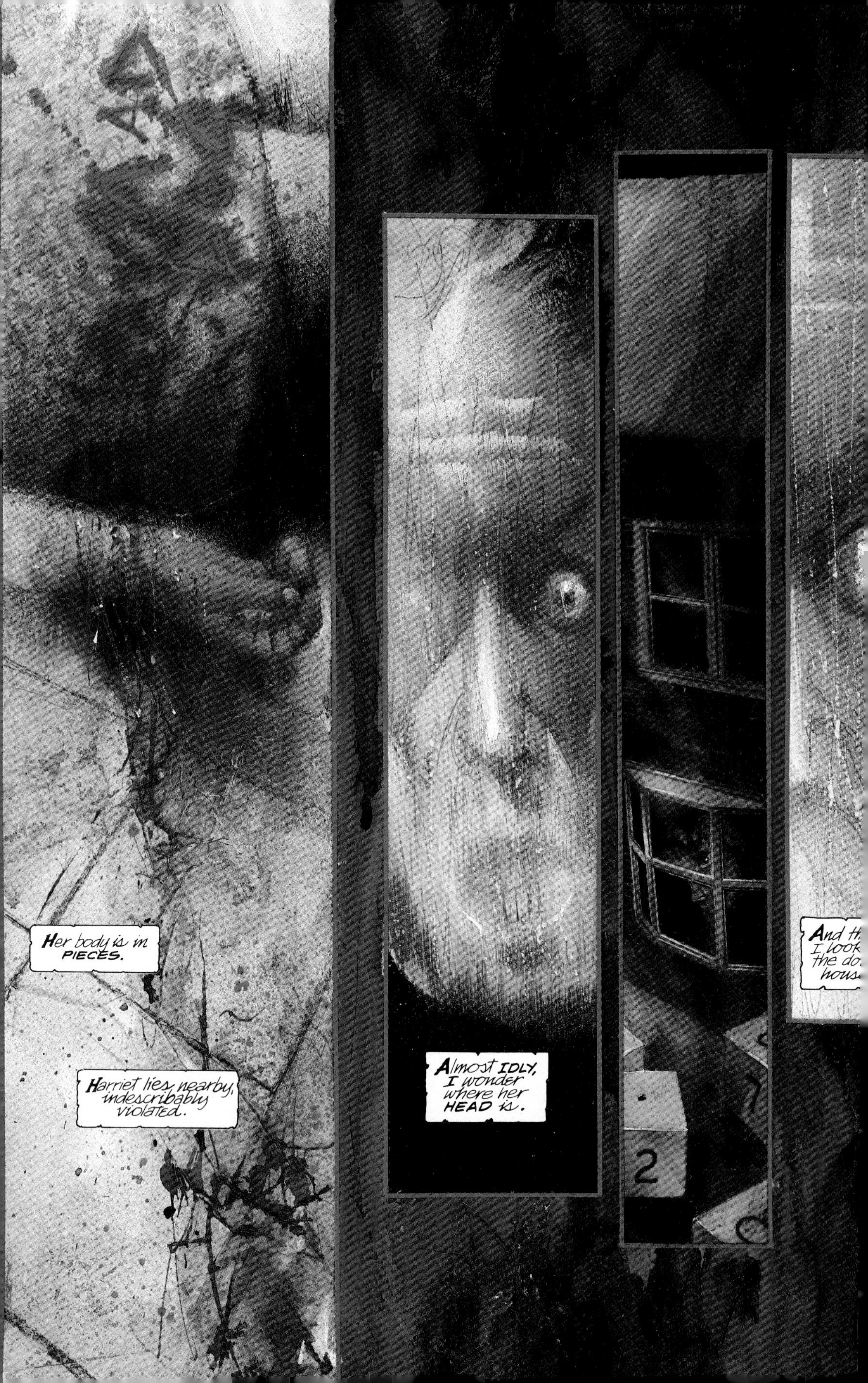
Her body is in PIECES.
Harriet lies nearby, indescribably violated.
Almost IDLY, I wonder where her HEAD is.

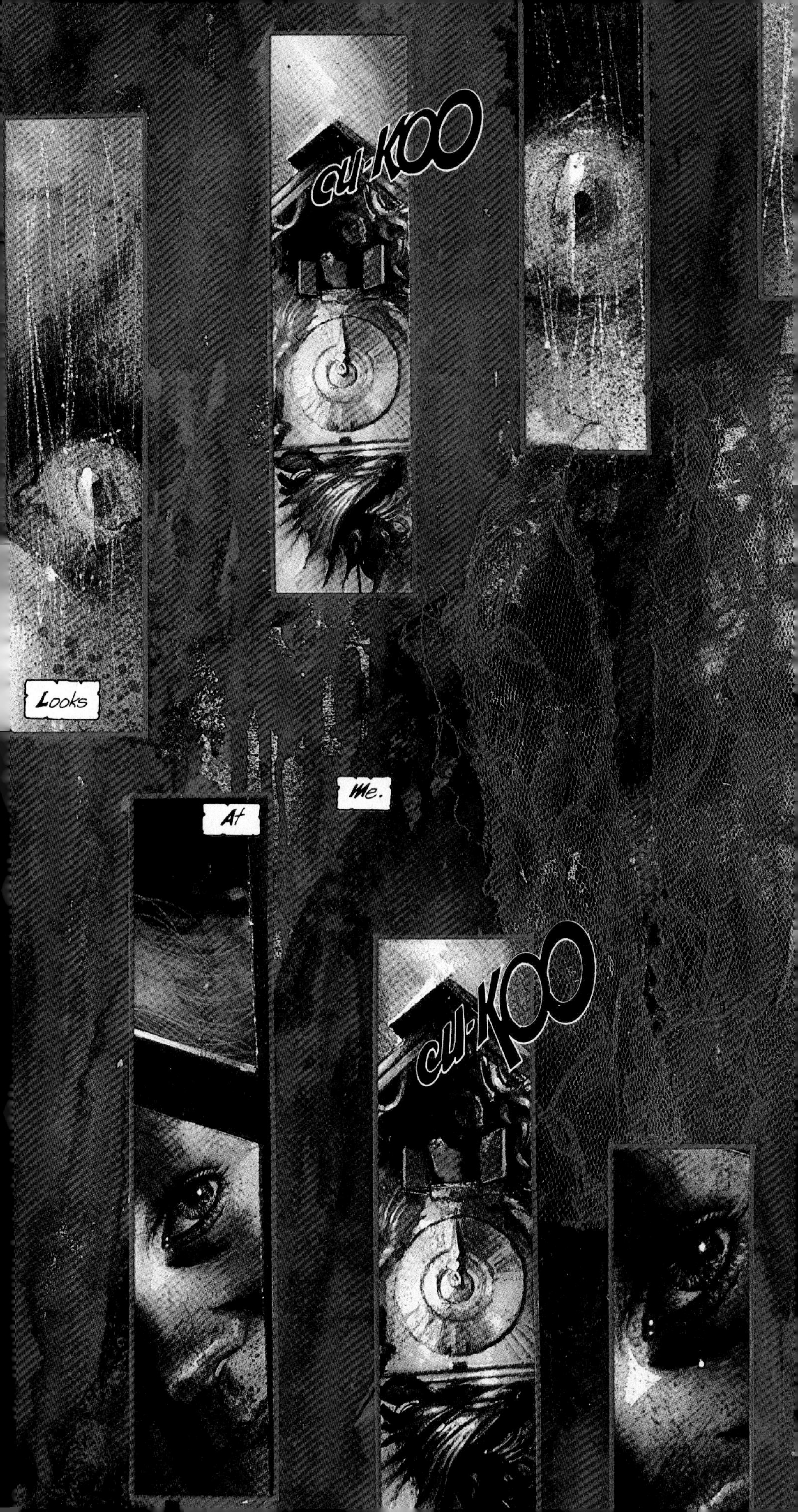
CU-KOO
Looks
At
Me.
CU-KOO

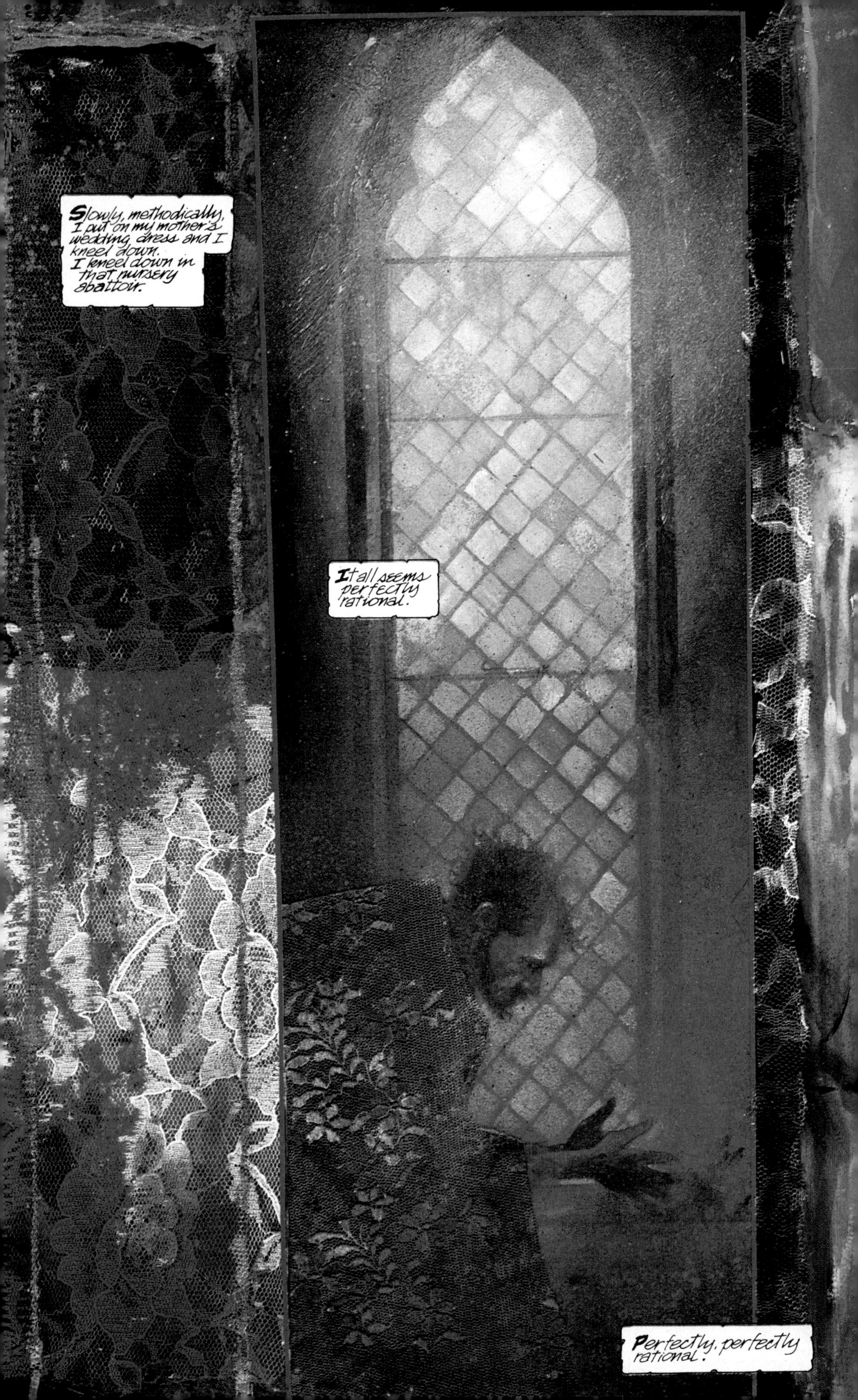
Slowly, methodically, I put on my mother's wedding dress and I kneel down. I kneel down in that nursery abattoir.
It all seems perfectly rational.
Perfectly, perfectly rational.

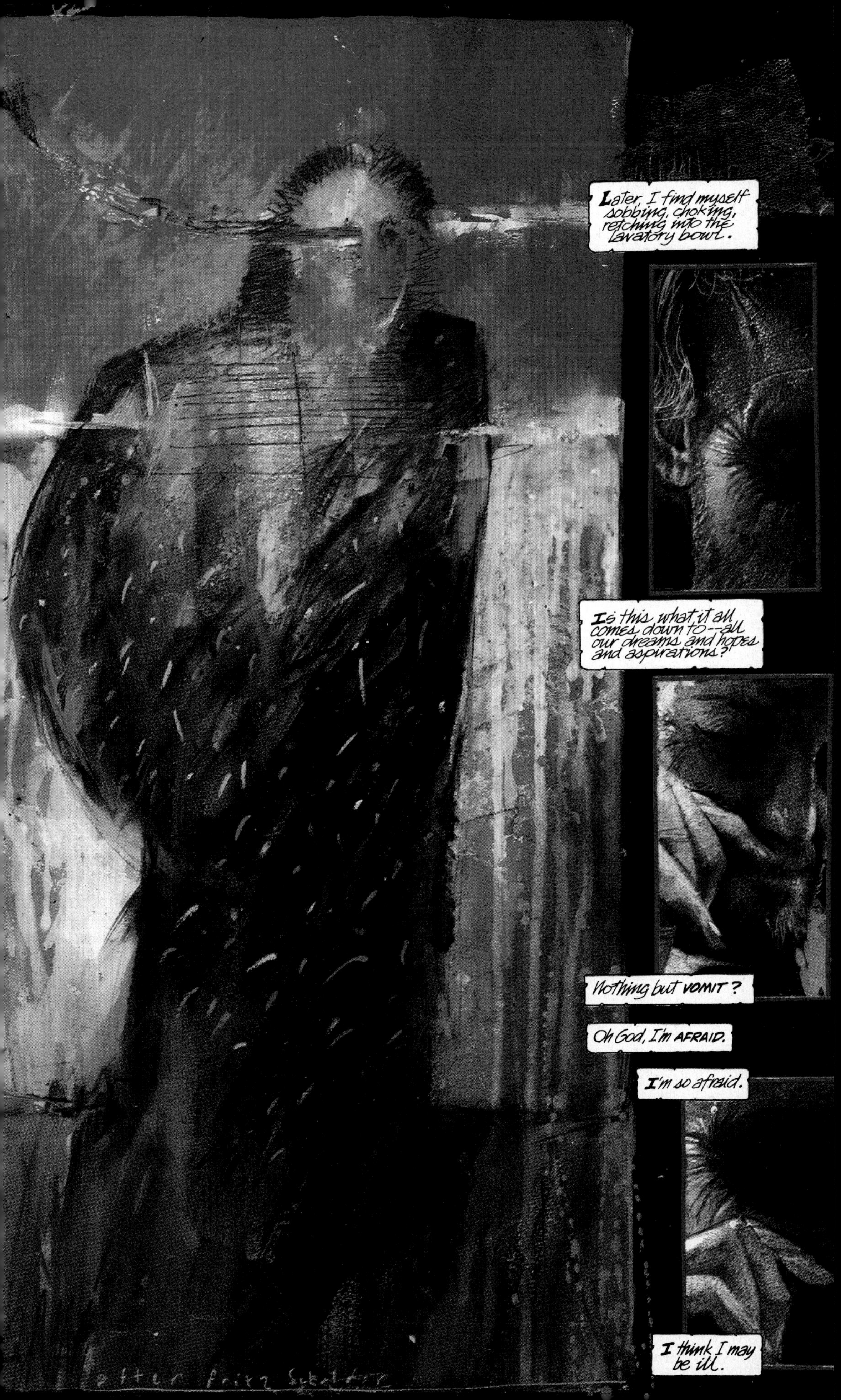
Later, I find myself sobbing, choking, retching into the lavatory bowl.
Is this what it all comes down to--all our dreams and hopes and aspirations?
Nothing but VOMIT?
Oh God, I'm AFRAID.
I'm so afraid.
I think I may be ill.

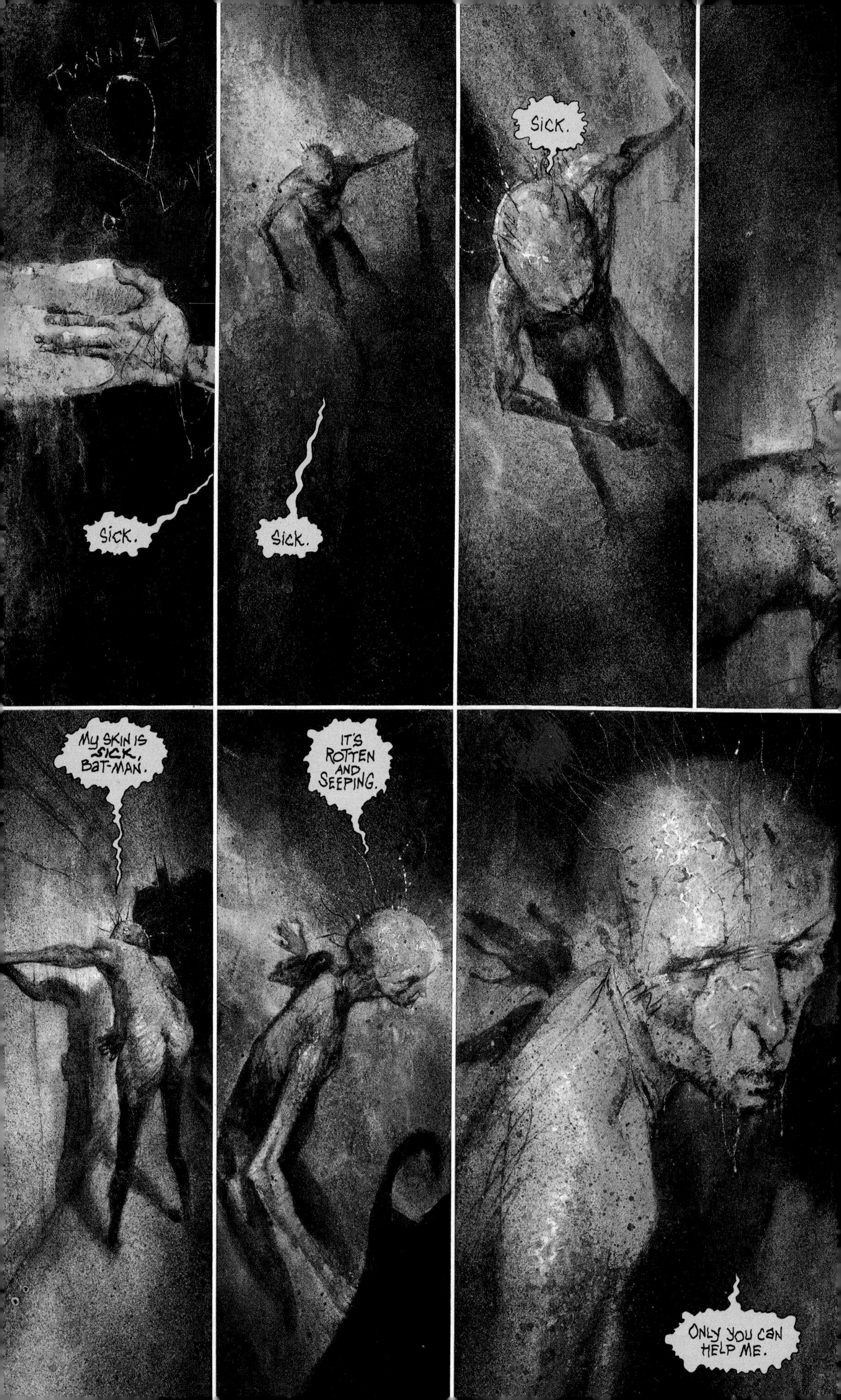
SICK.
SICK.
SICK.
MY SKIN IS SICK, BAT-MAN.
IT'S ROTTEN AND SEEPING.
ONLY YOU CAN HELP ME.

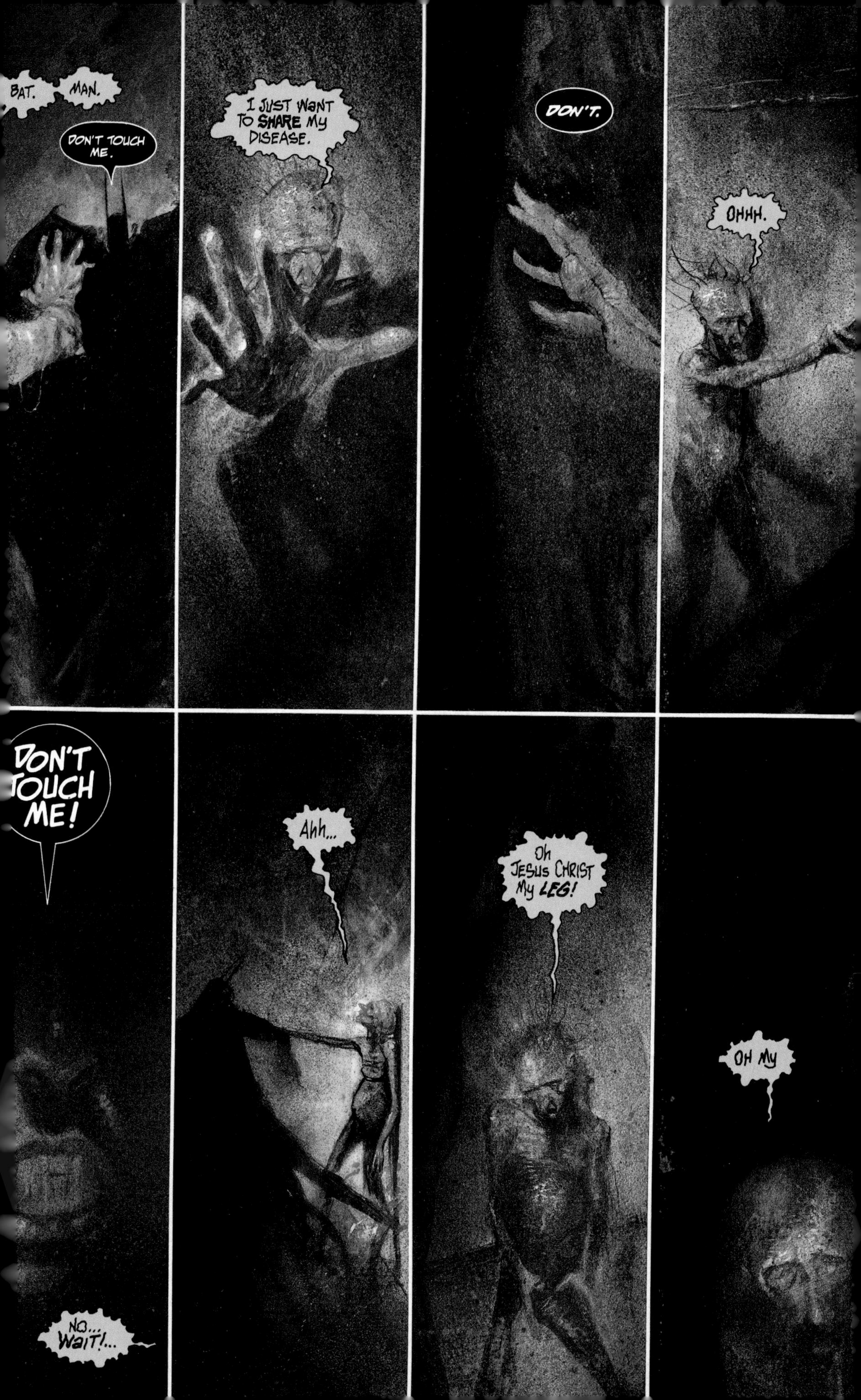
BAT.
MAN.
DON'T TOUCH ME.
I JUST WANT TO SHARE MY DISEASE.
DON'T.
OHHH.
DON'T TOUCH ME!
NO... WAIT!...
Ahh...
Oh JESUS CHRIST MY LEG!
OH MY

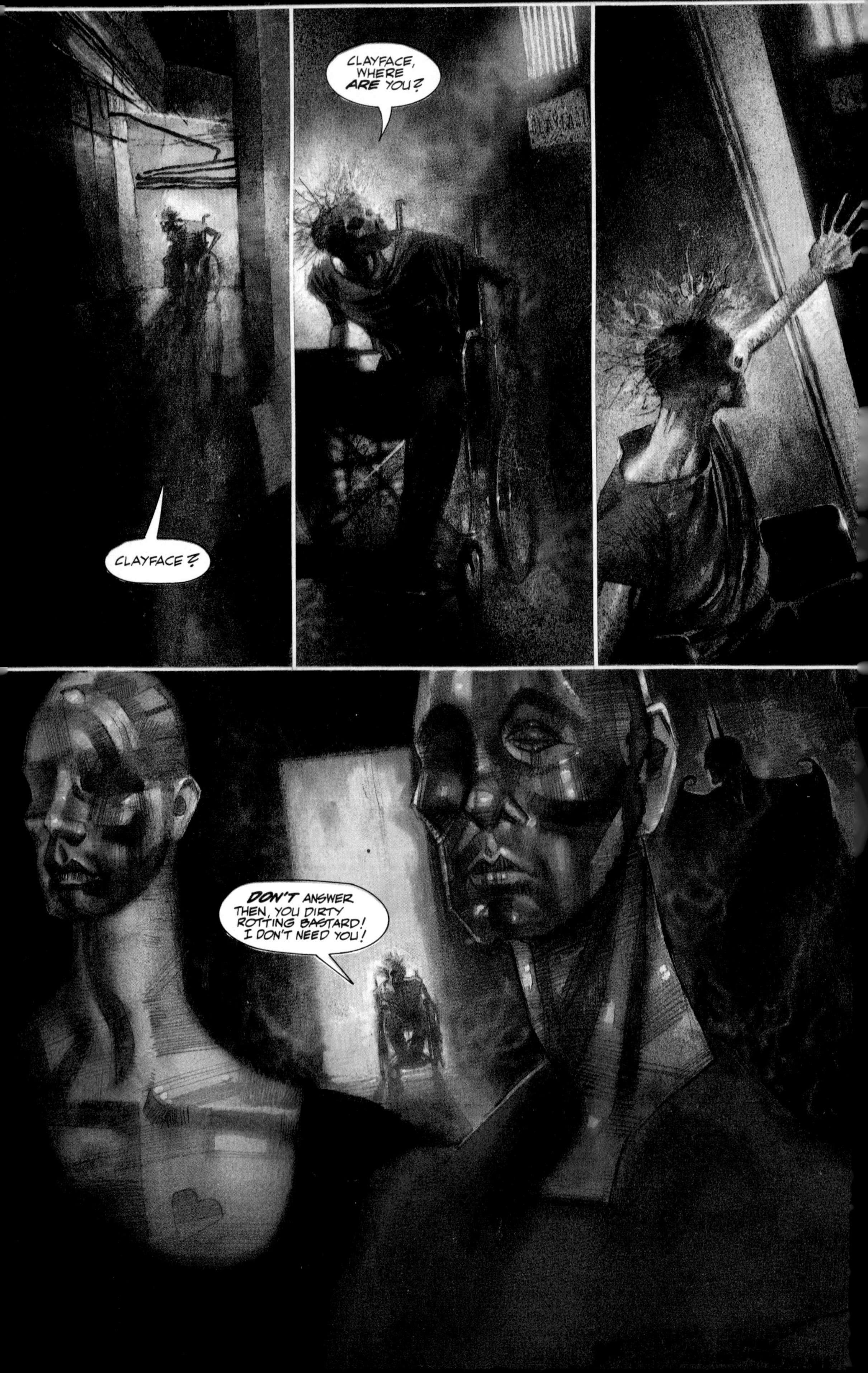
CLAYFACE?
CLAYFACE, WHERE ARE YOU?
DON'T ANSWER THEN, YOU DIRTY ROTTING BASTARD! I DON'T NEED YOU!

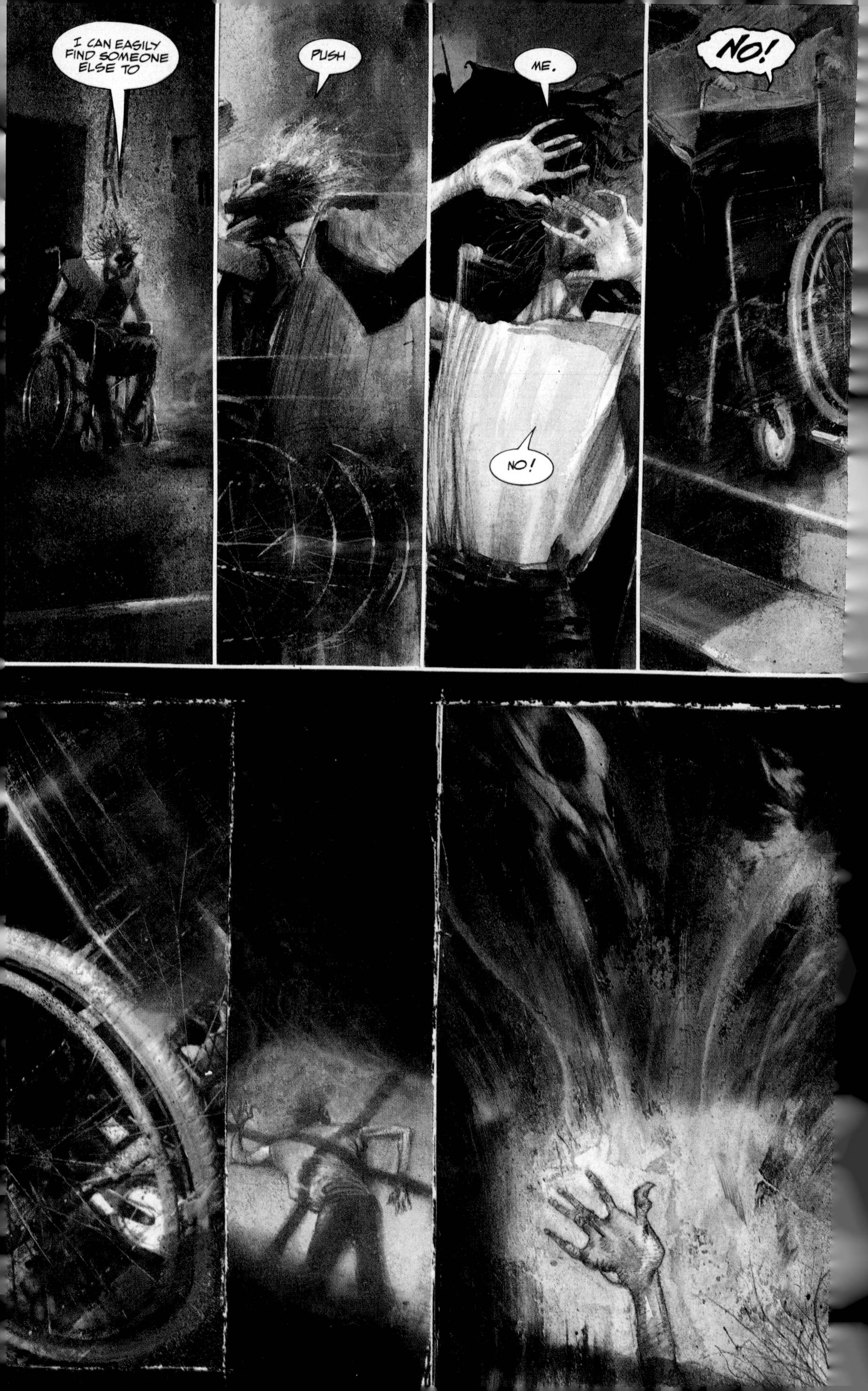
I CAN EASILY FIND SOMEONE ELSE TO
PUSH
ME.
NO!
NO!

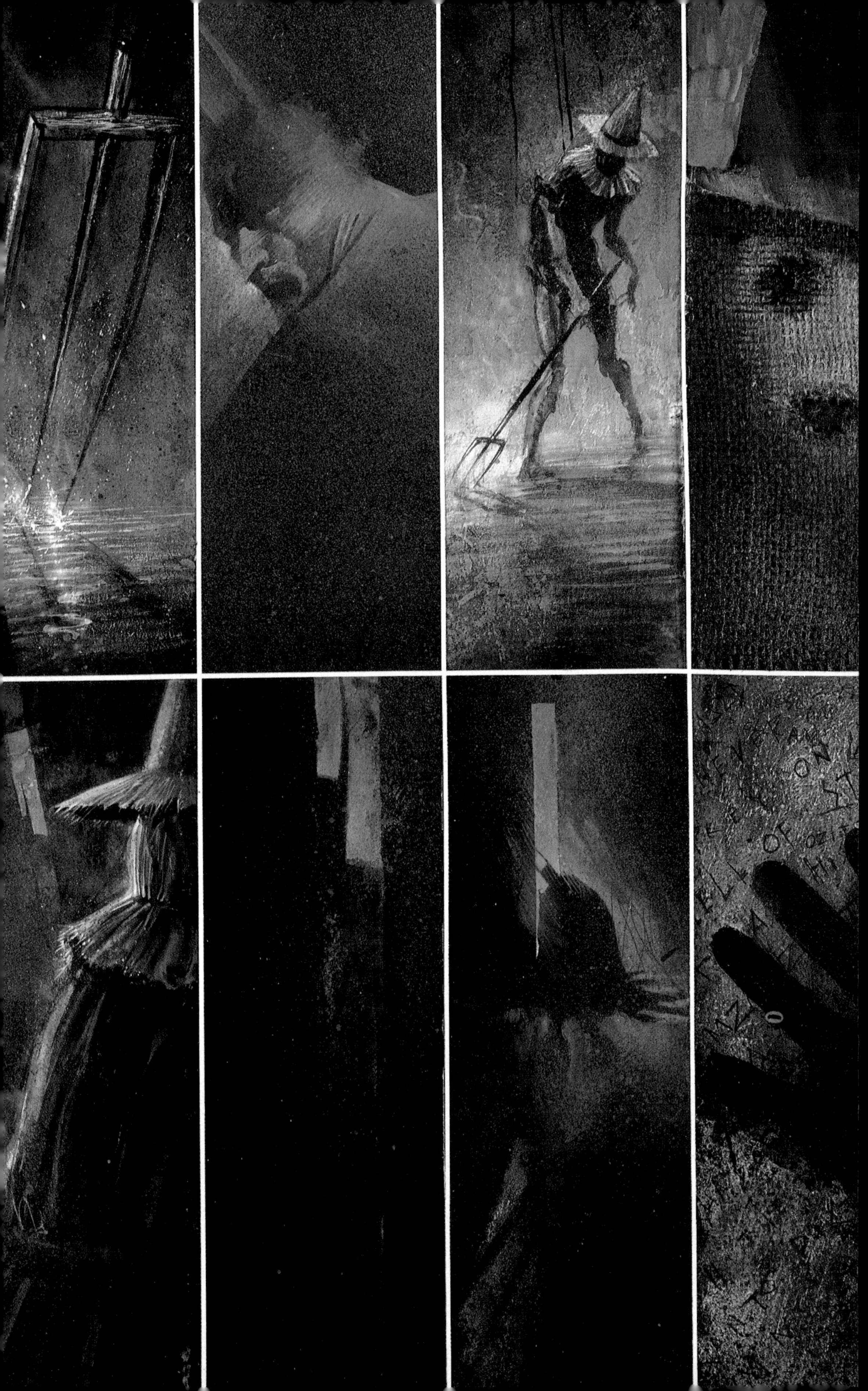

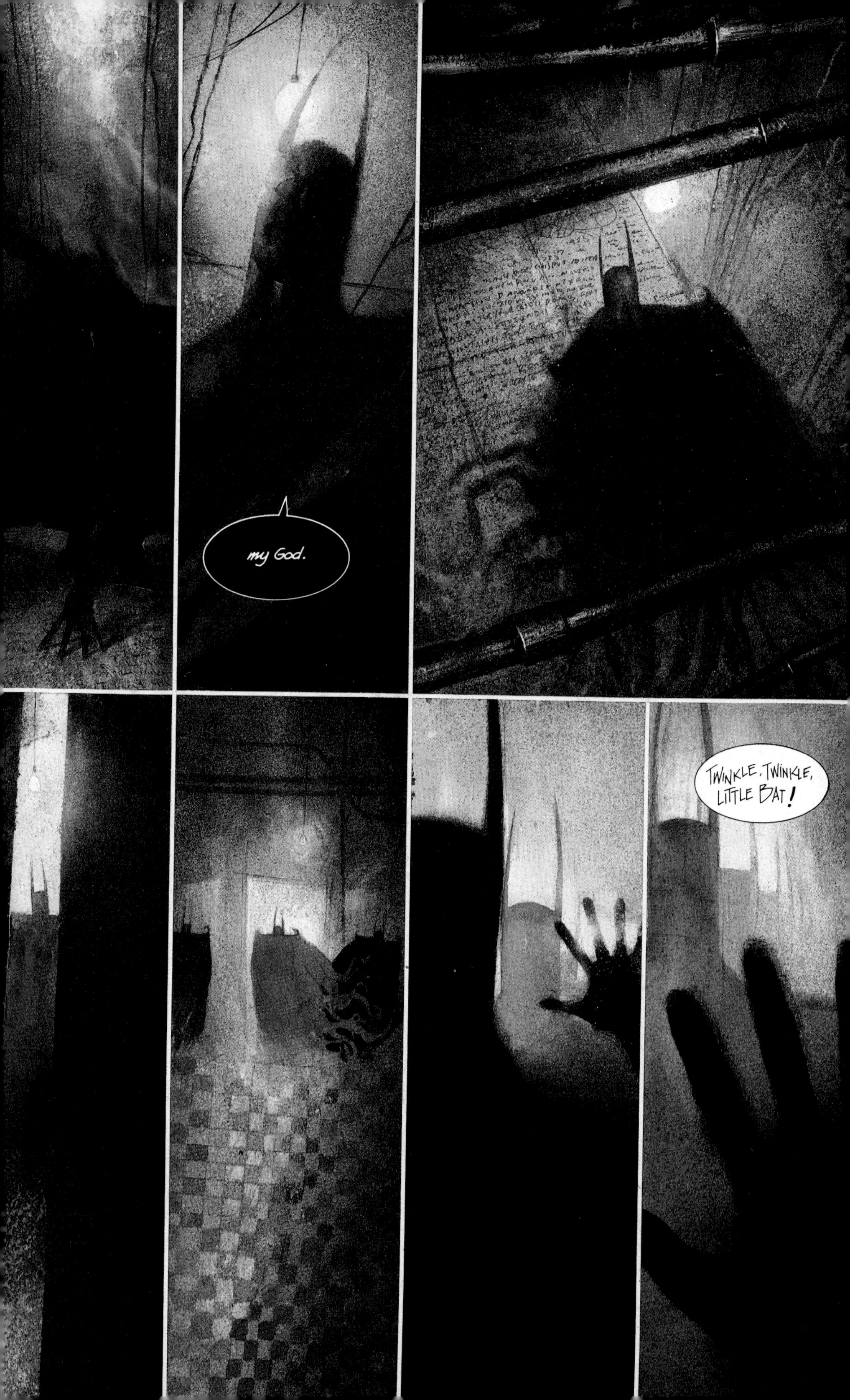
my God.
TWINKLE, TWINKLE, LITTLE BAT!

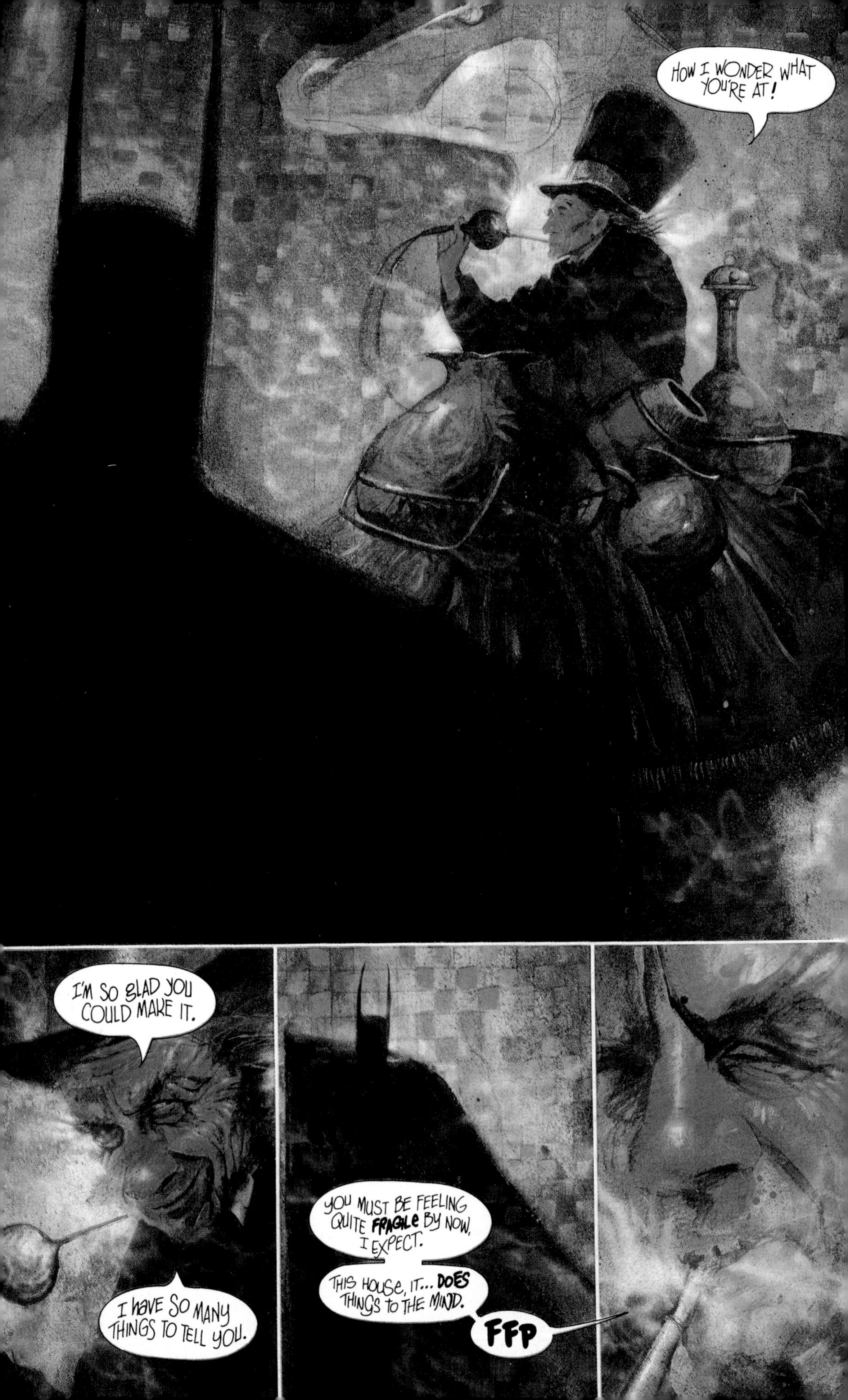
HOW I WONDER WHAT YOU'RE AT!
I'M SO GLAD YOU COULD MAKE IT.
I have SO MANY THINGS TO TELL YOU.
YOU MUST BE FEELING QUITE FRAGILE BY NOW, I EXPECT.
THIS HOUSE, IT... DOES THINGS TO THE MIND.
FFP

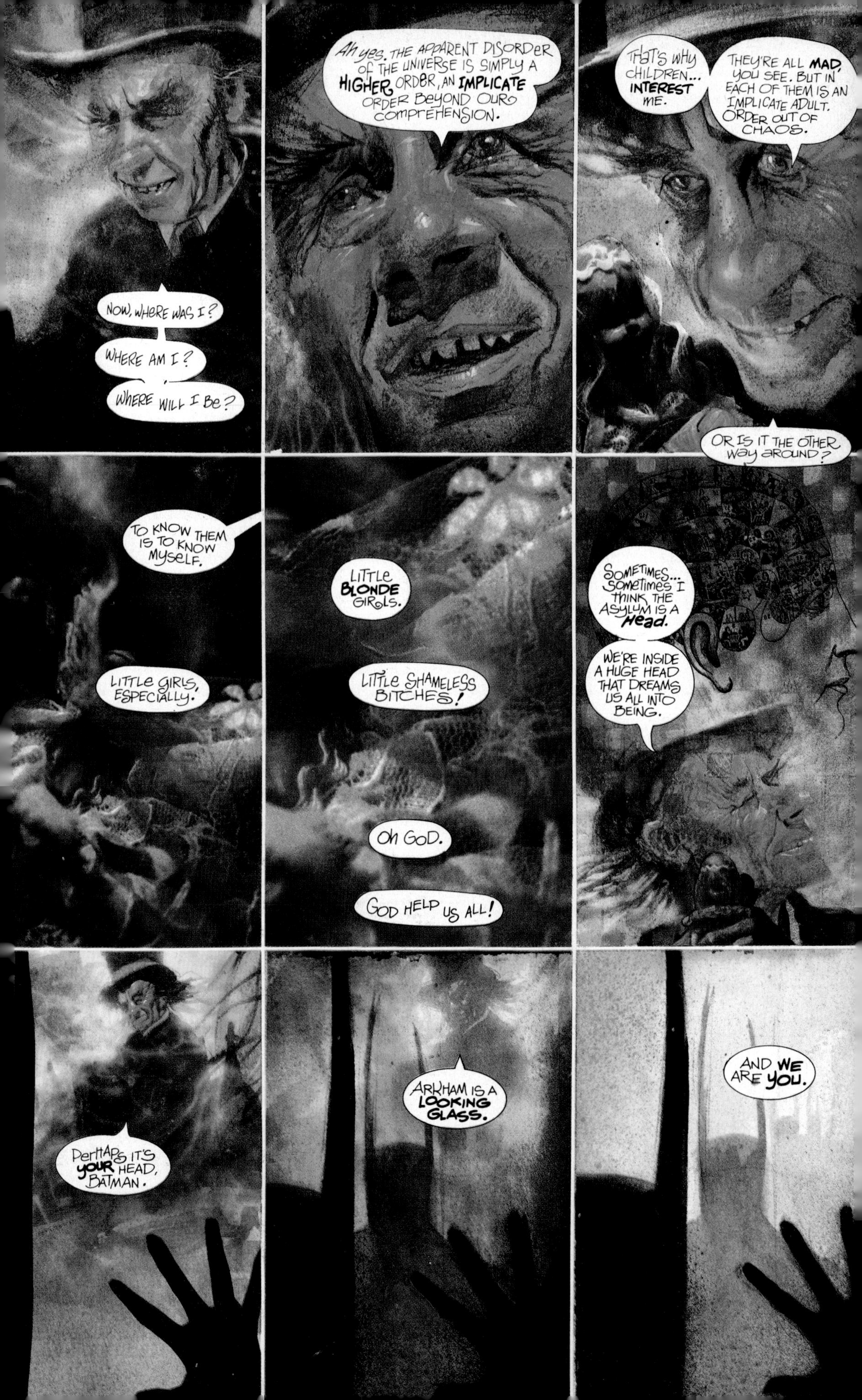
NOW, WHERE WAS I?
WHERE AM I?
WHERE WILL I BE?
Ah yes. THE APPARENT DISORDER OF THE UNIVERSE IS SIMPLY A HIGHER ORDER, AN IMPLICATE ORDER BEYOND OUR COMPREHENSION.
THAT'S WHY CHILDREN... INTEREST ME.
THEY'RE ALL MAD, YOU SEE. BUT IN EACH OF THEM IS AN IMPLICATE ADULT. ORDER OUT OF CHAOS.
OR IS IT THE OTHER WAY AROUND?
TO KNOW THEM IS TO KNOW MYSELF.
LITTLE GIRLS, ESPECIALLY.
LITTLE BLONDE GIRLS.
LITTLE SHAMELESS BITCHES!
Oh GOD.
GOD HELP US ALL!
SOMETIMES... SOMETIMES I THINK THE ASYLUM IS A HEAD.
WE'RE INSIDE A HUGE HEAD THAT DREAMS US ALL INTO BEING.
PERHAPS IT'S YOUR HEAD, BATMAN.
ARKHAM IS A LOOKING GLASS.
AND WE ARE YOU.

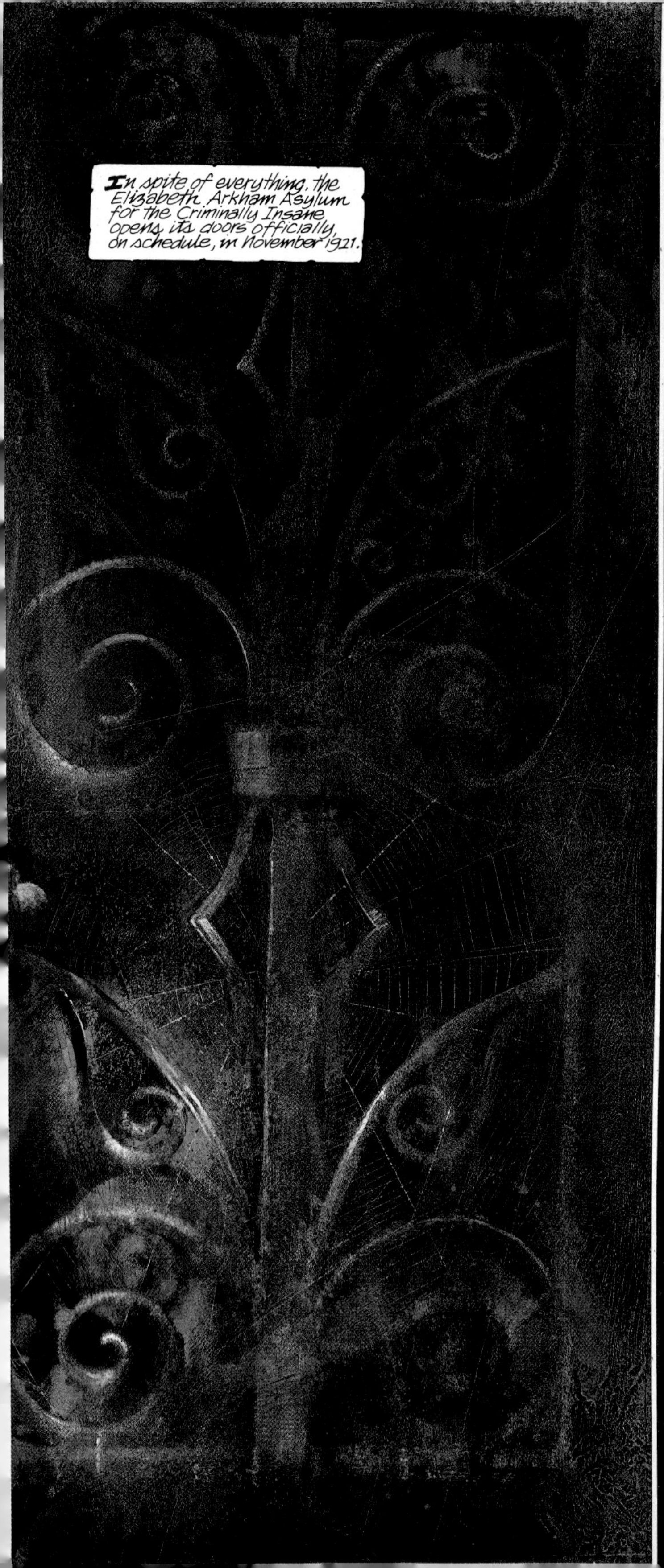
In spite of everything, the Elizabeth Arkham Asylum for the Criminally Insane opens its doors officially, on schedule, in November 1921.

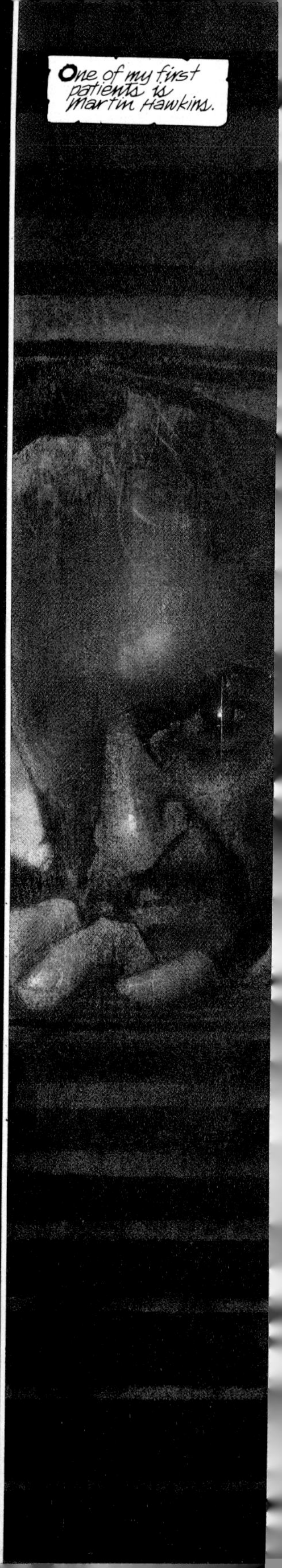
One of my first patients is Martin Hawkins.

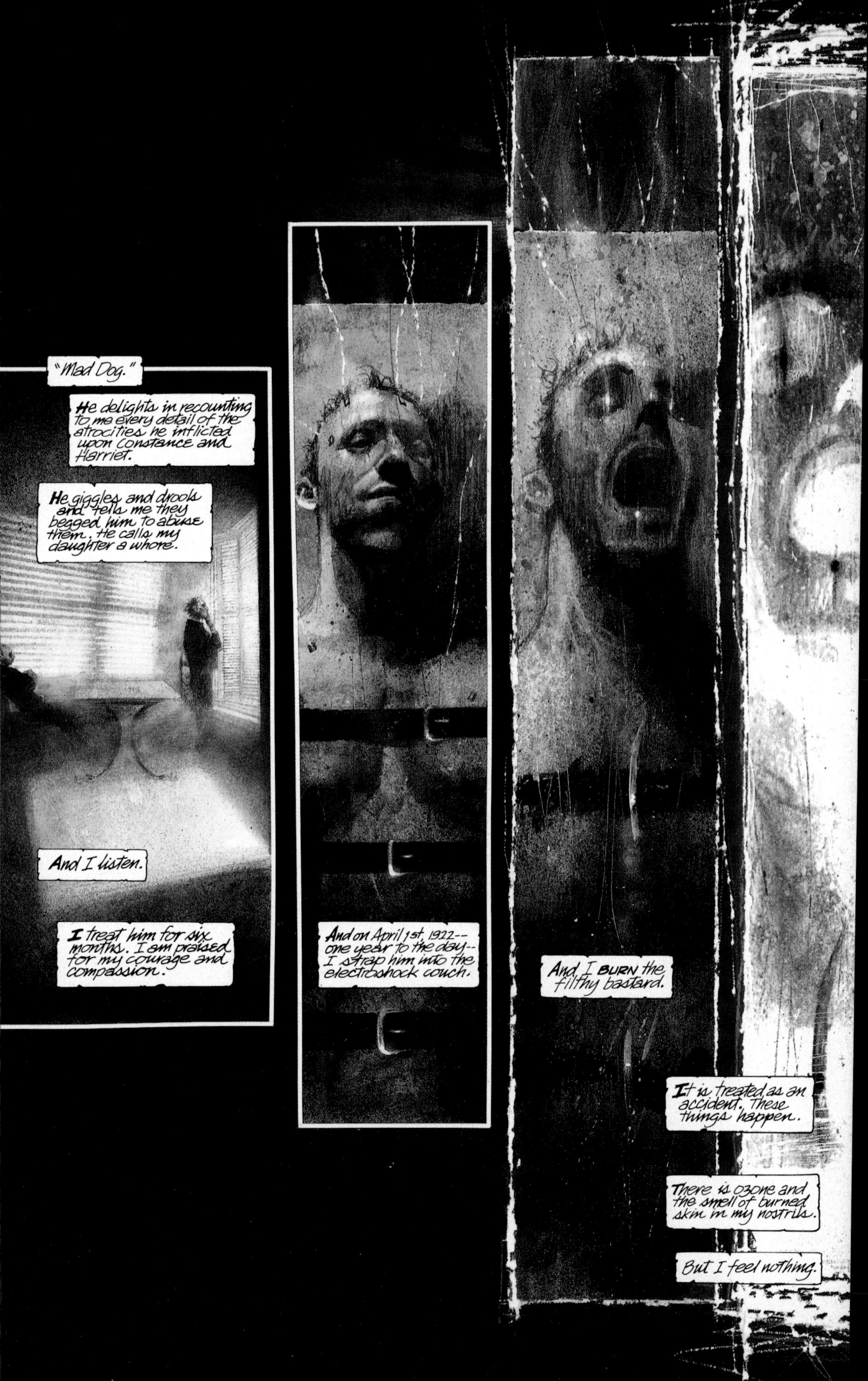
"Mad Dog."
He delights in recounting to me every detail of the atrocities he inflicted upon Constance and Harriet.
He giggles and drools and tells me they begged him to abuse them. He calls my daughter a whore.
And I listen.
I treat him for six months. I am praised for my courage and compassion.
And on April 1st, 1922-- one year to the day-- I strap him into the electroshock couch.
And I BURN the filthy bastard.
It is treated as an accident. These things happen.
There is ozone and the smell of burned skin in my nostrils.
But I feel nothing.

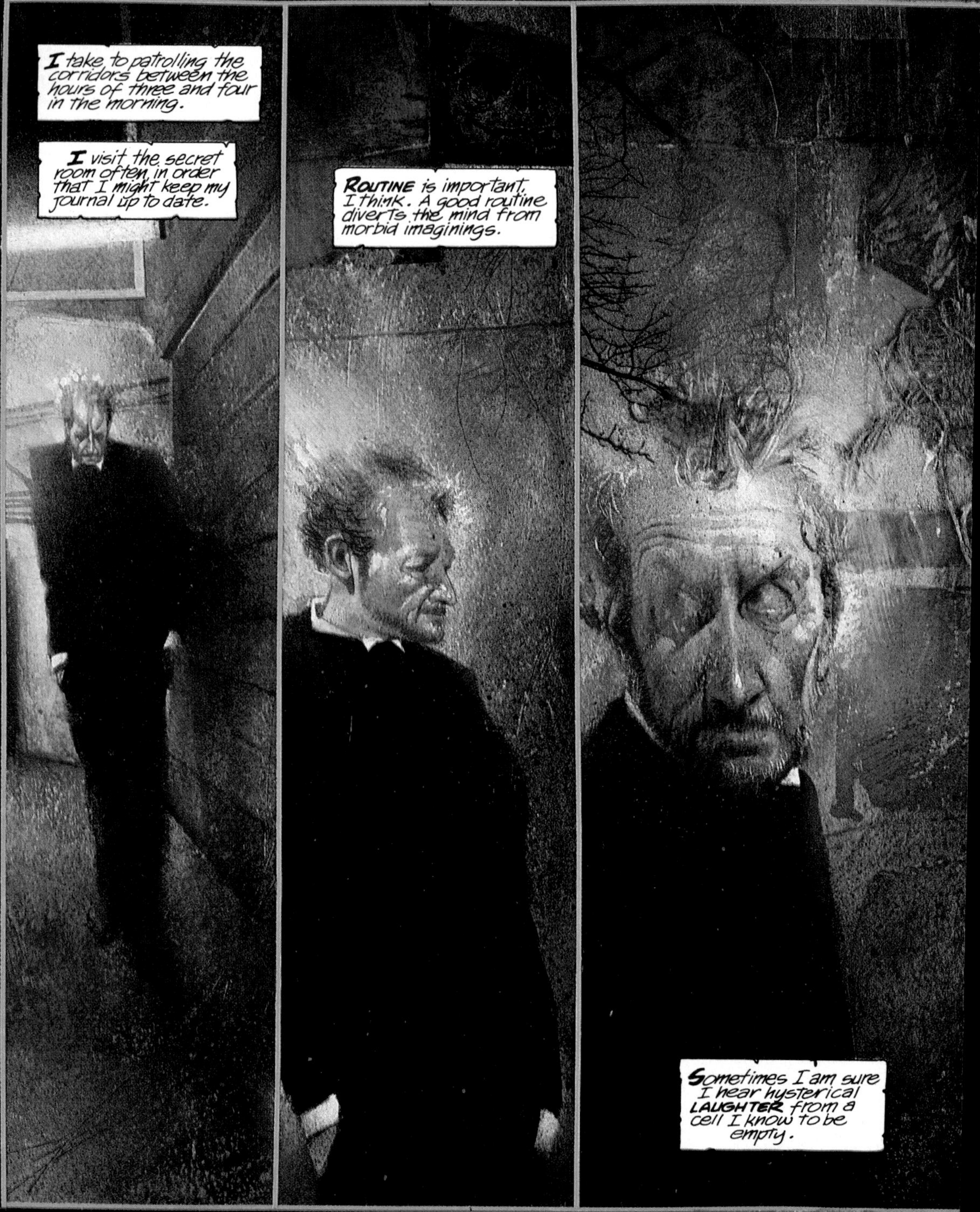
I take to patrolling the corridors between the hours of three and four in the morning.
I visit the secret room often in order that I might keep my journal up to date.
ROUTINE is important, I think. A good routine diverts the mind from morbid imaginings.
Sometimes I am sure I hear hysterical LAUGHTER from a cell I know to be empty.

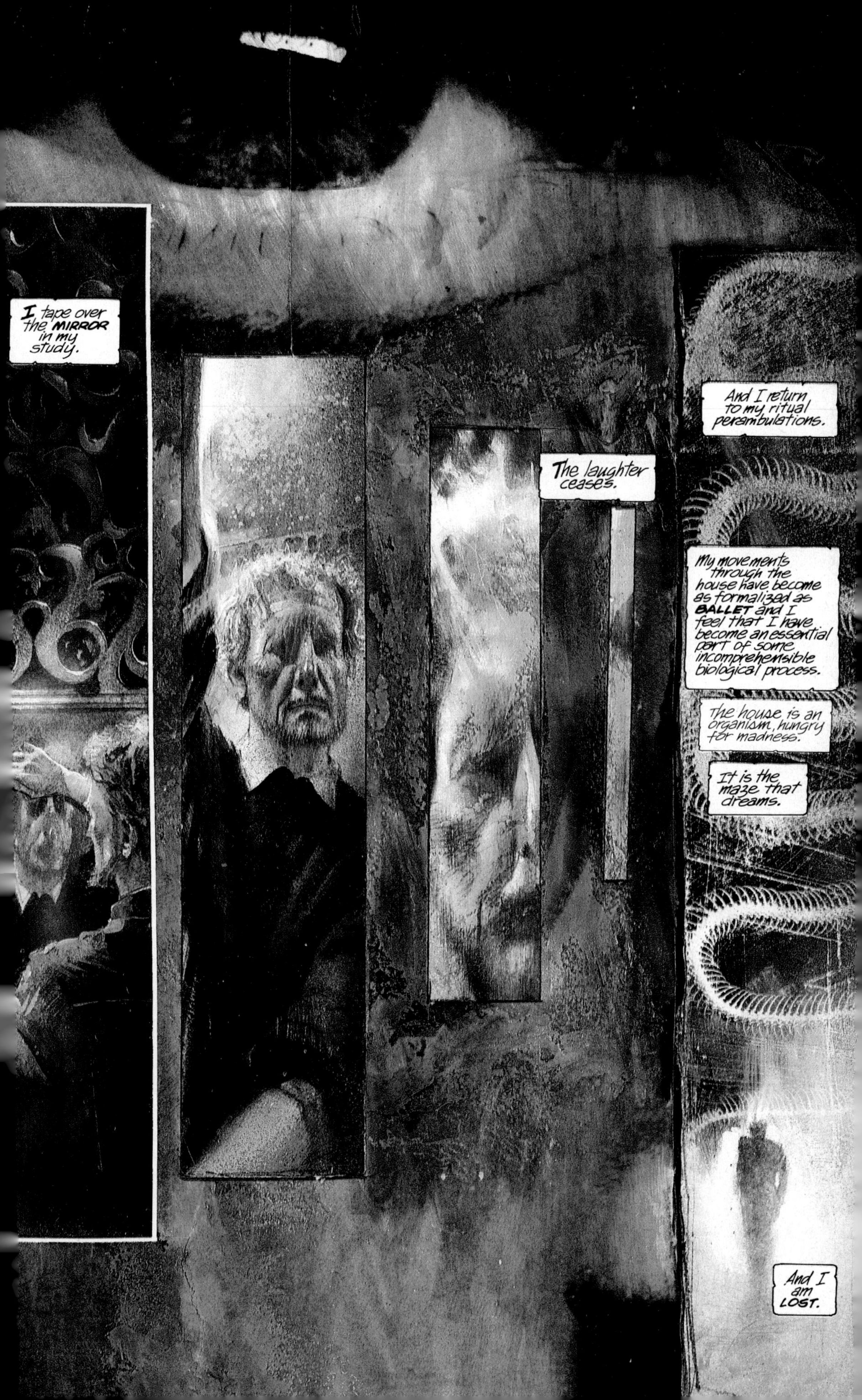
I tape over the MIRROR in my study.
The laughter ceases.
And I return to my ritual perambulations.
My movements through the house have become as formalized as BALLET and I feel that I have become an essential part of some incomprehensible biological process.
The house is an organism, hungry for madness.
It is the maze that dreams.
And I am LOST.

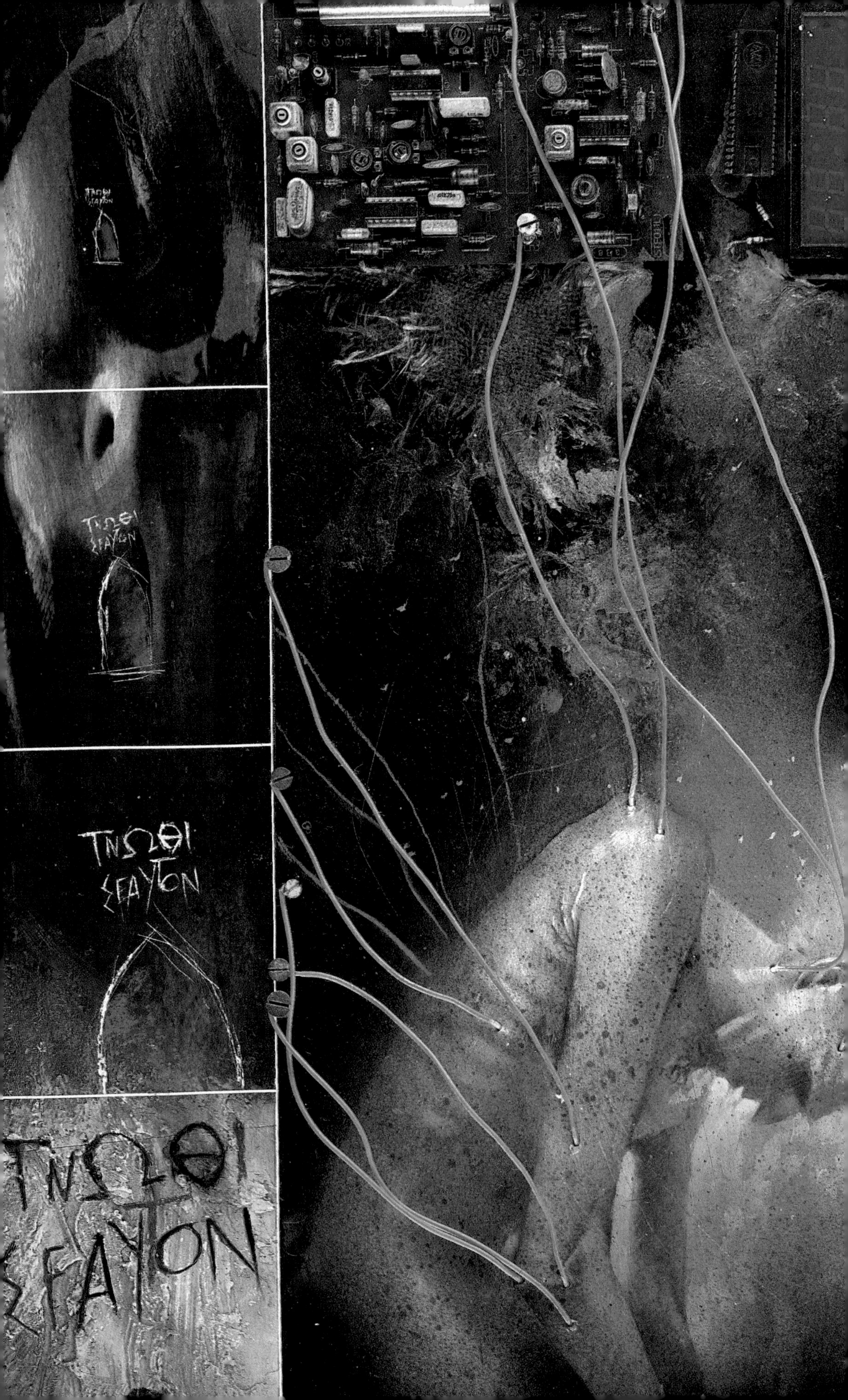
ΓΝΩΘΙ
ΣΕΑΥΤΟΝ
ΓΝΩΘΙ
ΣΕΑΥΤΟΝ
ΓΝΩΘΙ
ΣΕΑΥΤΟΝ

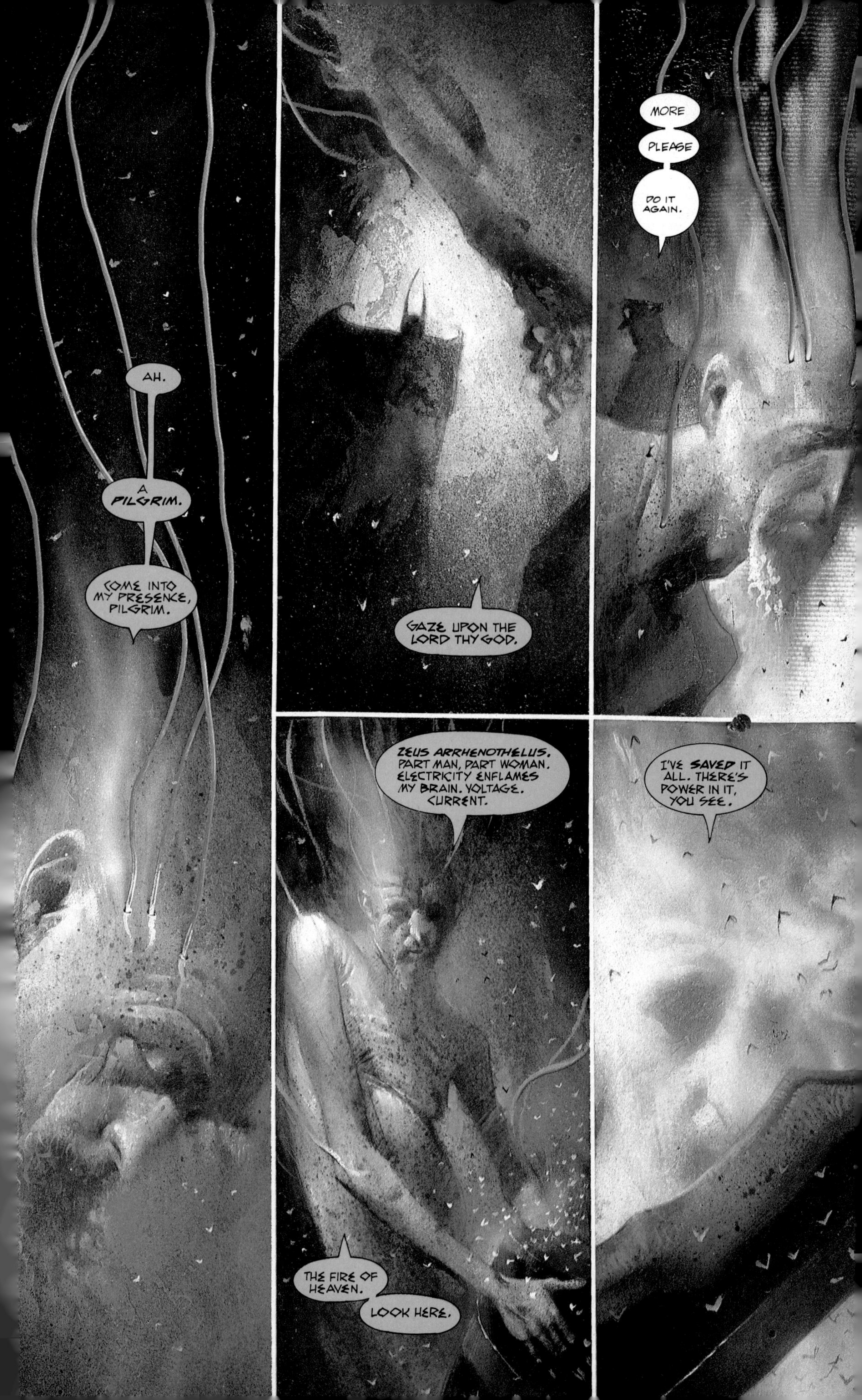
AH.
A PILGRIM.
COME INTO MY PRESENCE, PILGRIM.
GAZE UPON THE LORD THY GOD.
MORE
PLEASE
DO IT AGAIN.
ZEUS ARRHENOTHELUS. PART MAN, PART WOMAN. ELECTRICITY ENFLAMES MY BRAIN. VOLTAGE. CURRENT.
THE FIRE OF HEAVEN.
LOOK HERE.
I'VE SAVED IT ALL. THERE'S POWER IN IT, YOU SEE.

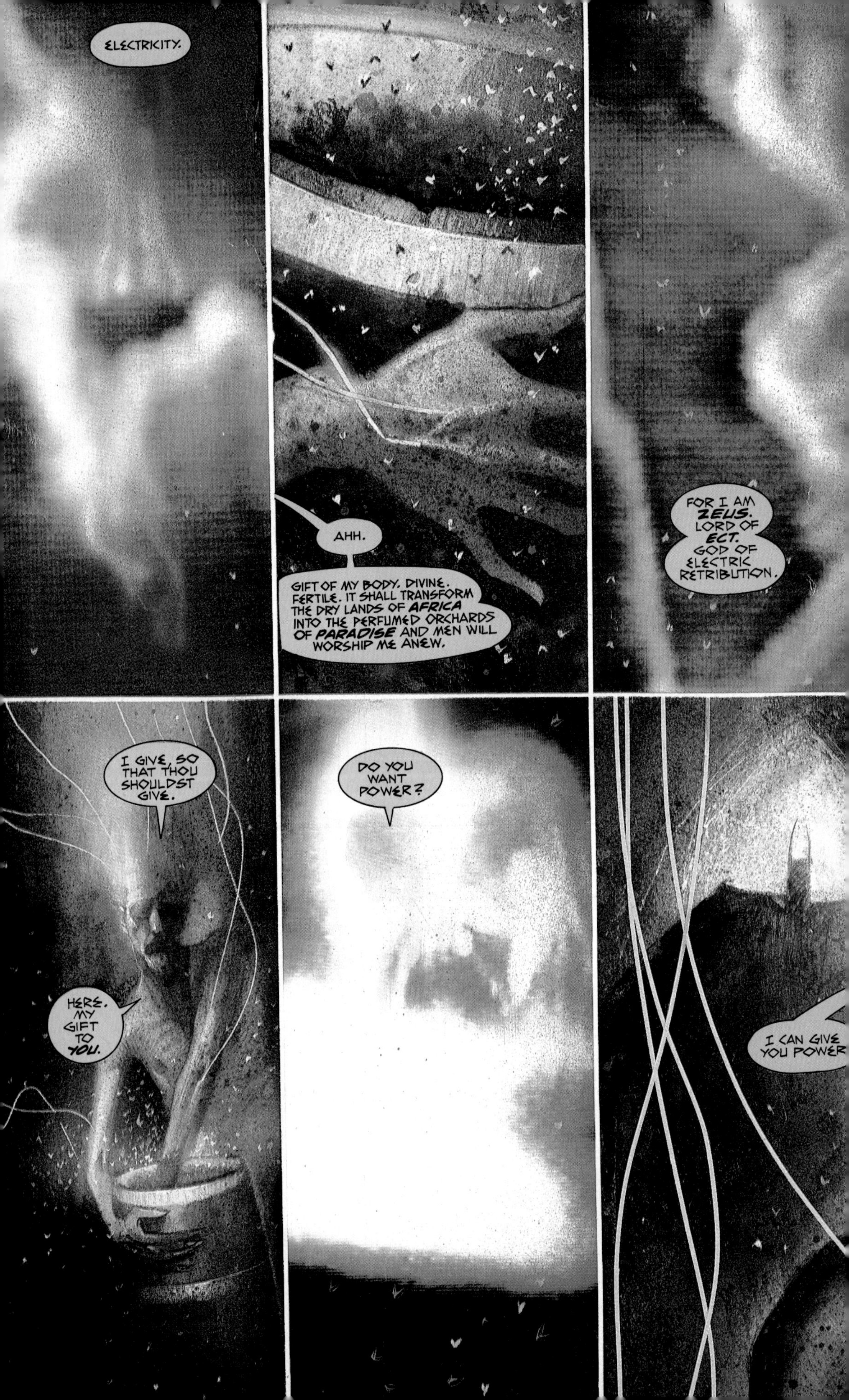
ELECTRICITY.
AHH.
GIFT OF MY BODY. DIVINE. FERTILE. IT SHALL TRANSFORM THE DRY LANDS OF AFRICA INTO THE PERFUMED ORCHARDS OF PARADISE AND MEN WILL WORSHIP ME ANEW.
FOR I AM ZEUS. LORD OF ECT.
GOD OF ELECTRIC RETRIBUTION.
I GIVE, SO THAT THOU SHOULDST GIVE.
HERE. MY GIFT TO YOU.
DO YOU WANT POWER?
I CAN GIVE YOU POWER

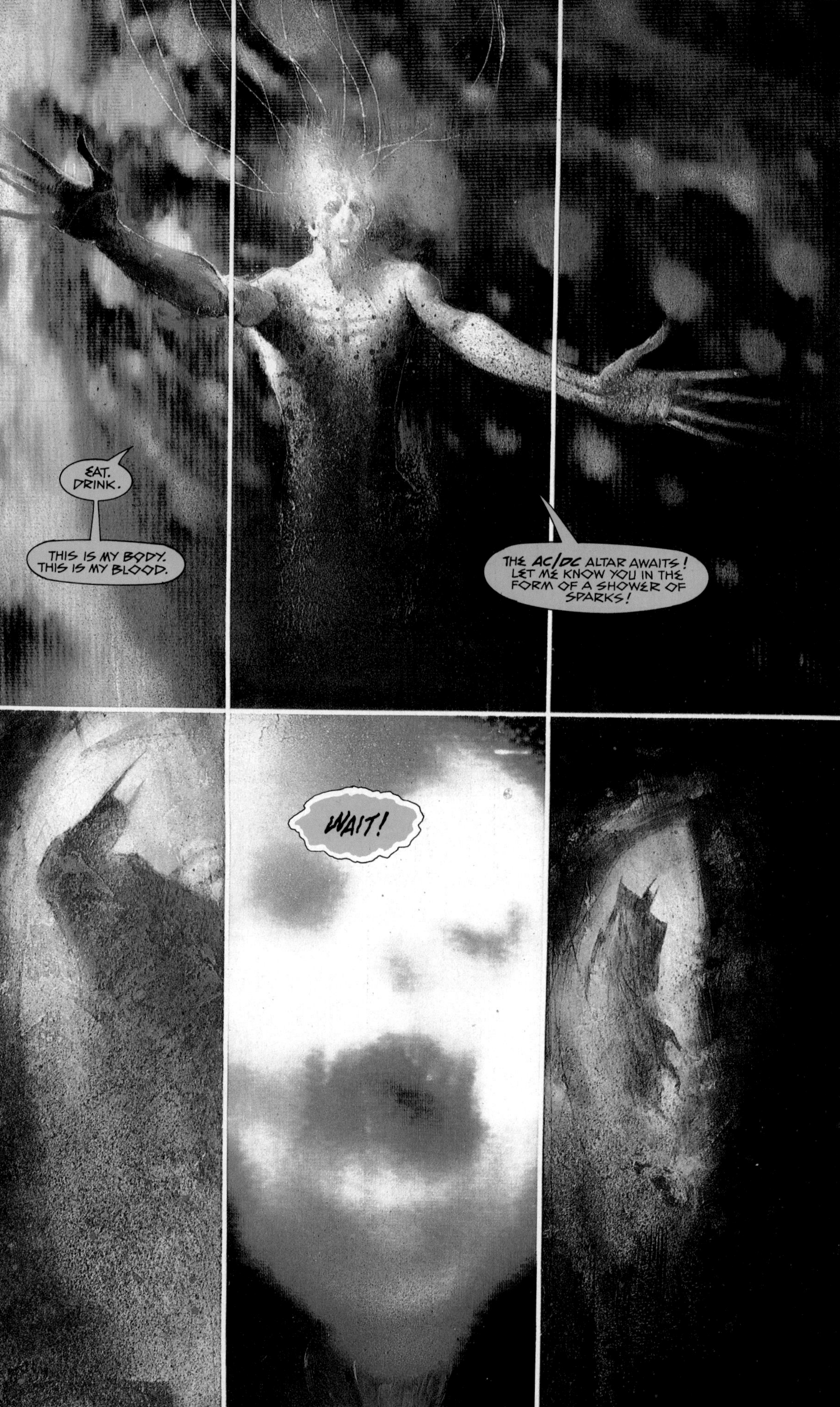
EAT. DRINK.
THIS IS MY BODY. THIS IS MY BLOOD.
THE AC/DC ALTAR AWAITS! LET ME KNOW YOU IN THE FORM OF A SHOWER OF SPARKS!
WAIT!

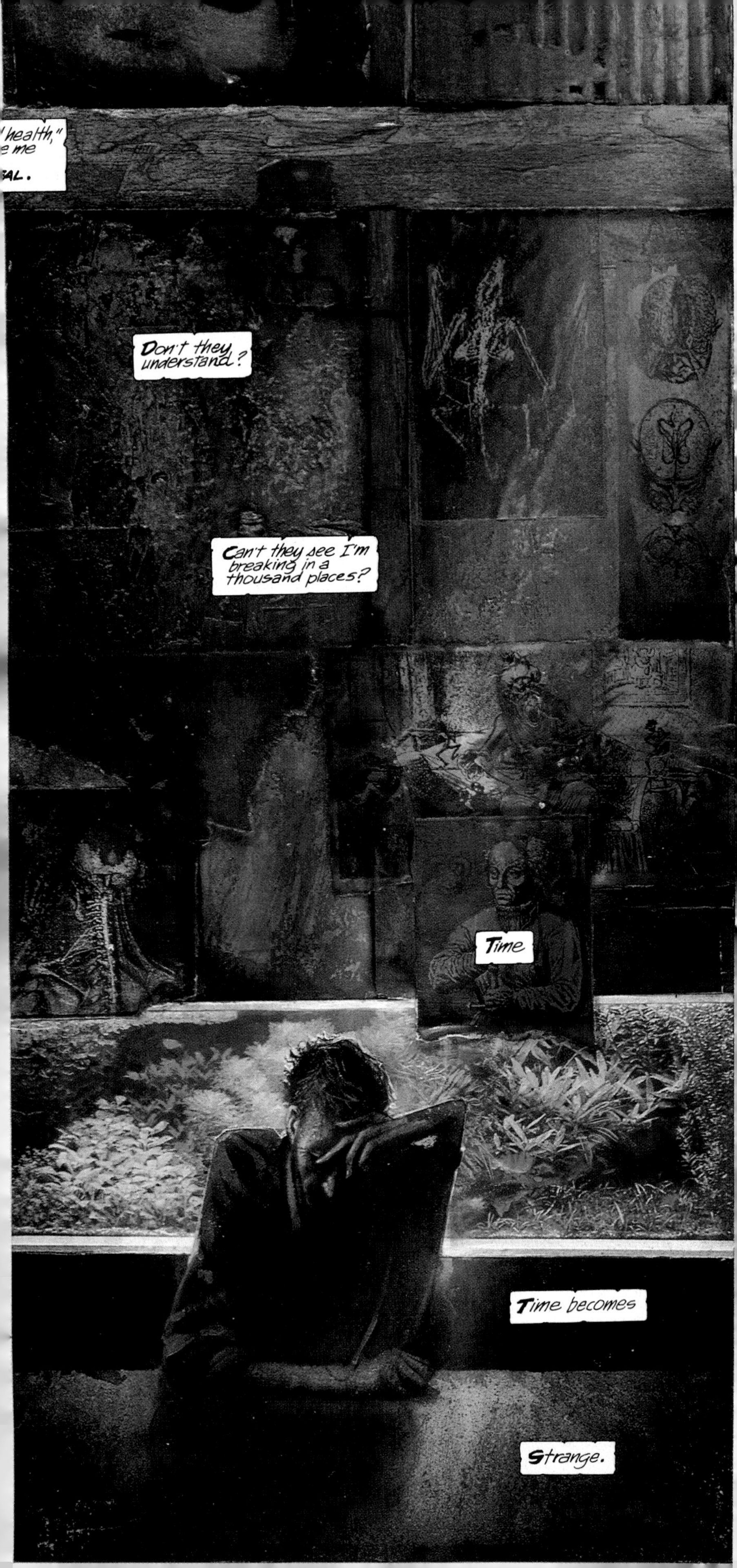
health,"
Don't they understand?
Can't they see I'm breaking in a thousand places?
Time
Time becomes
Strange.

Forty minutes have passed since I ingested three portions of the **AMANITA** mushroom.

So far, no effect.

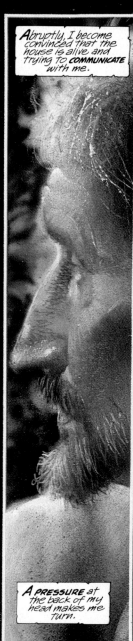

Abruptly, I become convinced that the house is alive and trying to **COMMUNICATE** with me.

A **PRESSURE** at the back of my head makes me turn.

In their tiny, contained universe, two vast and shimmering clown fish glide toward one another.

And make the sign of **PISCES.**

PISCES!
The astrological attribution of the moon card in the Tarot pack!

The symbol of trial and initiation. Death and rebirth.

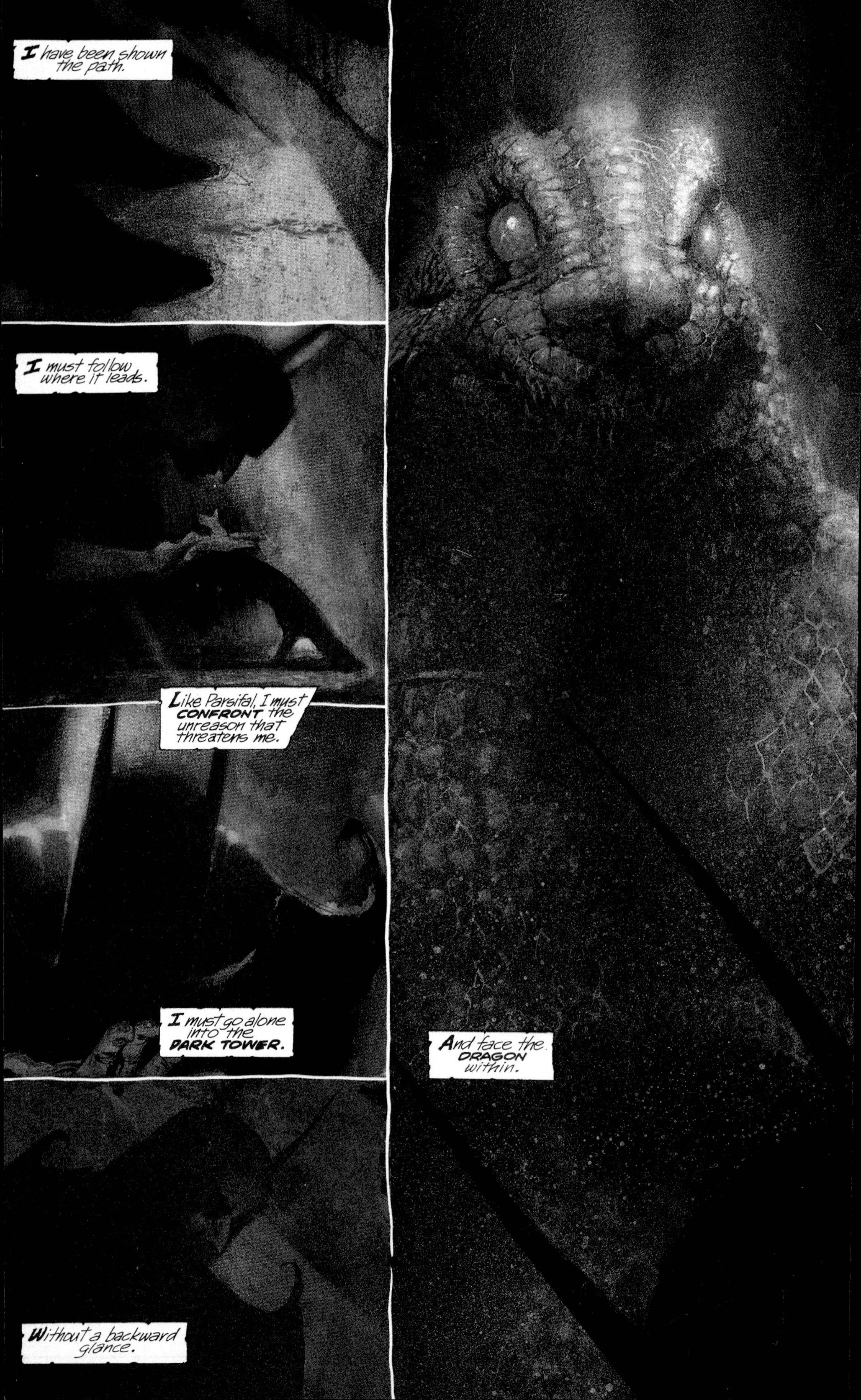
I have been shown the path.
I must follow where it leads.
Like Parsifal, I must CONFRONT the unreason that threatens me.
I must go alone into the DARK TOWER.
Without a backward glance.
And face the DRAGON within.

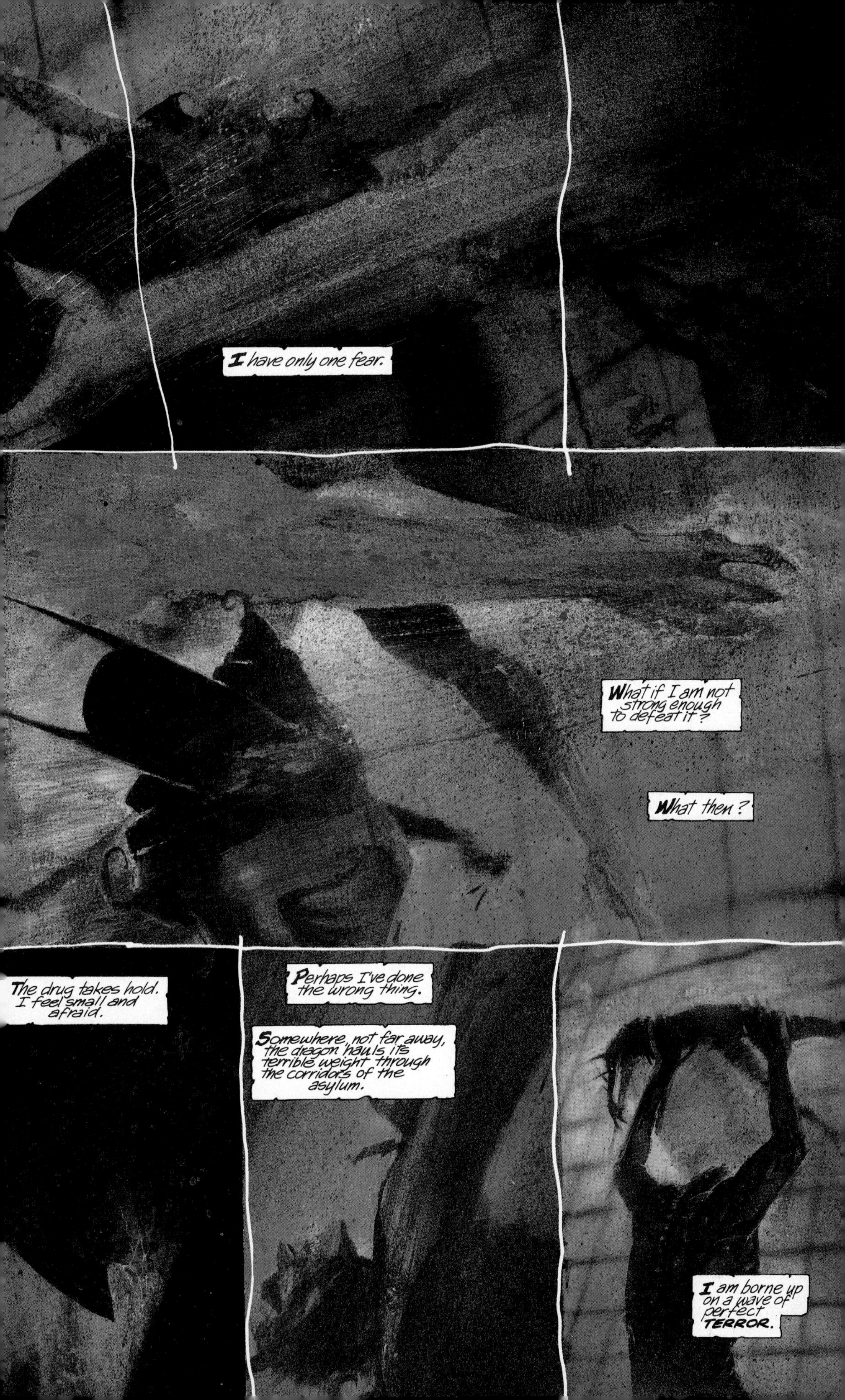
I have only one fear.
What if I am not strong enough to defeat it?
What then?
The drug takes hold. I feel small and afraid.
Perhaps I've done the wrong thing.
Somewhere, not far away, the dragon hauls its terrible weight through the corridors of the asylum.
I am borne up on a wave of perfect TERROR.

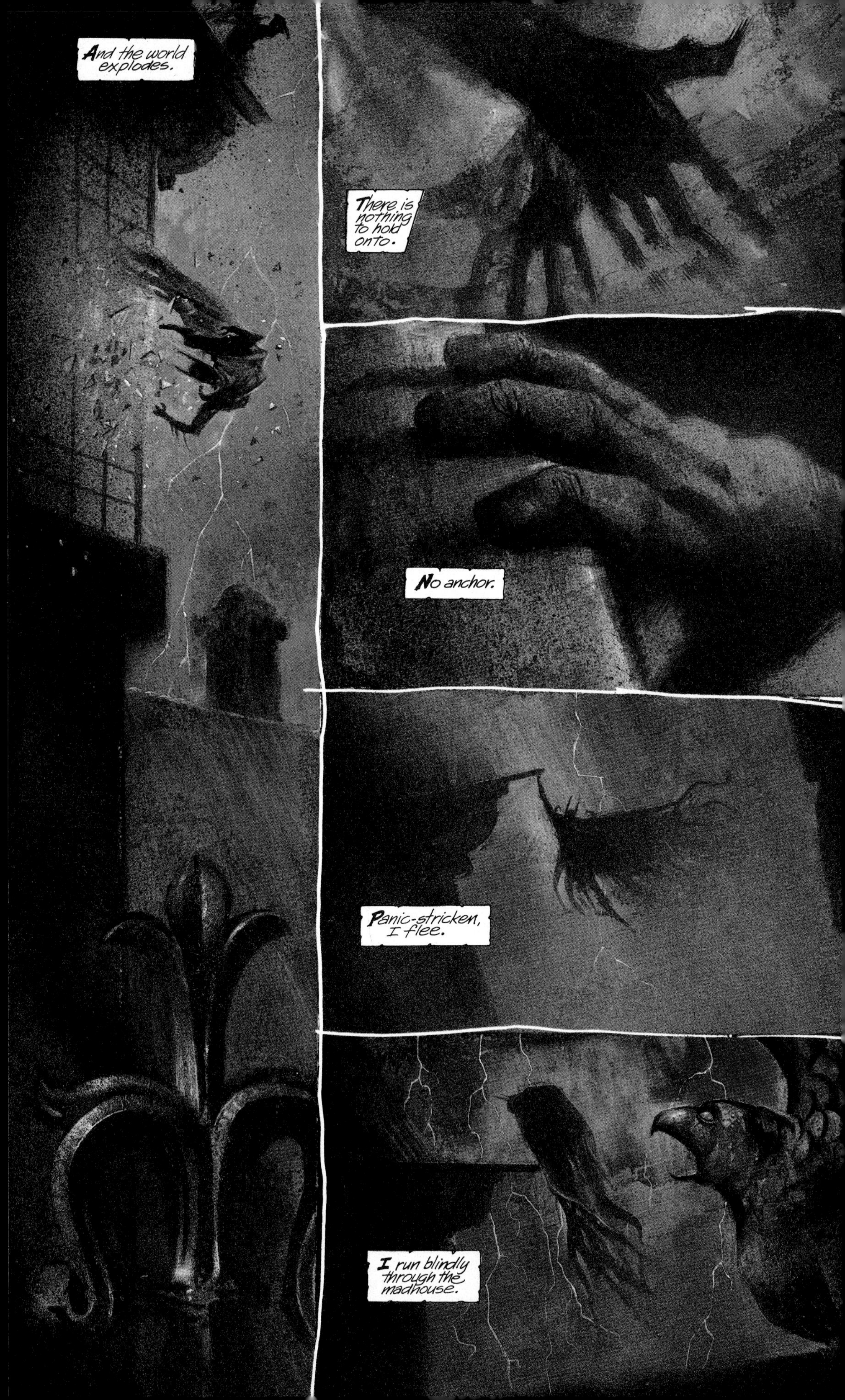
And the world explodes.
There is nothing to hold onto.
No anchor.
Panic-stricken, I flee.
I run blindly through the madhouse.

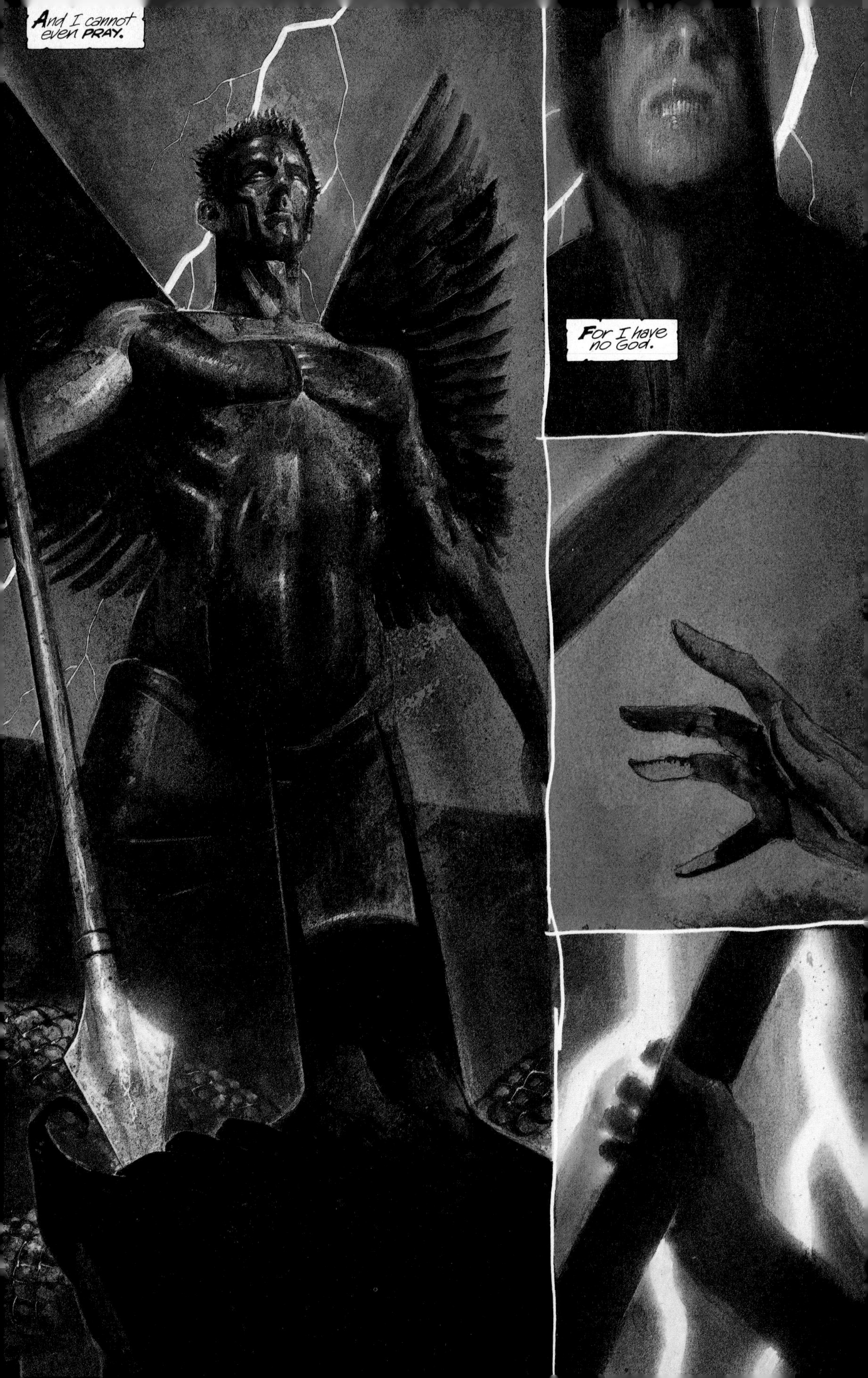
And I cannot even PRAY.
For I have no God.

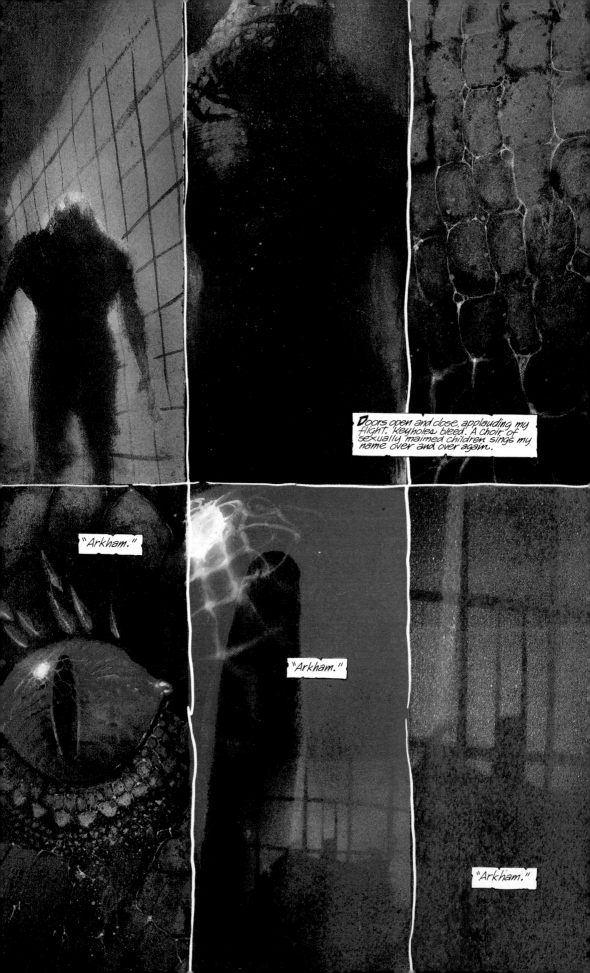

Doors open and close, applauding my flight. Keyholes bleed. A choir of sexually maimed children sings my name over and over again.

"Arkham."

"Arkham."

"Arkham."

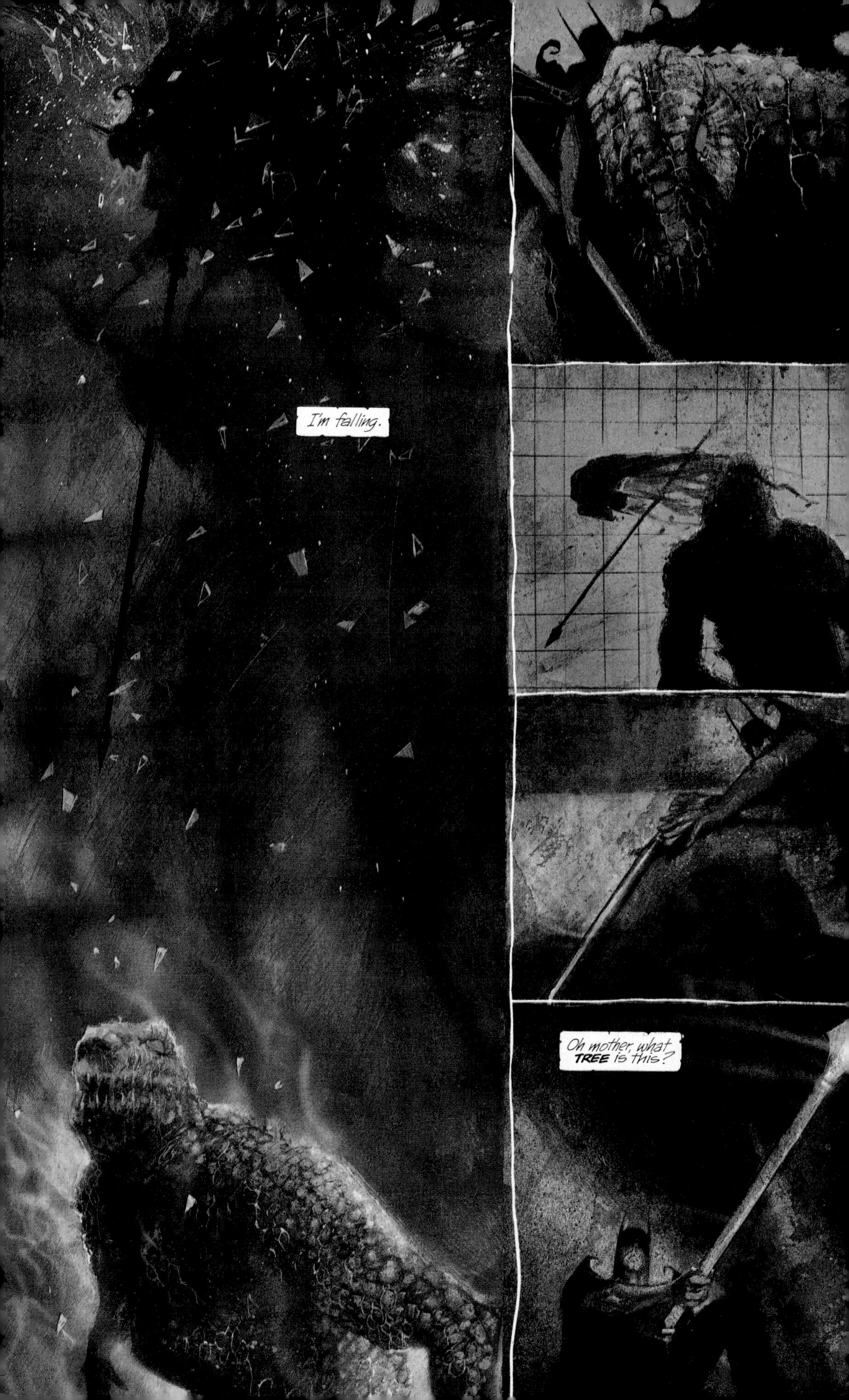
I'm falling.
Oh mother, what TREE is this?

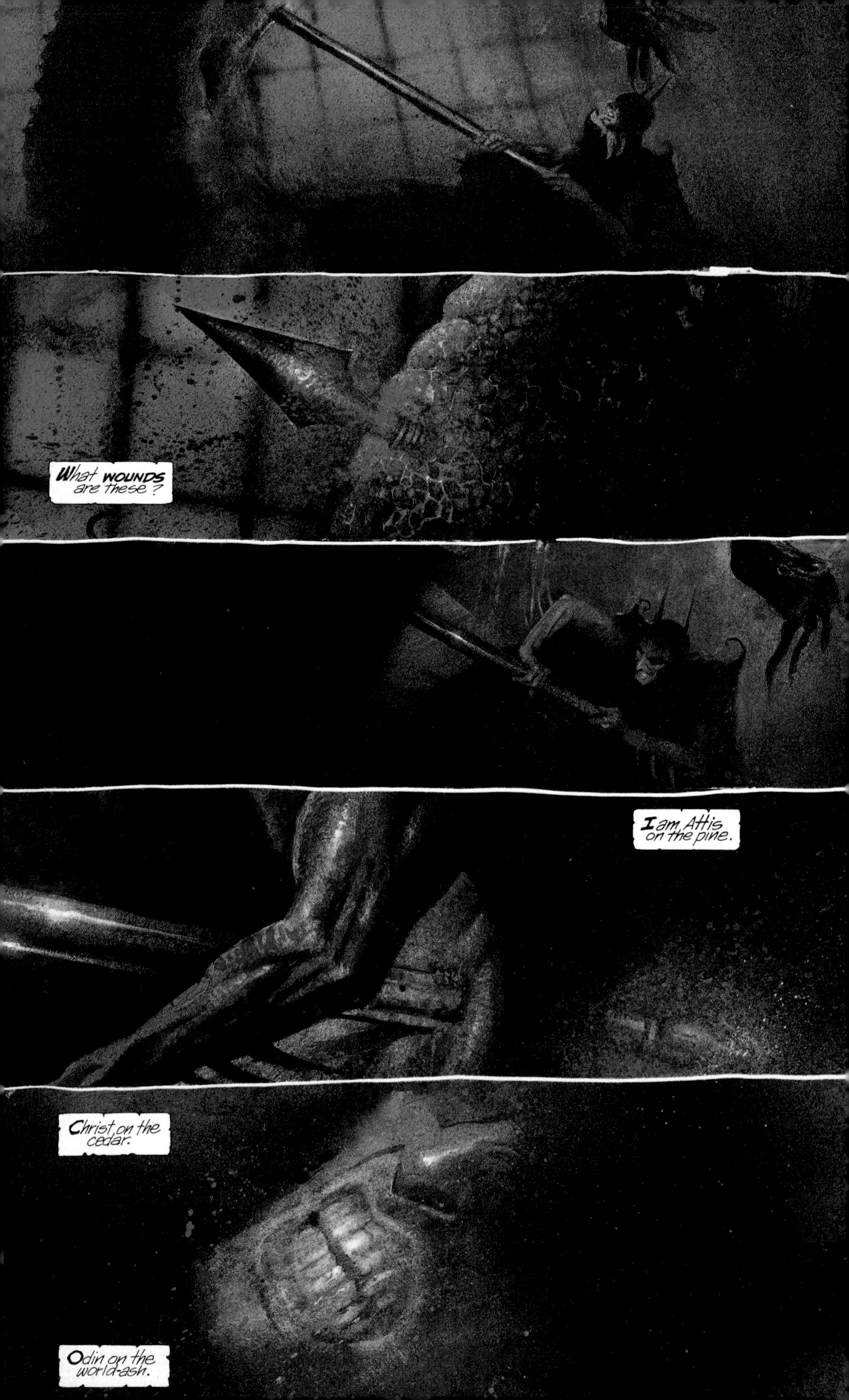
What WOUNDS are these?
I am Attis on the pine.
Christ on the cedar.
Odin on the world-ash.

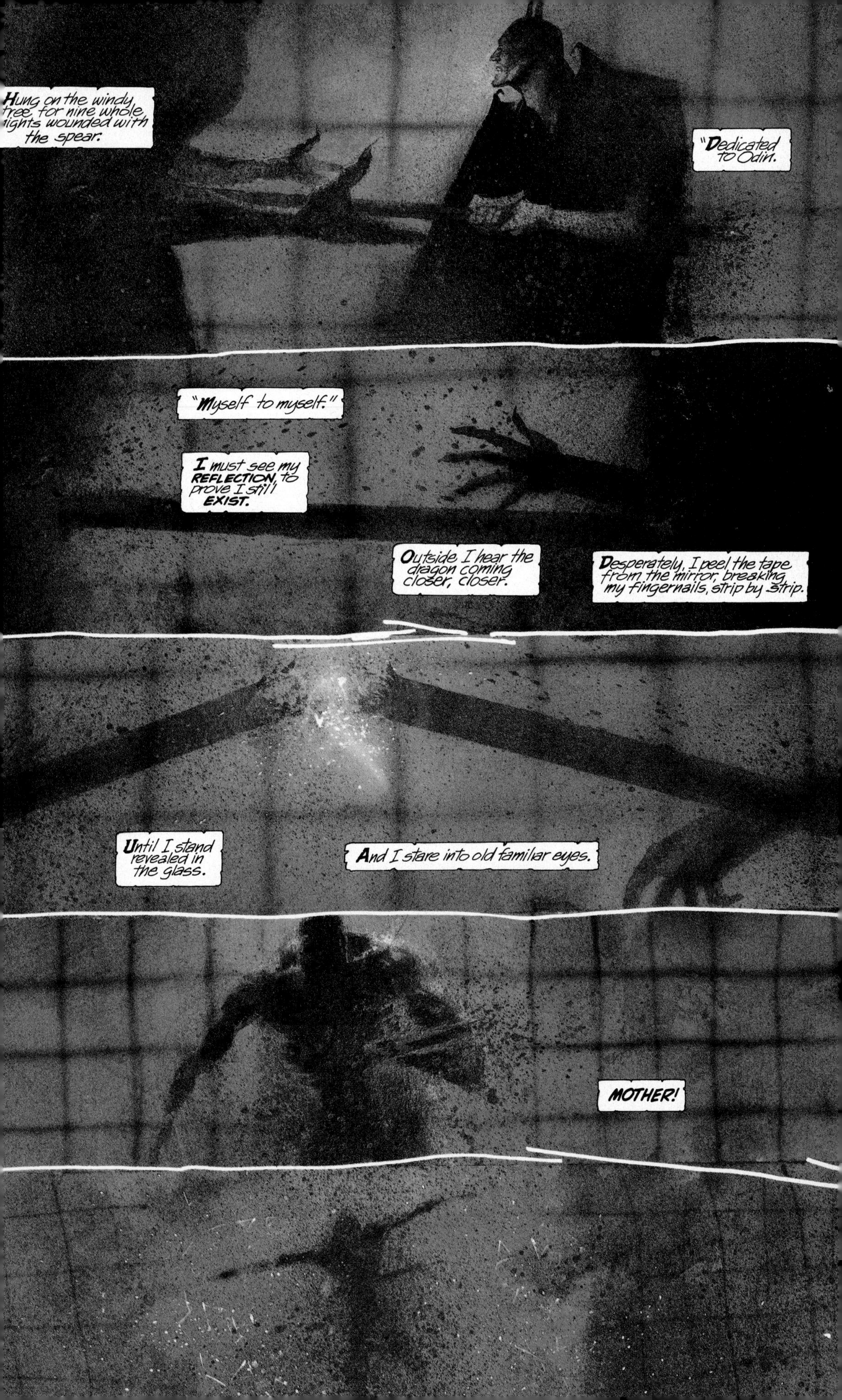
Hung on the windy tree, for nine whole nights wounded with the spear.
"Dedicated to Odin.
"Myself to myself."
I must see my REFLECTION, to prove I still EXIST.
Outside I hear the dragon coming closer, closer.
Desperately, I peel the tape from the mirror, breaking my fingernails, strip by strip.
Until I stand revealed in the glass.
And I stare into old familiar eyes.
MOTHER!

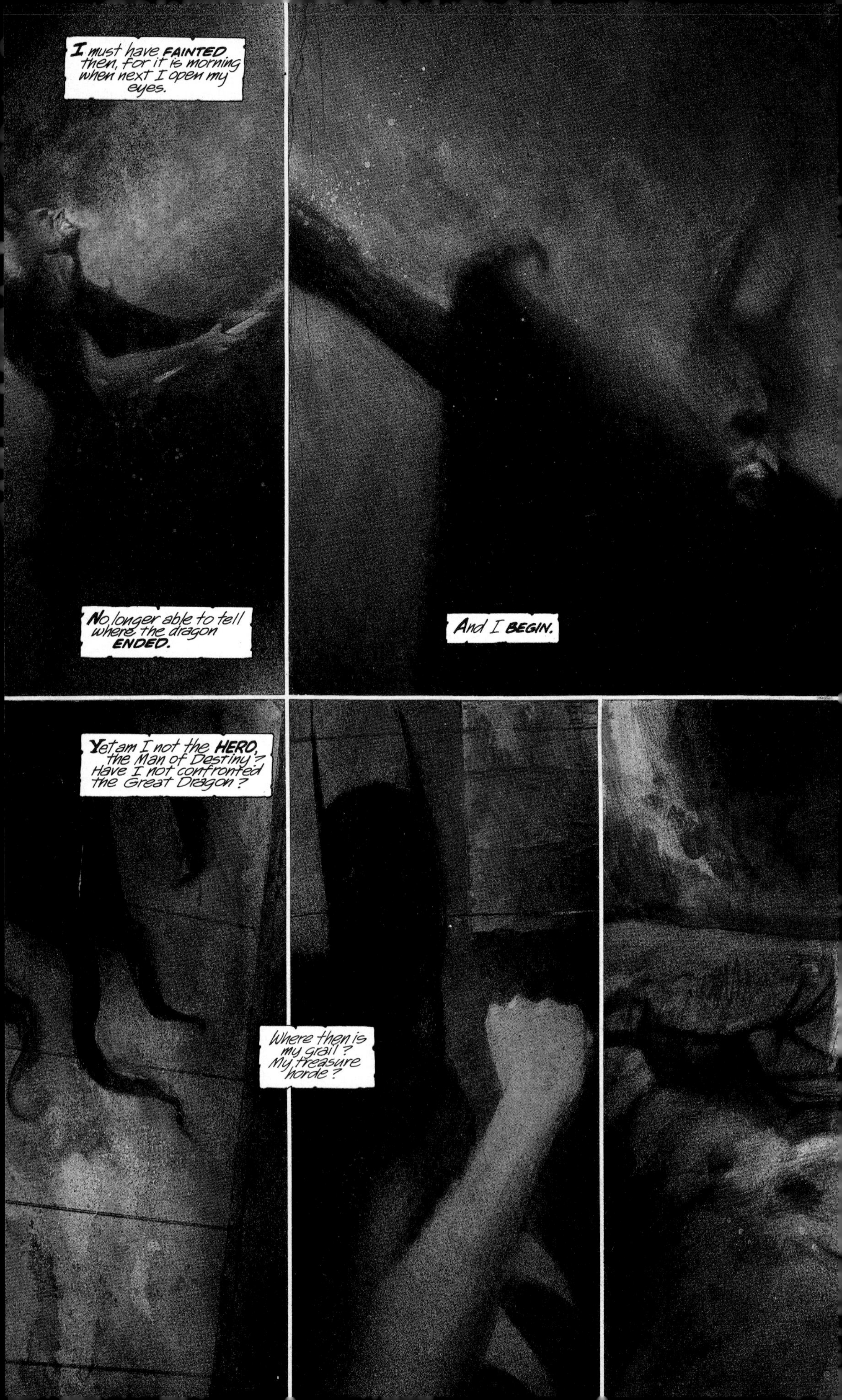
I must have FAINTED then, for it is morning when next I open my eyes.
No longer able to tell where the dragon ENDED.
And I BEGIN.
Yet am I not the HERO, the Man of Destiny? Have I not confronted the Great Dragon?
Where then is my grail? My treasure horde?

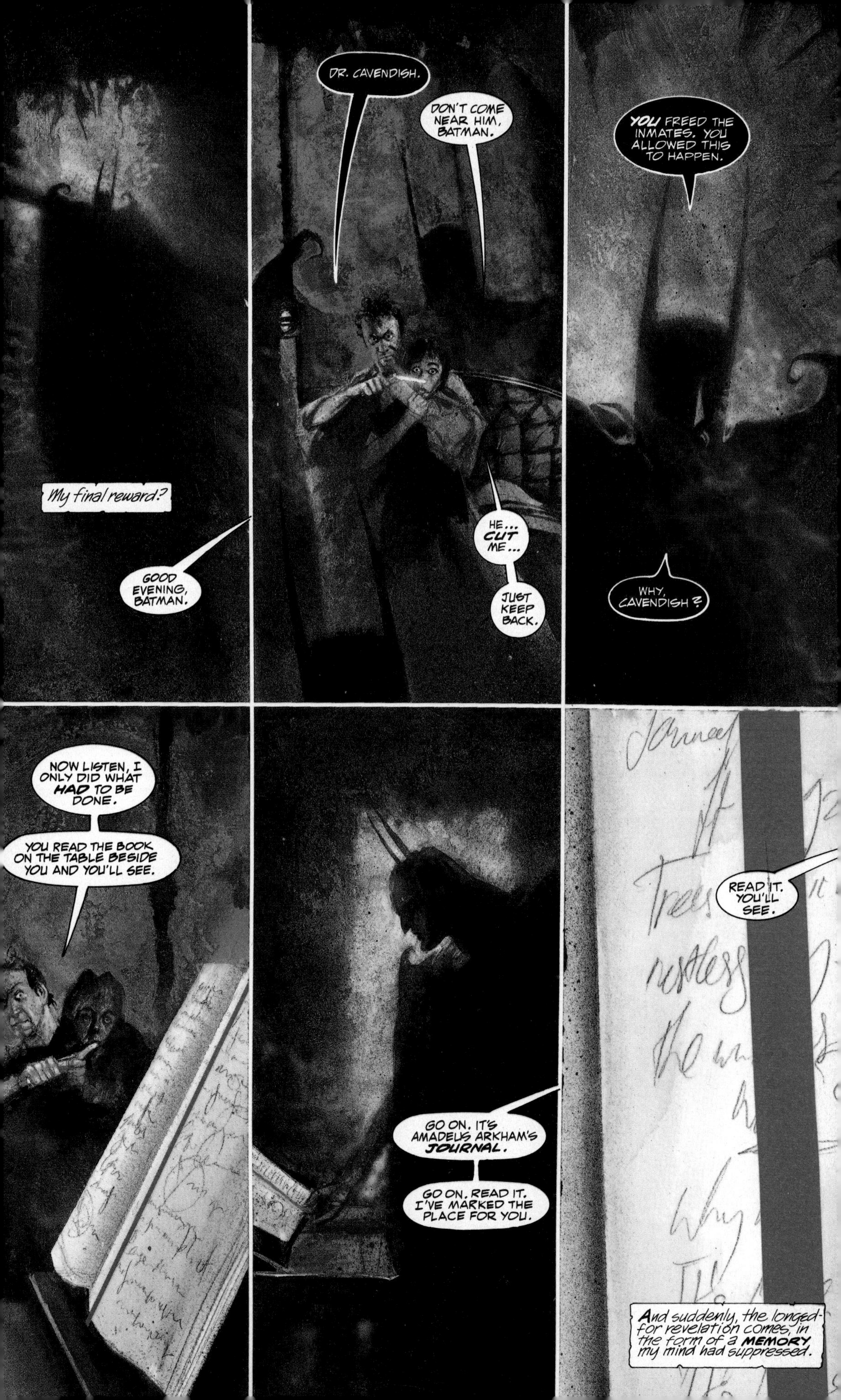

My final reward?
GOOD EVENING, BATMAN.
DR. CAVENDISH.
DON'T COME NEAR HIM, BATMAN.
HE... CUT ME...
JUST KEEP BACK.
YOU FREED THE INMATES. YOU ALLOWED THIS TO HAPPEN.
WHY, CAVENDISH?
NOW LISTEN, I ONLY DID WHAT HAD TO BE DONE.
YOU READ THE BOOK ON THE TABLE BESIDE YOU AND YOU'LL SEE.
GO ON. IT'S AMADEUS ARKHAM'S JOURNAL.
GO ON. READ IT. I'VE MARKED THE PLACE FOR YOU.
READ IT. YOU'LL SEE.
And suddenly, the longed-for revelation comes, in the form of a MEMORY my mind had suppressed.

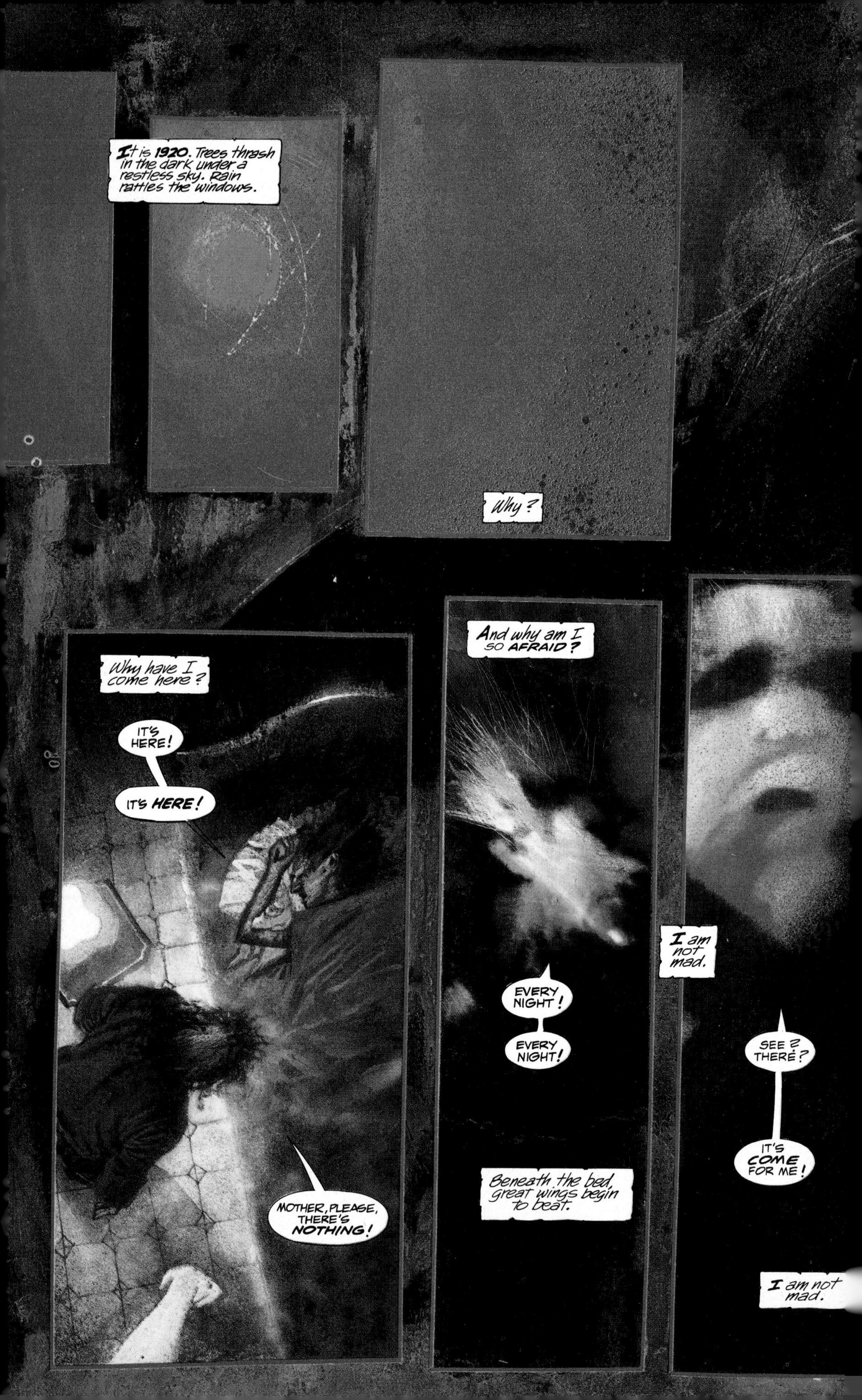
It is 1920. Trees thrash in the dark under a restless sky. Rain rattles the windows.
Why?
Why have I come here?
IT'S HERE!
IT'S HERE!
MOTHER, PLEASE, THERE'S NOTHING!
And why am I so AFRAID?
EVERY NIGHT!
EVERY NIGHT!
Beneath the bed, great wings begin to beat.
I am not mad.
SEE? THERE?
IT'S COME FOR ME!
I am not mad.

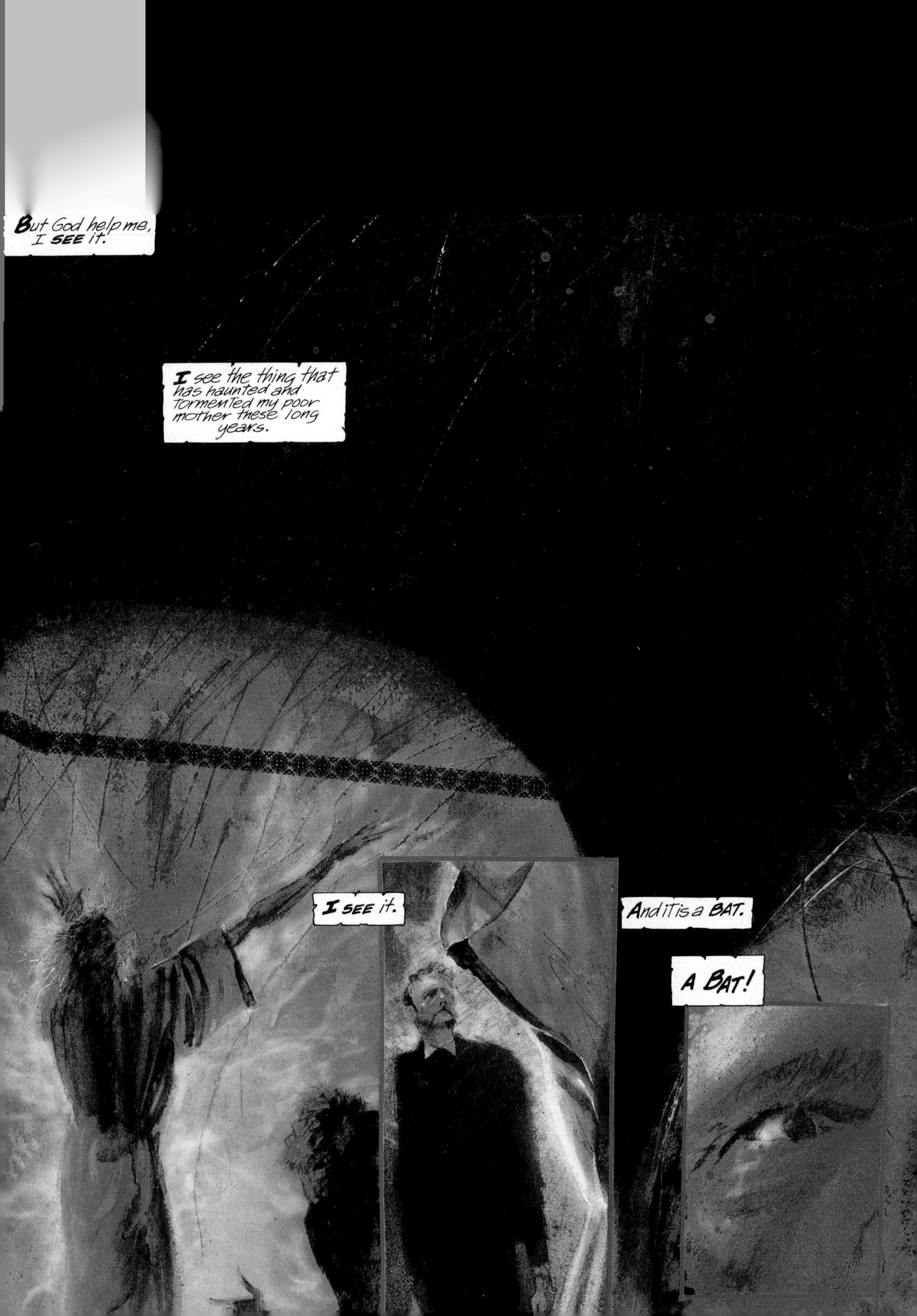
But God help me, I SEE it.
I see the thing that has haunted and tormented my poor mother these long years.
I SEE it.
And it is a BAT.
A BAT!

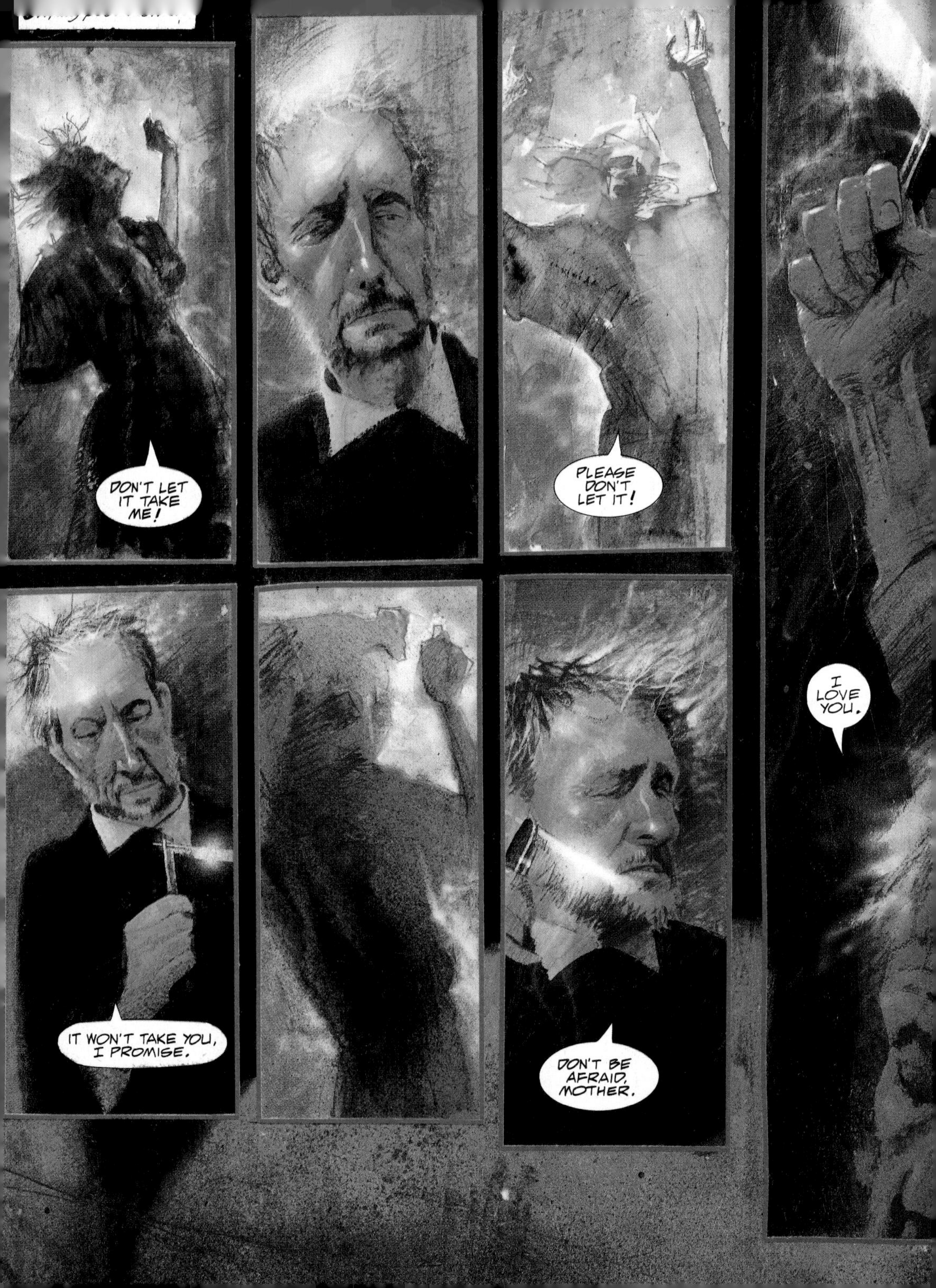
DON'T LET IT TAKE ME!
PLEASE DON'T LET IT!
I LOVE YOU.
IT WON'T TAKE YOU, I PROMISE.
DON'T BE AFRAID, MOTHER.

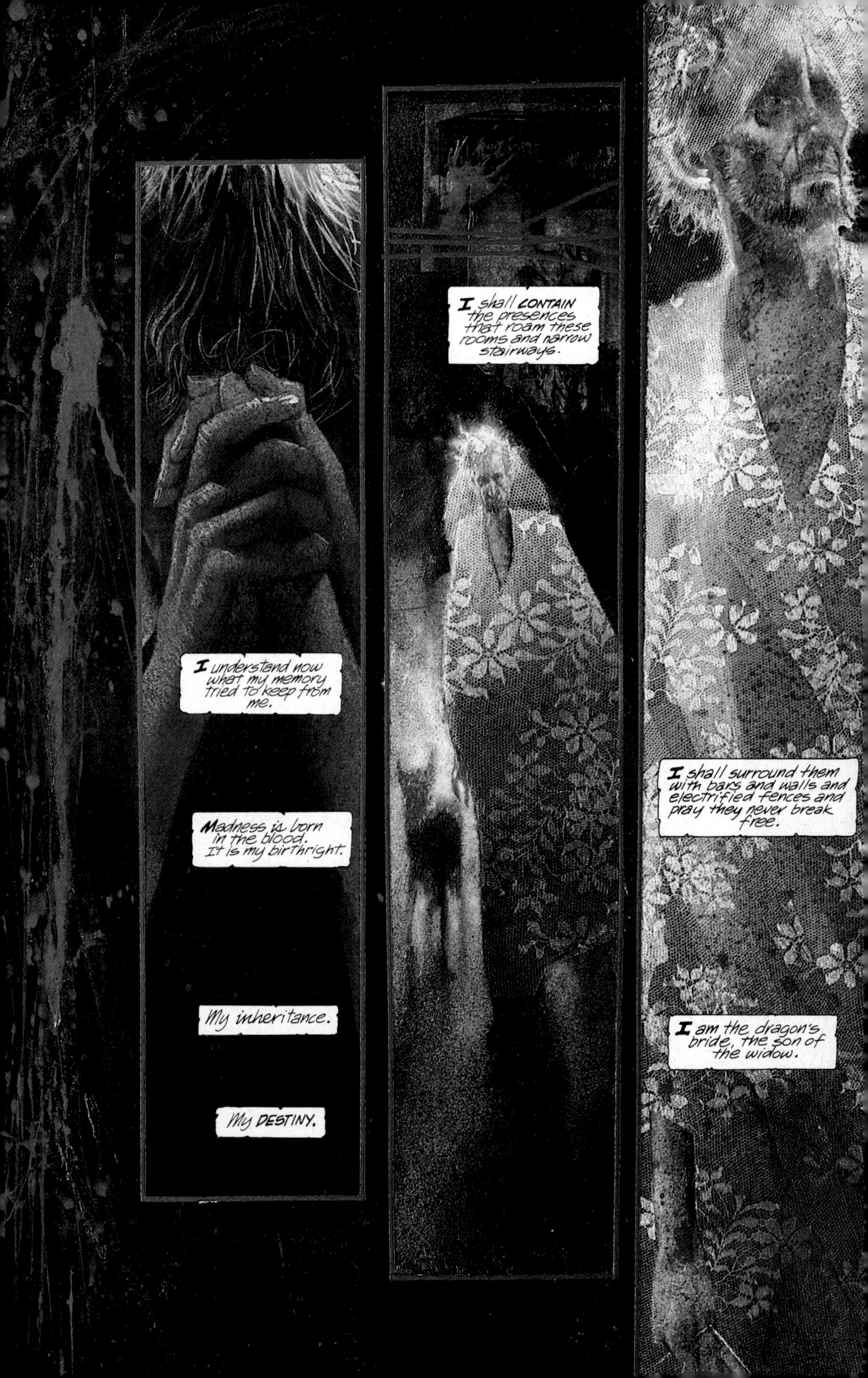
I understand now what my memory tried to keep from me.
Madness is born in the blood. It is my birthright.
My inheritance.
My DESTINY.
I shall CONTAIN the presences that roam these rooms and narrow stairways.
I shall surround them with bars and walls and electrified fences and pray they never break free.
I am the dragon's bride, the son of the widow.

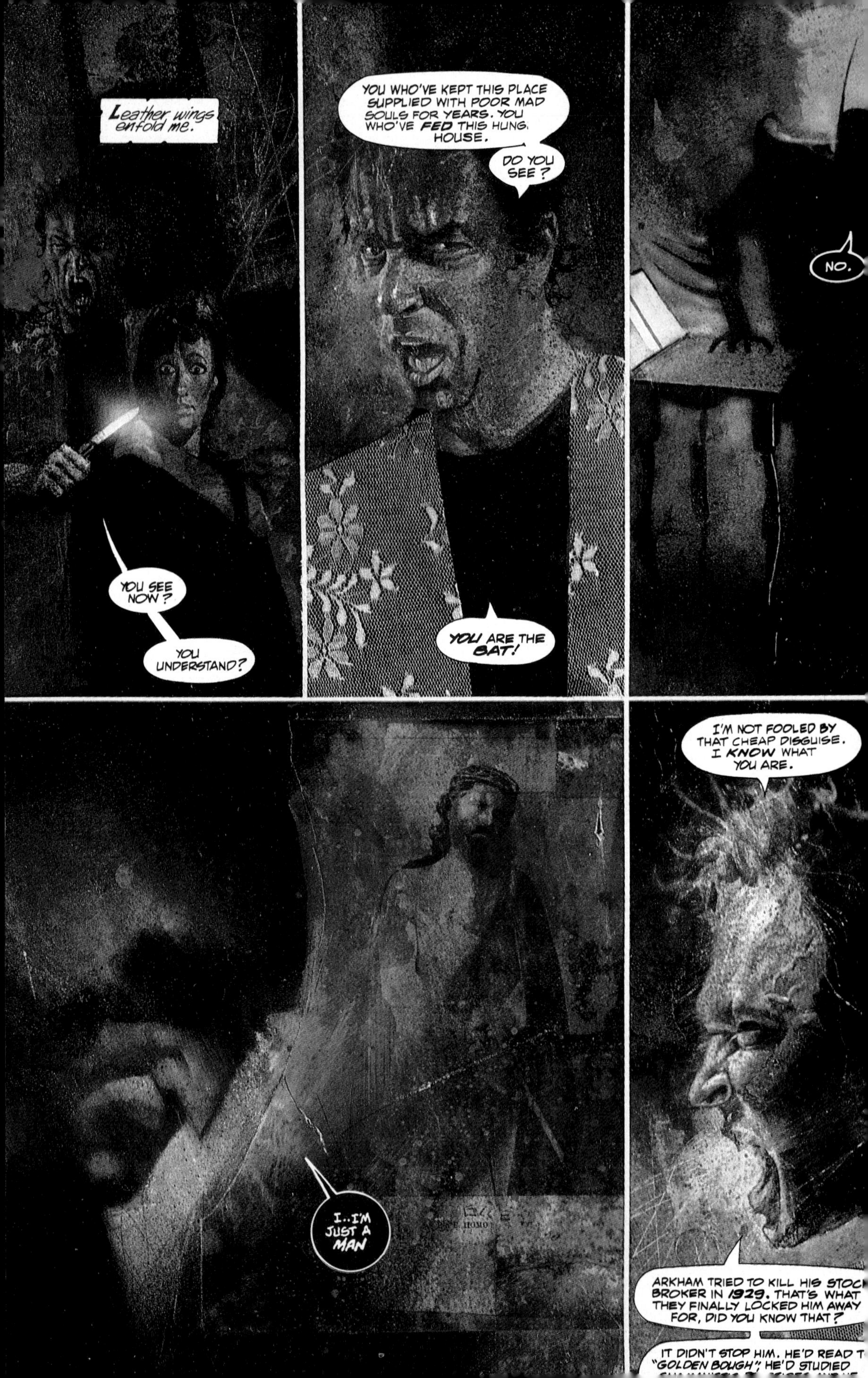
Leather wings enfold me.
YOU SEE NOW?
YOU UNDERSTAND?
YOU WHO'VE KEPT THIS PLACE SUPPLIED WITH POOR MAD SOULS FOR YEARS. YOU WHO'VE FED THIS HUNG. HOUSE.
DO YOU SEE?
YOU ARE THE BAT!
NO.
I..I'M JUST A MAN
I'M NOT FOOLED BY THAT CHEAP DISGUISE. I KNOW WHAT YOU ARE.
ARKHAM TRIED TO KILL HIS STOC BROKER IN 1929. THAT'S WHAT THEY FINALLY LOCKED HIM AWAY FOR, DID YOU KNOW THAT?
IT DIDN'T STOP HIM. HE'D READ T "GOLDEN BOUGH", HE'D STUDIED

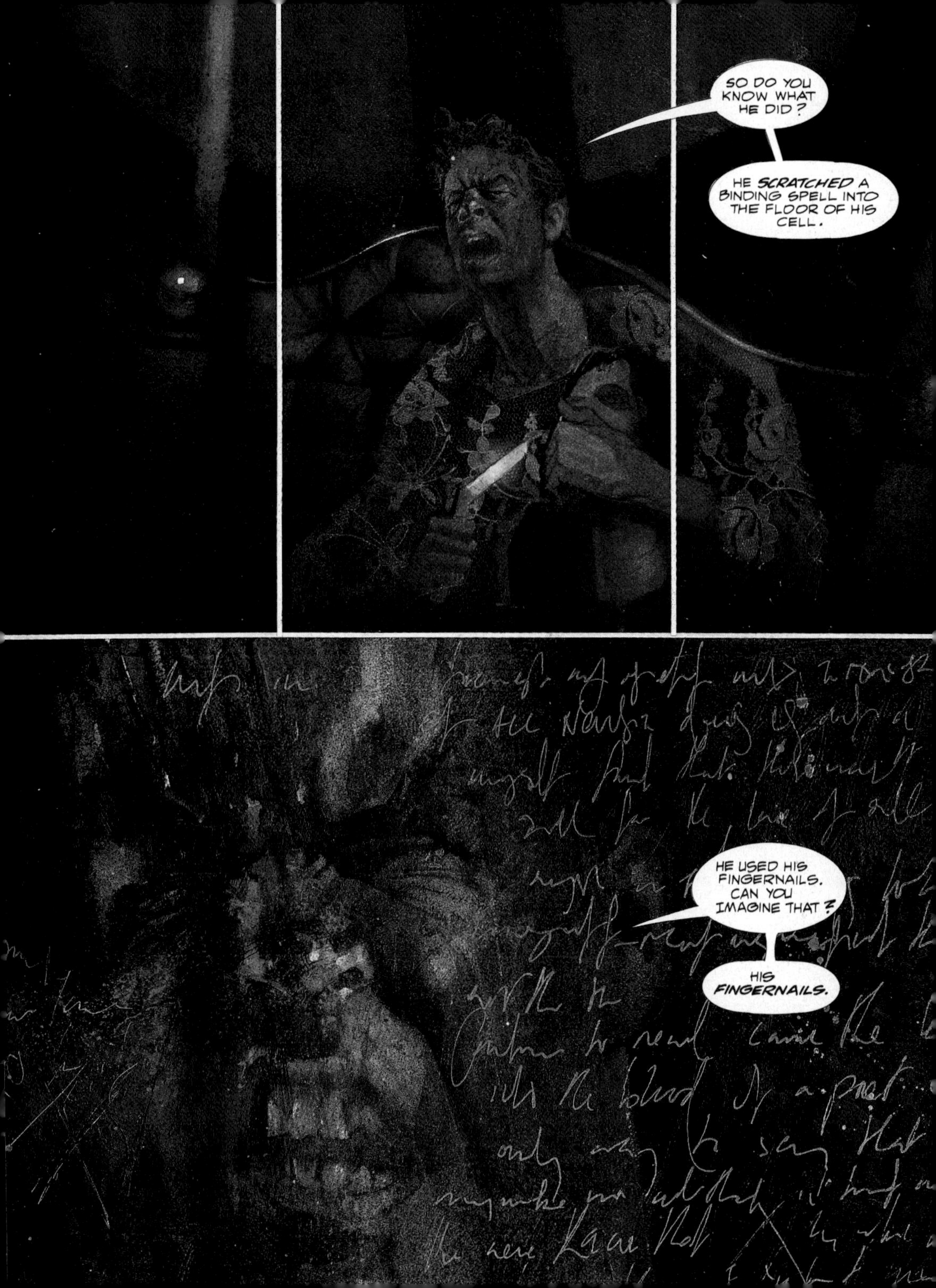
SO DO YOU KNOW WHAT HE DID?
HE SCRATCHED A BINDING SPELL INTO THE FLOOR OF HIS CELL.
HE USED HIS FINGERNAILS. CAN YOU IMAGINE THAT?
HIS FINGERNAILS.

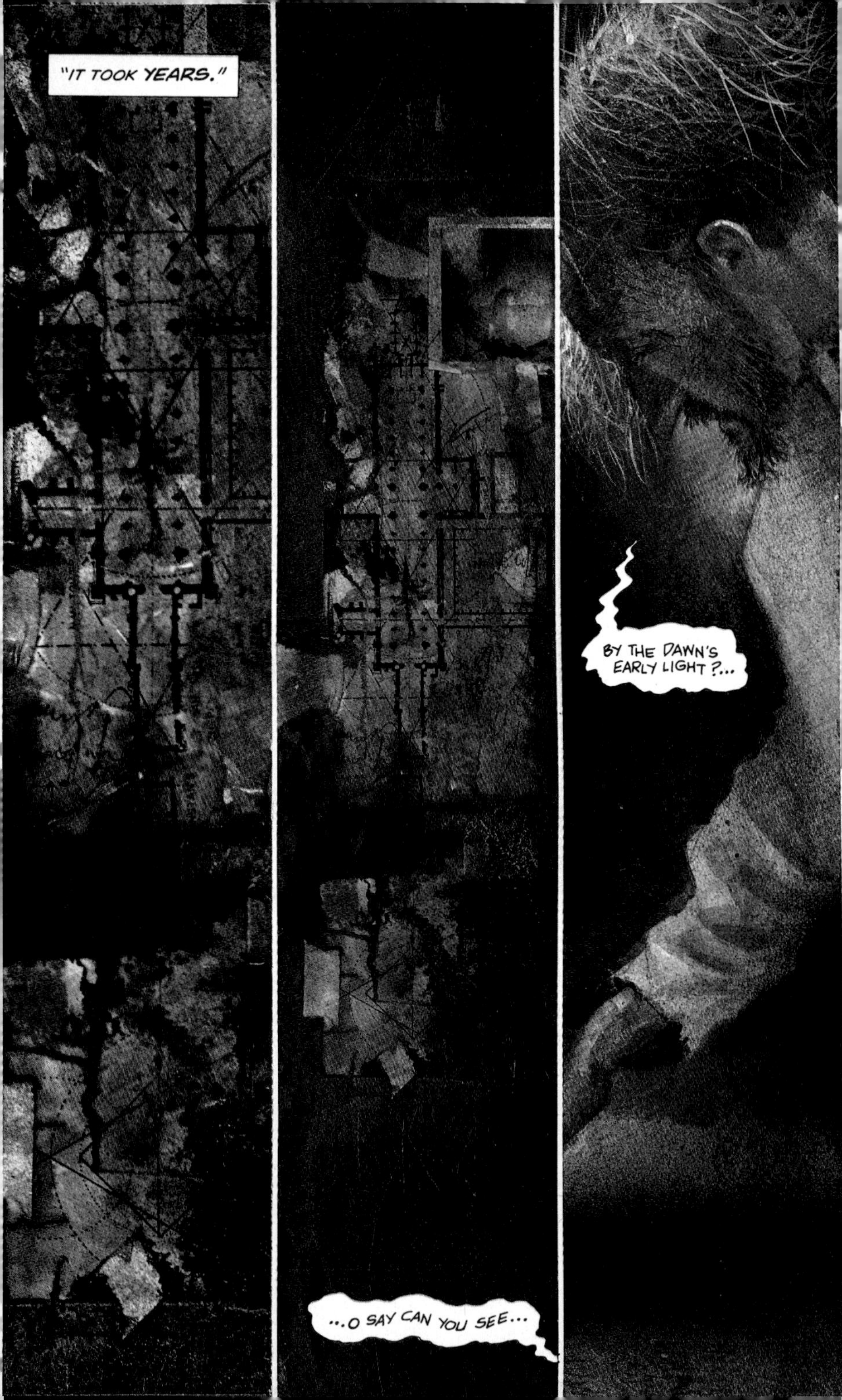
"IT TOOK YEARS."
...O SAY CAN YOU SEE...
BY THE DAWN'S EARLY LIGHT?...

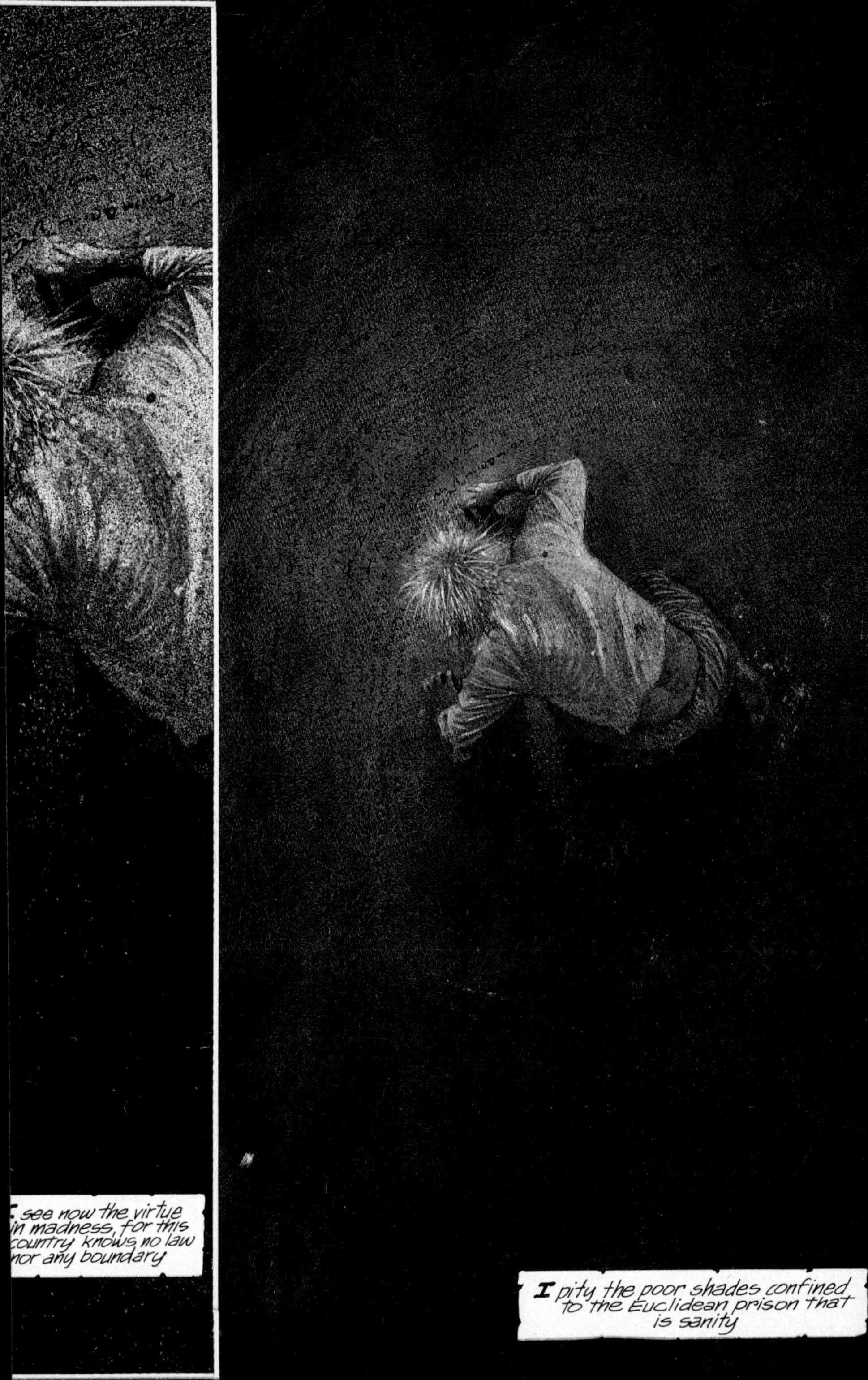
I see now the virtue in madness, for this country knows no law nor any boundary
I pity the poor shades confined to the Euclidean prison that is sanity

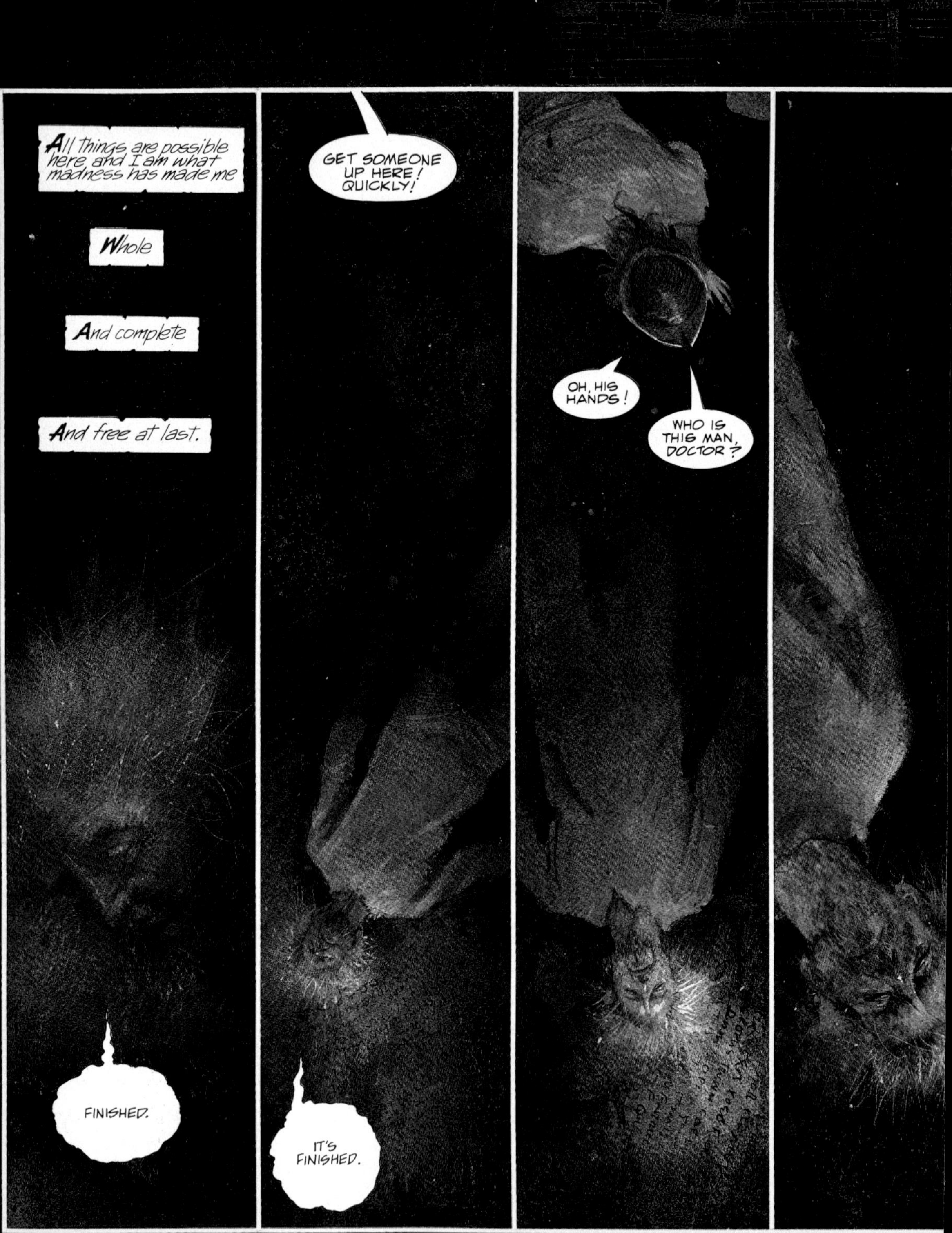
All things are possible here, and I am what madness has made me
Whole
And complete
And free at last.
FINISHED.
GET SOMEONE UP HERE! QUICKLY!
IT'S FINISHED.
OH, HIS HANDS!
WHO IS THIS MAN, DOCTOR?

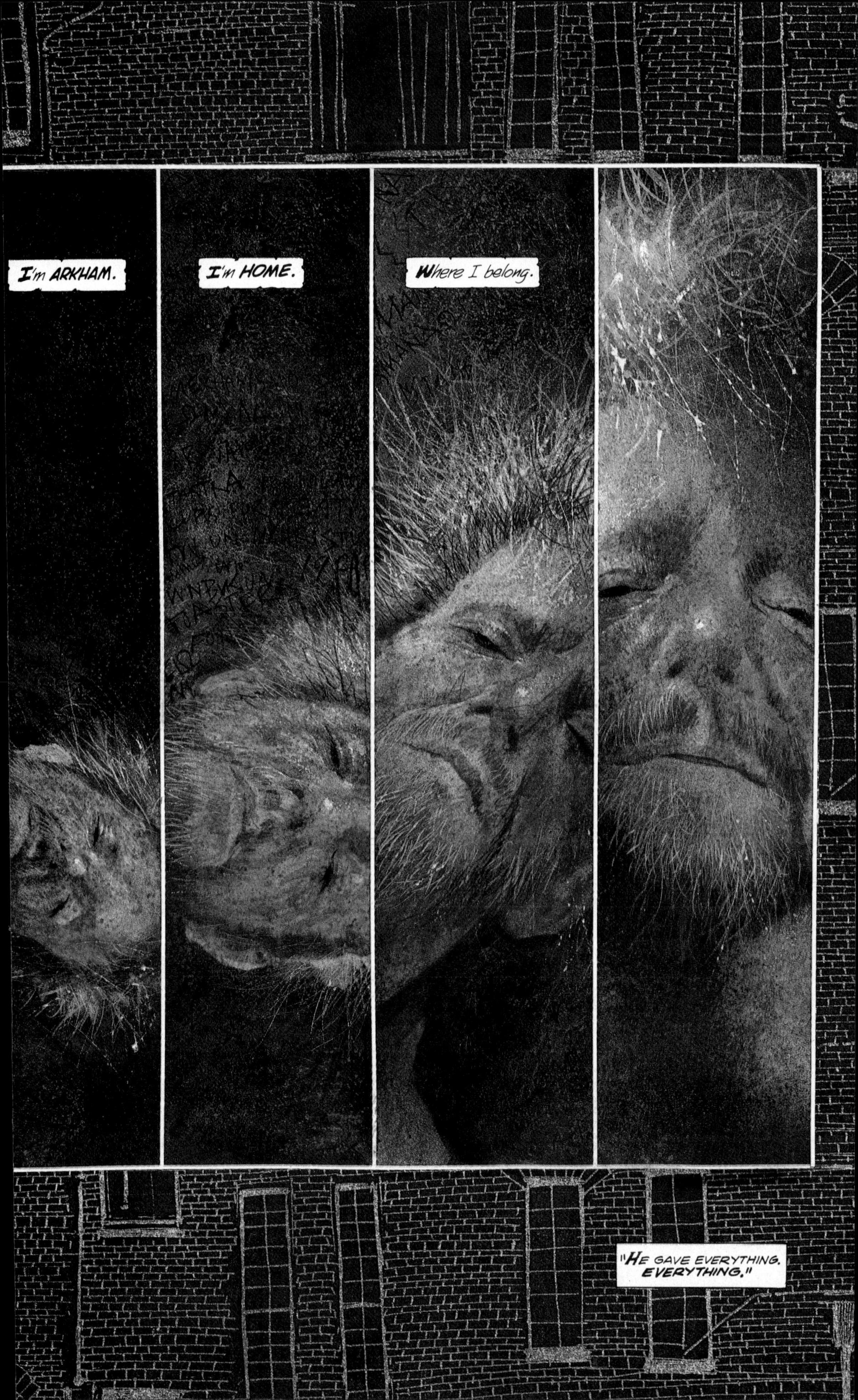
I'm ARKHAM.
I'm HOME.
Where I belong.
"HE GAVE EVERYTHING. EVERYTHING."

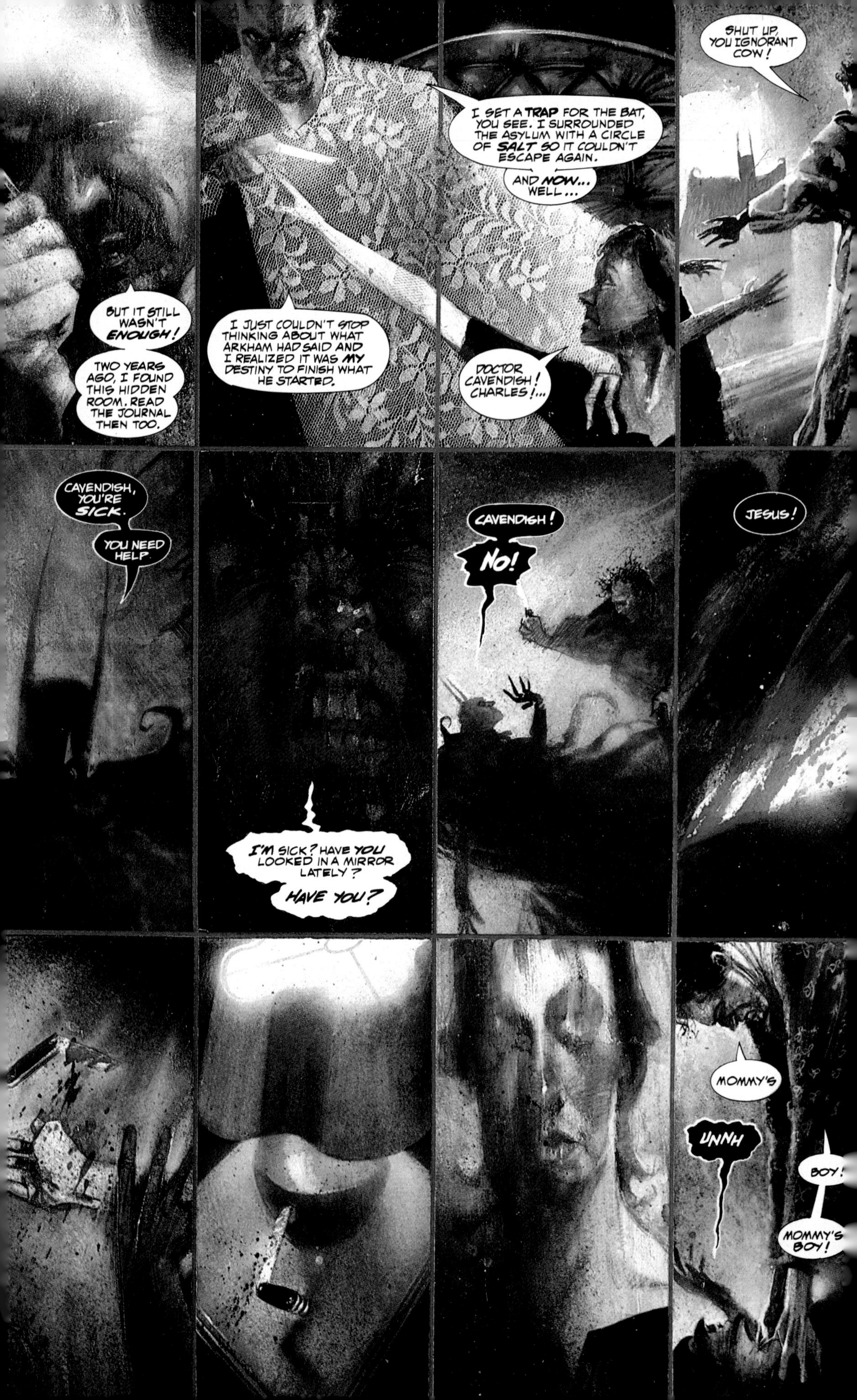
BUT IT STILL WASN'T ENOUGH!
TWO YEARS AGO, I FOUND THIS HIDDEN ROOM. READ THE JOURNAL THEN TOO.
I JUST COULDN'T STOP THINKING ABOUT WHAT ARKHAM HAD SAID AND I REALIZED IT WAS MY DESTINY TO FINISH WHAT HE STARTED.
I SET A TRAP FOR THE BAT, YOU SEE. I SURROUNDED THE ASYLUM WITH A CIRCLE OF SALT SO IT COULDN'T ESCAPE AGAIN.
AND NOW... WELL...
DOCTOR CAVENDISH! CHARLES!...
SHUT UP, YOU IGNORANT COW!
CAVENDISH, YOU'RE SICK.
YOU NEED HELP.
I'M SICK? HAVE YOU LOOKED IN A MIRROR LATELY?
HAVE YOU?
CAVENDISH!
NO!
JESUS!
MOMMY'S
UNNH
BOY!
MOMMY'S BOY!

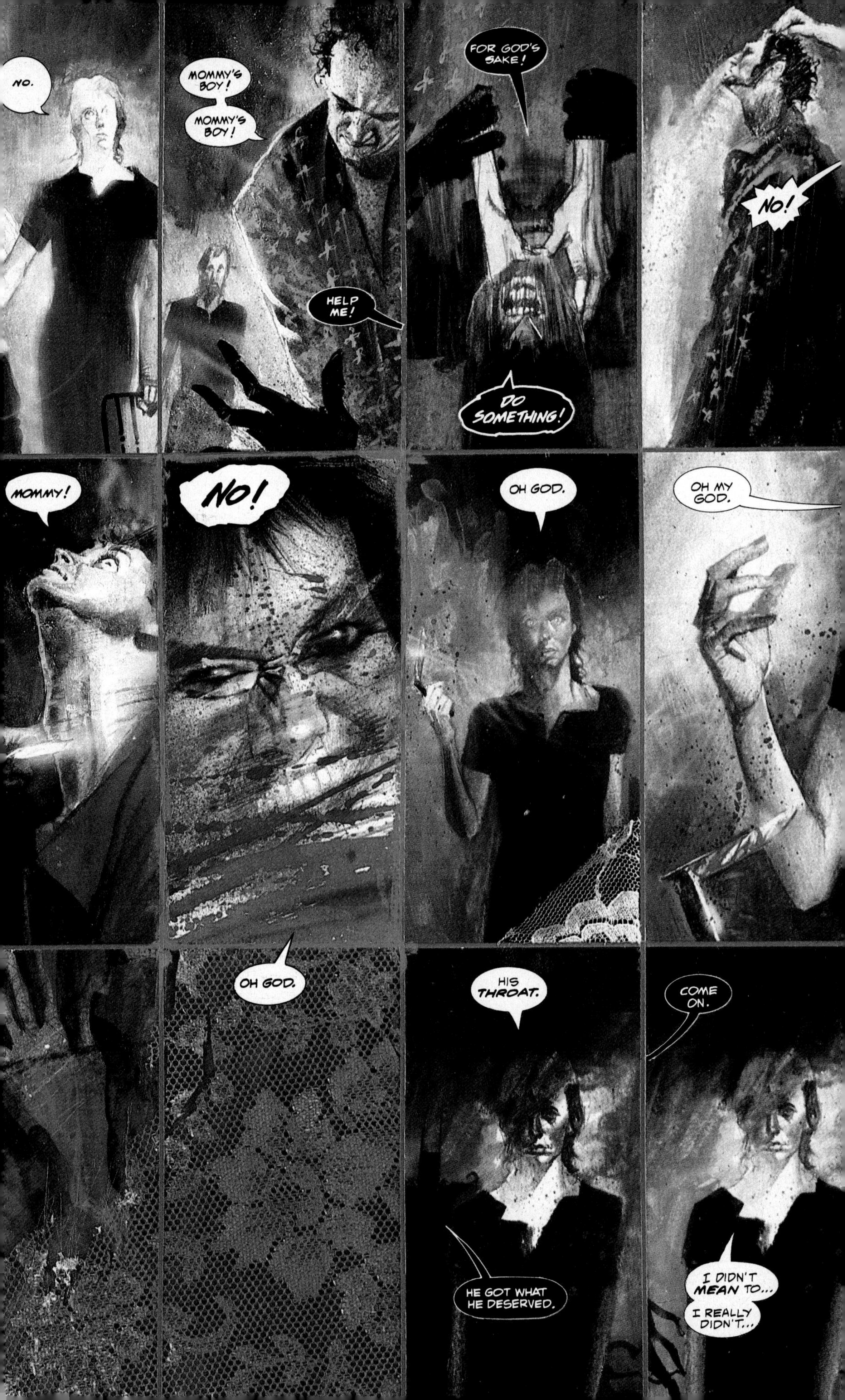
NO.
MOMMY'S BOY!
MOMMY'S BOY!
HELP ME!
FOR GOD'S SAKE!
DO SOMETHING!
NO!
MOMMY!
NO!
OH GOD.
OH MY GOD.
OH GOD.
HIS THROAT.
HE GOT WHAT HE DESERVED.
COME ON.
I DIDN'T MEAN TO...
I REALLY DIDN'T...

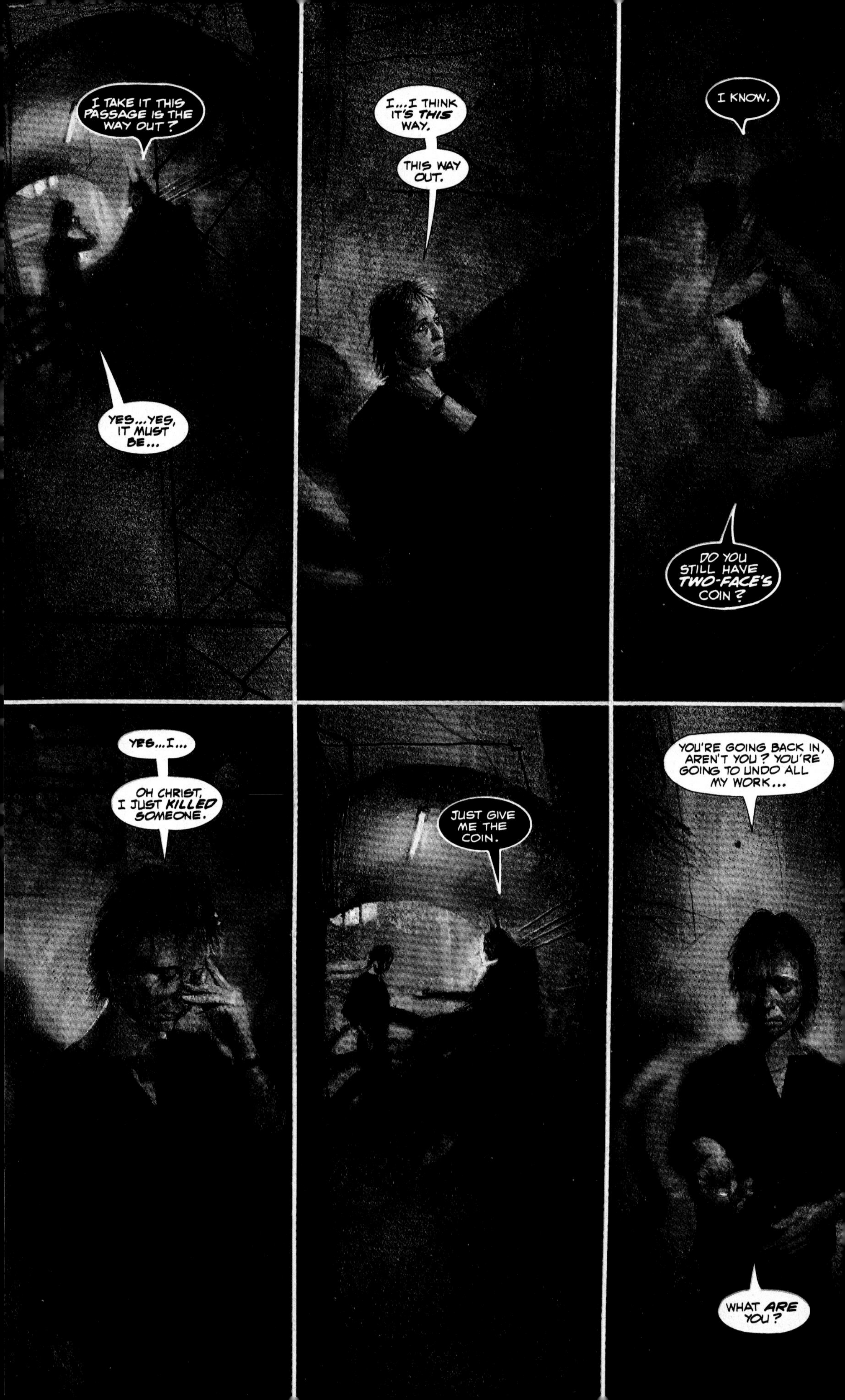
I TAKE IT THIS PASSAGE IS THE WAY OUT?
YES...YES, IT MUST BE...
I...I THINK IT'S THIS WAY.
THIS WAY OUT.
I KNOW.
DO YOU STILL HAVE TWO-FACE'S COIN?
YES...I...
OH CHRIST, I JUST KILLED SOMEONE.
JUST GIVE ME THE COIN.
YOU'RE GOING BACK IN, AREN'T YOU? YOU'RE GOING TO UNDO ALL MY WORK...
WHAT ARE YOU?

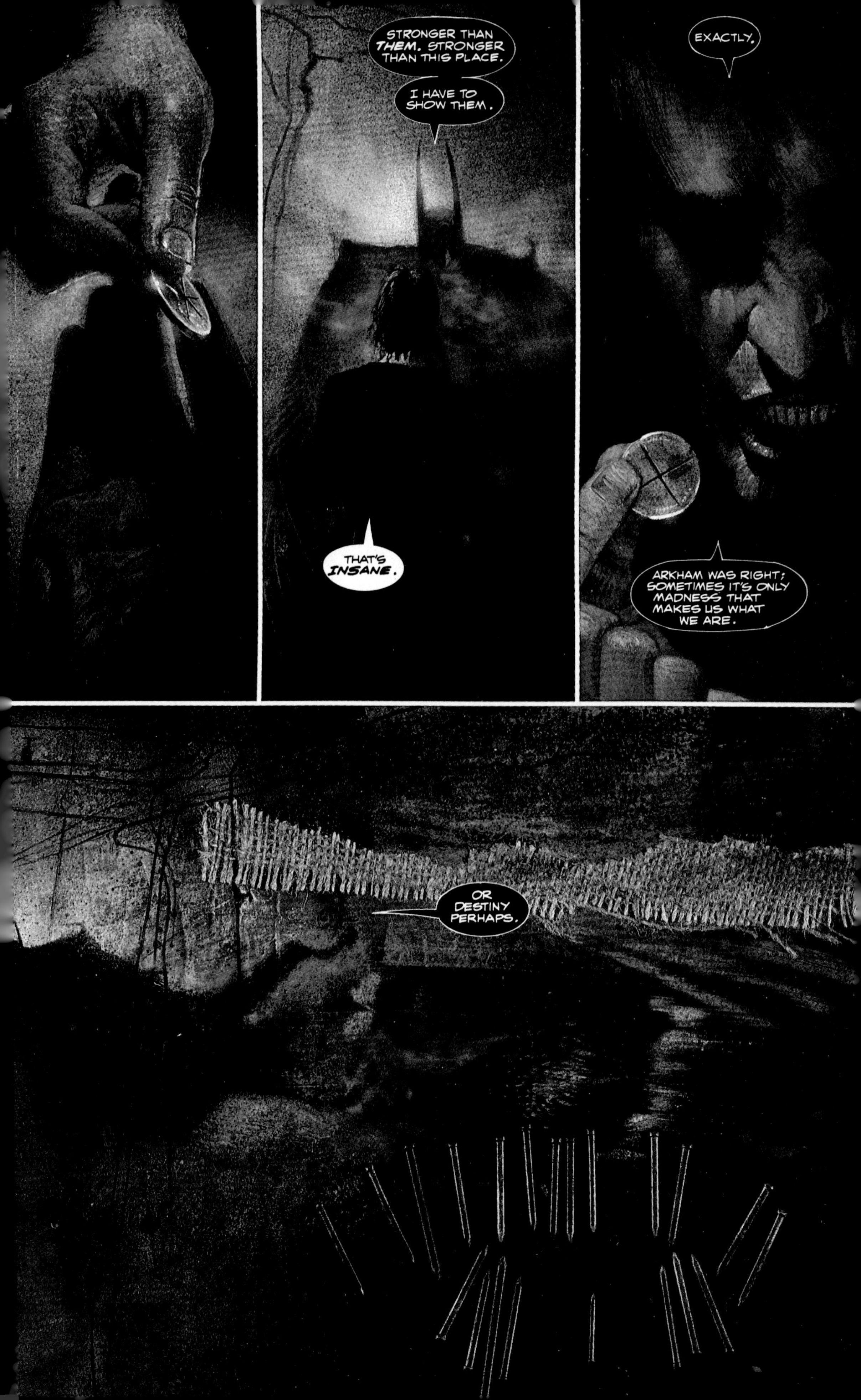
STRONGER THAN THEM. STRONGER THAN THIS PLACE.
I HAVE TO SHOW THEM.
THAT'S INSANE.
EXACTLY.
ARKHAM WAS RIGHT; SOMETIMES IT'S ONLY MADNESS THAT MAKES US WHAT WE ARE.
OR DESTINY PERHAPS.

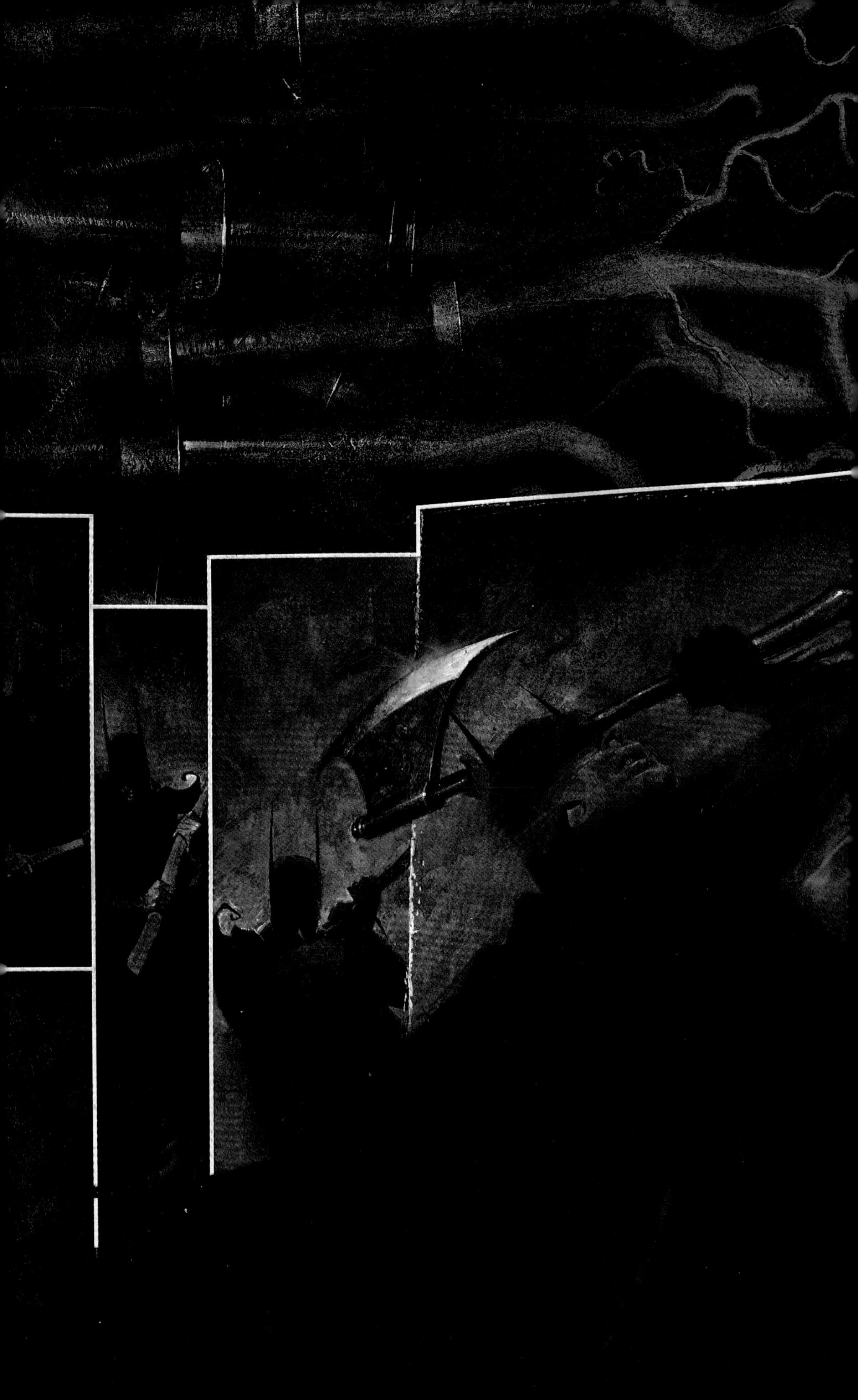

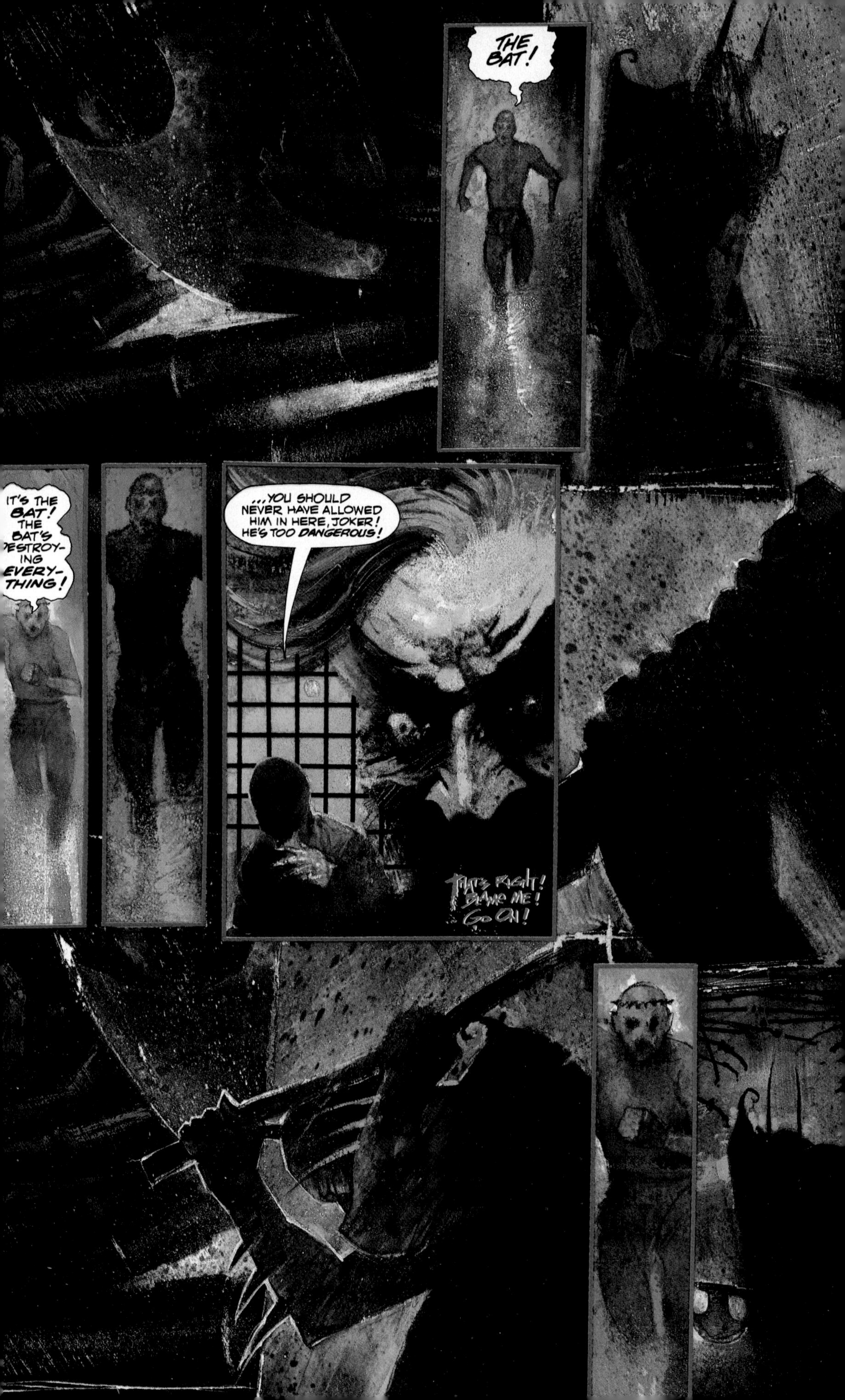
THE BAT!
IT'S THE BAT! THE BAT'S DESTROYING EVERYTHING!
...YOU SHOULD NEVER HAVE ALLOWED HIM IN HERE, JOKER! HE'S TOO DANGEROUS!
THAT'S RIGHT! BLAME ME! GO ON!

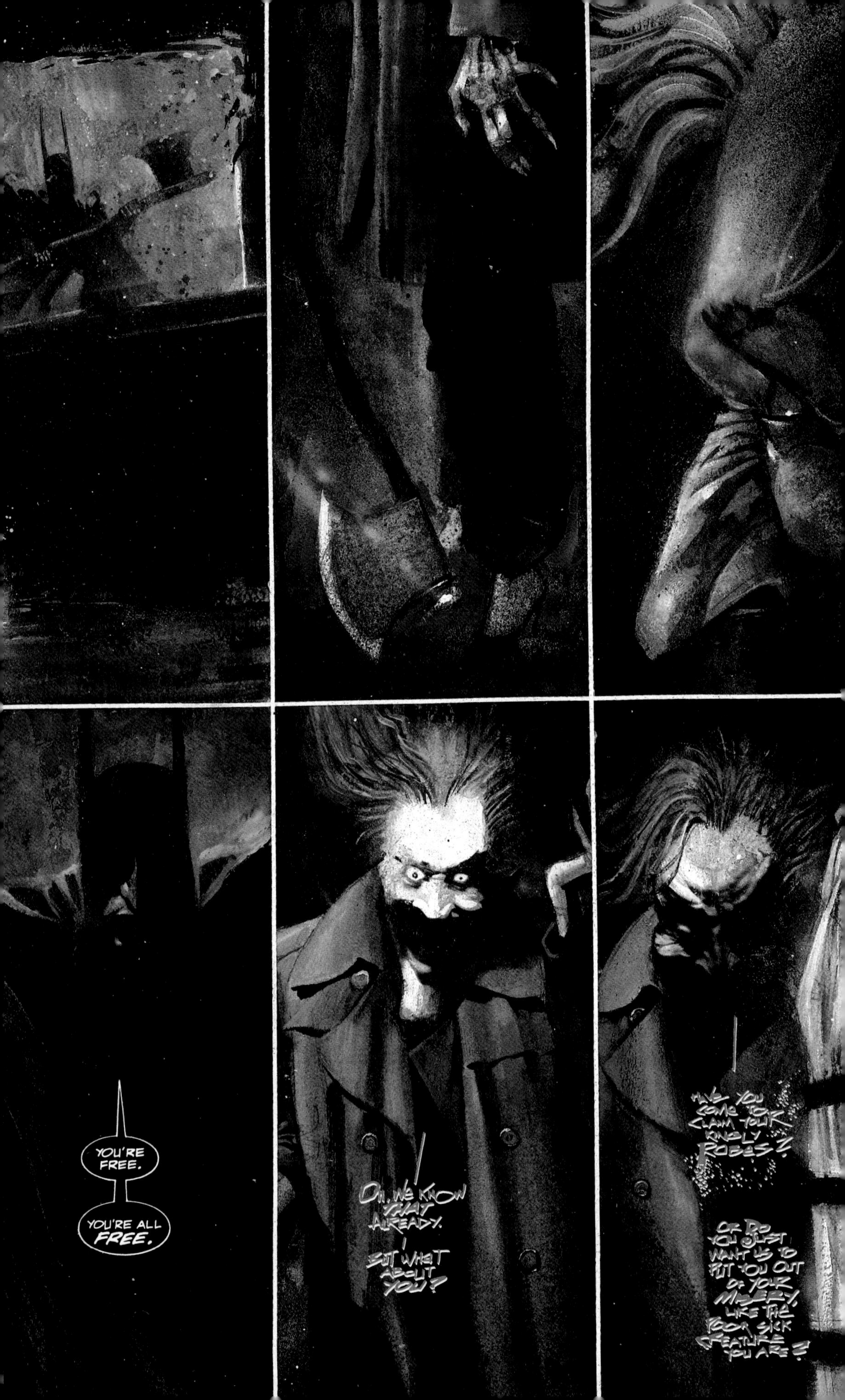

YOU'RE FREE.
YOU'RE ALL FREE.
OH, WE KNOW THAT ALREADY.
BUT WHAT ABOUT YOU?
HAVE YOU COME TO CLAIM YOUR KINGLY ROBES?
OR DO YOU JUST WANT US TO PUT YOU OUT OF YOUR MISERY, LIKE THE POOR SICK CREATURE YOU ARE?

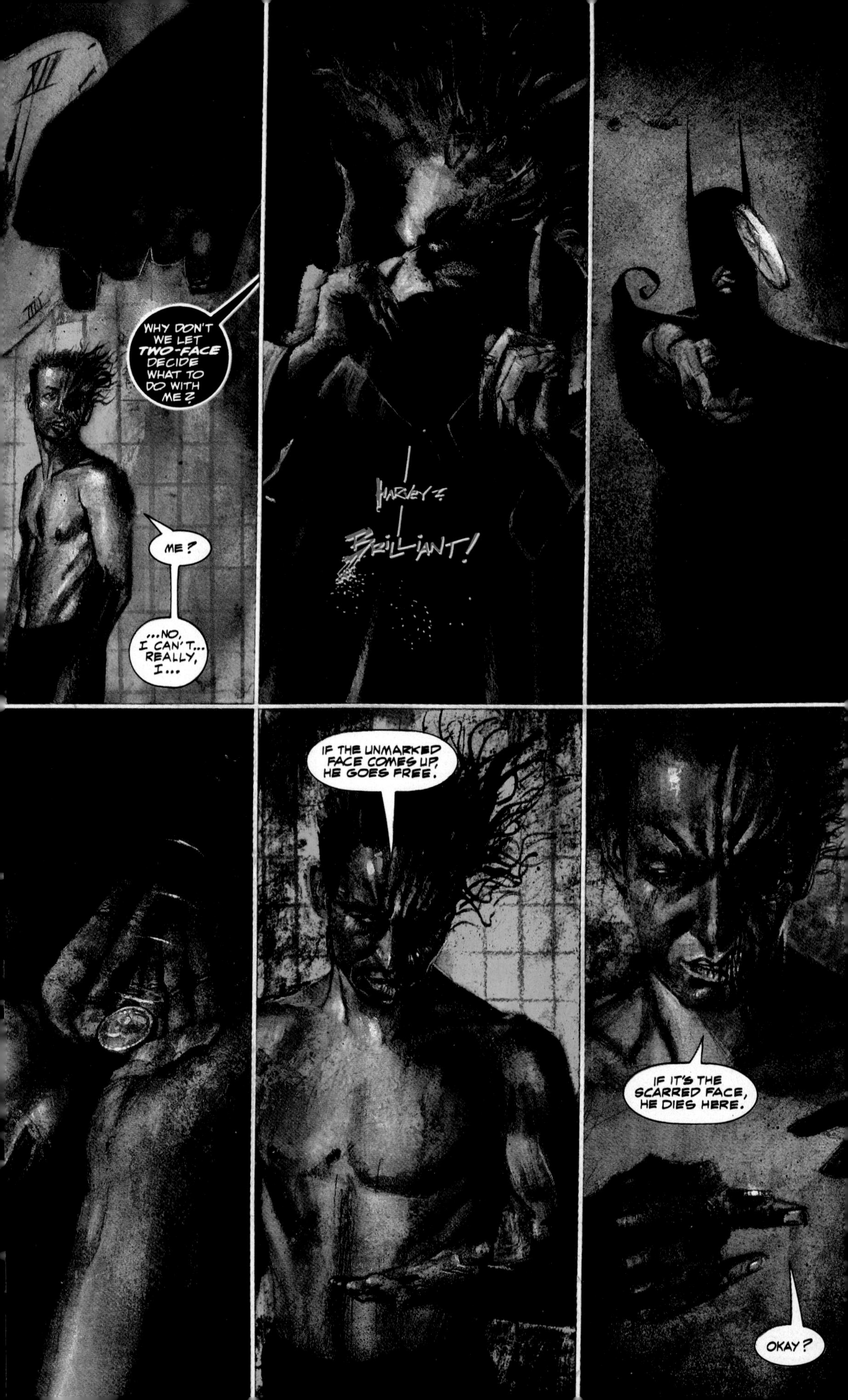
WHY DON'T WE LET TWO-FACE DECIDE WHAT TO DO WITH ME?
ME?
...NO, I CAN'T... REALLY, I...
HARVEY?
BRILLIANT!
IF THE UNMARKED FACE COMES UP HE GOES FREE.
IF IT'S THE SCARRED FACE, HE DIES HERE.
OKAY?

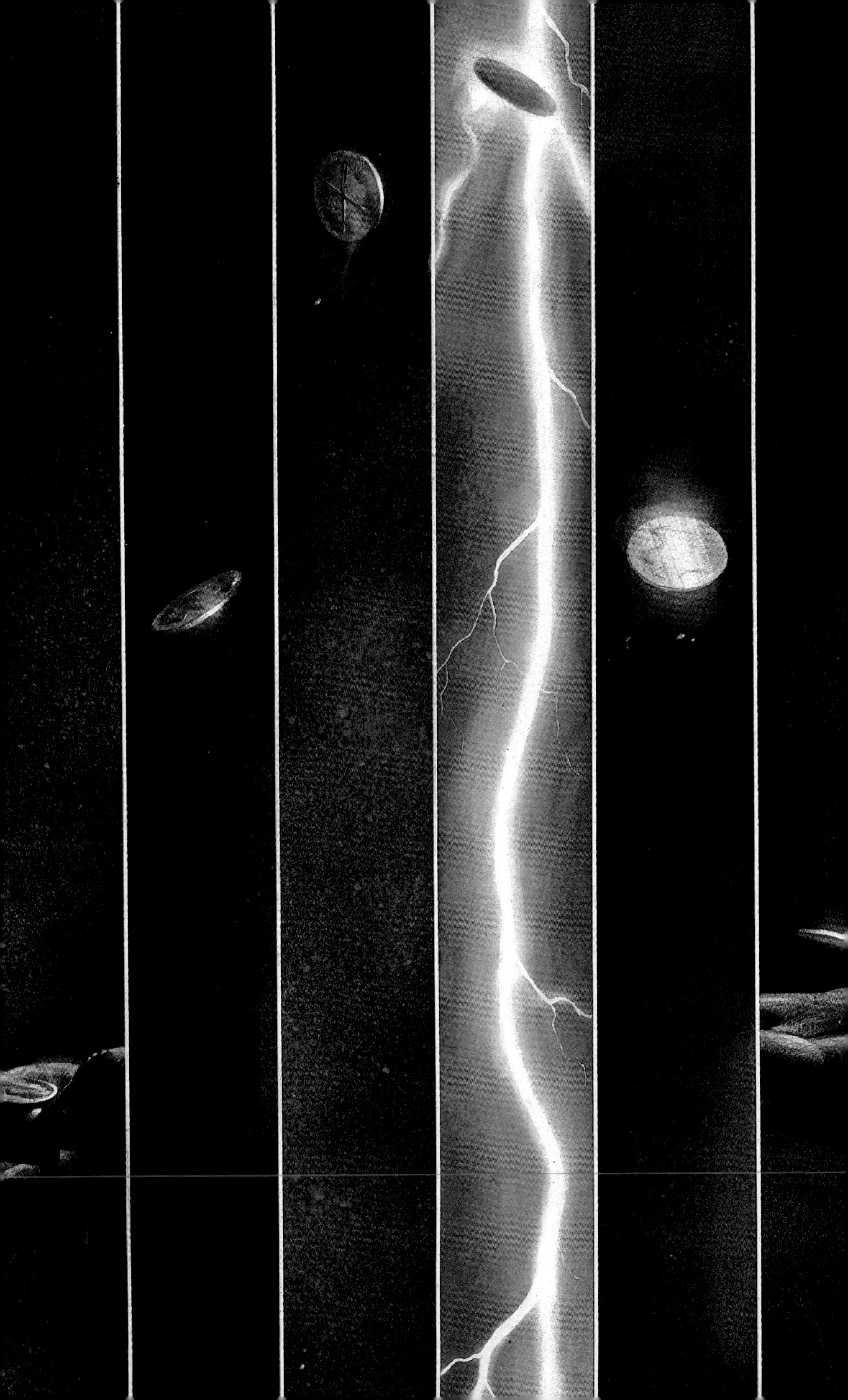

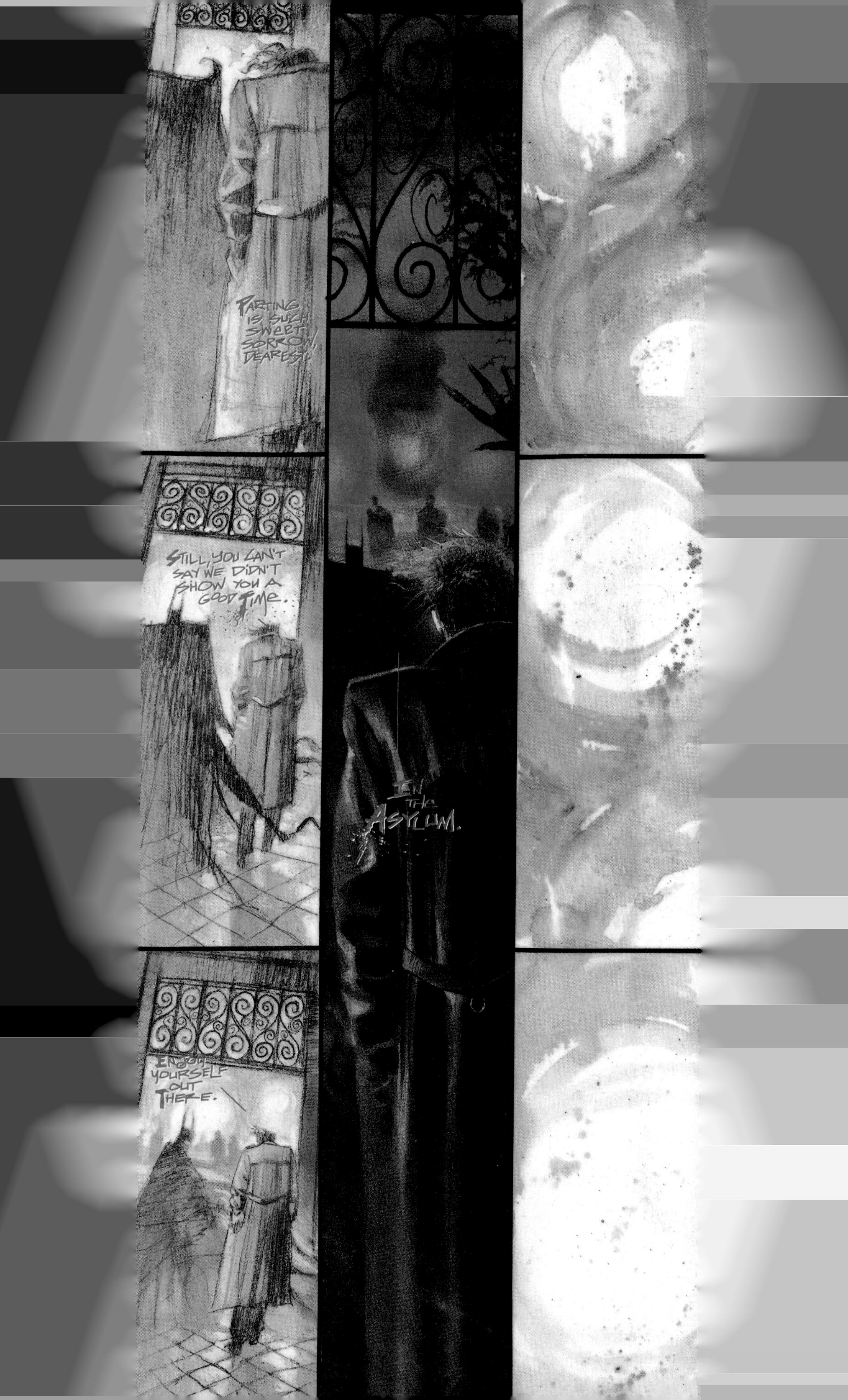
PARTING IS SUCH SWEET SORROW, DEAREST.
STILL, YOU CAN'T SAY WE DIDN'T SHOW YOU A GOOD TIME.
ENJOY YOURSELF OUT THERE.
IN THE ASYLUM.

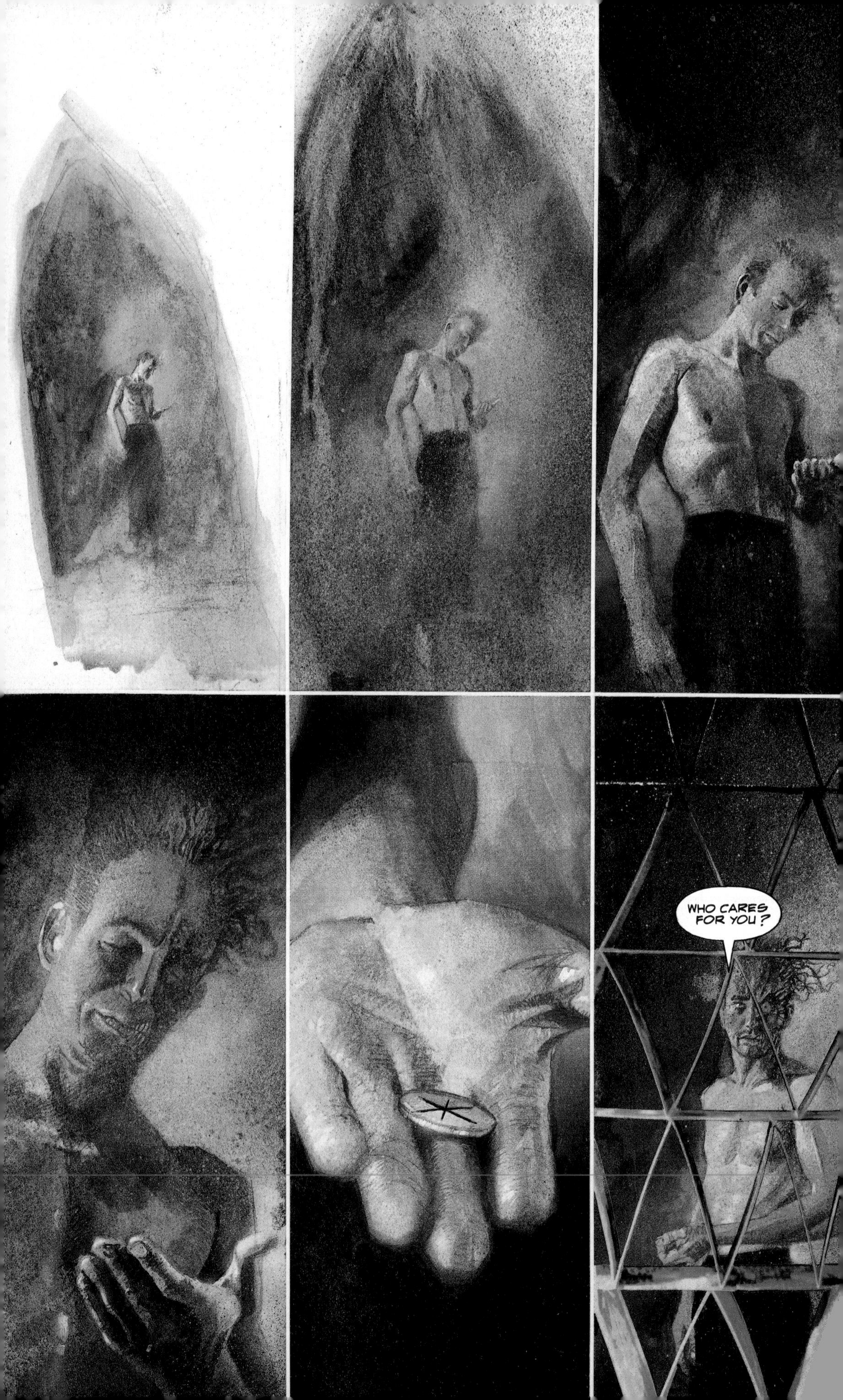
WHO CARES FOR YOU?

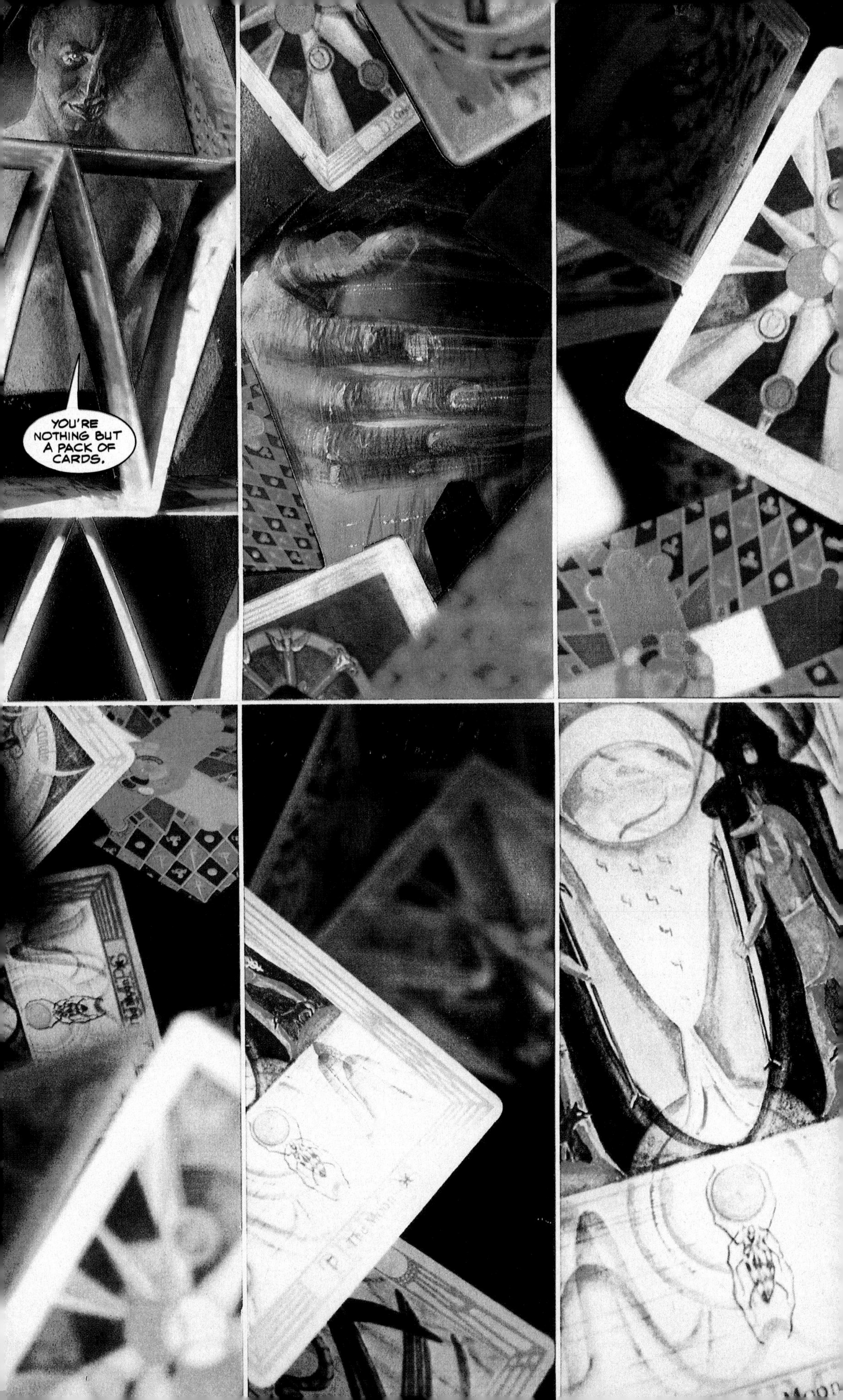
YOU'RE NOTHING BUT A PACK OF CARDS.

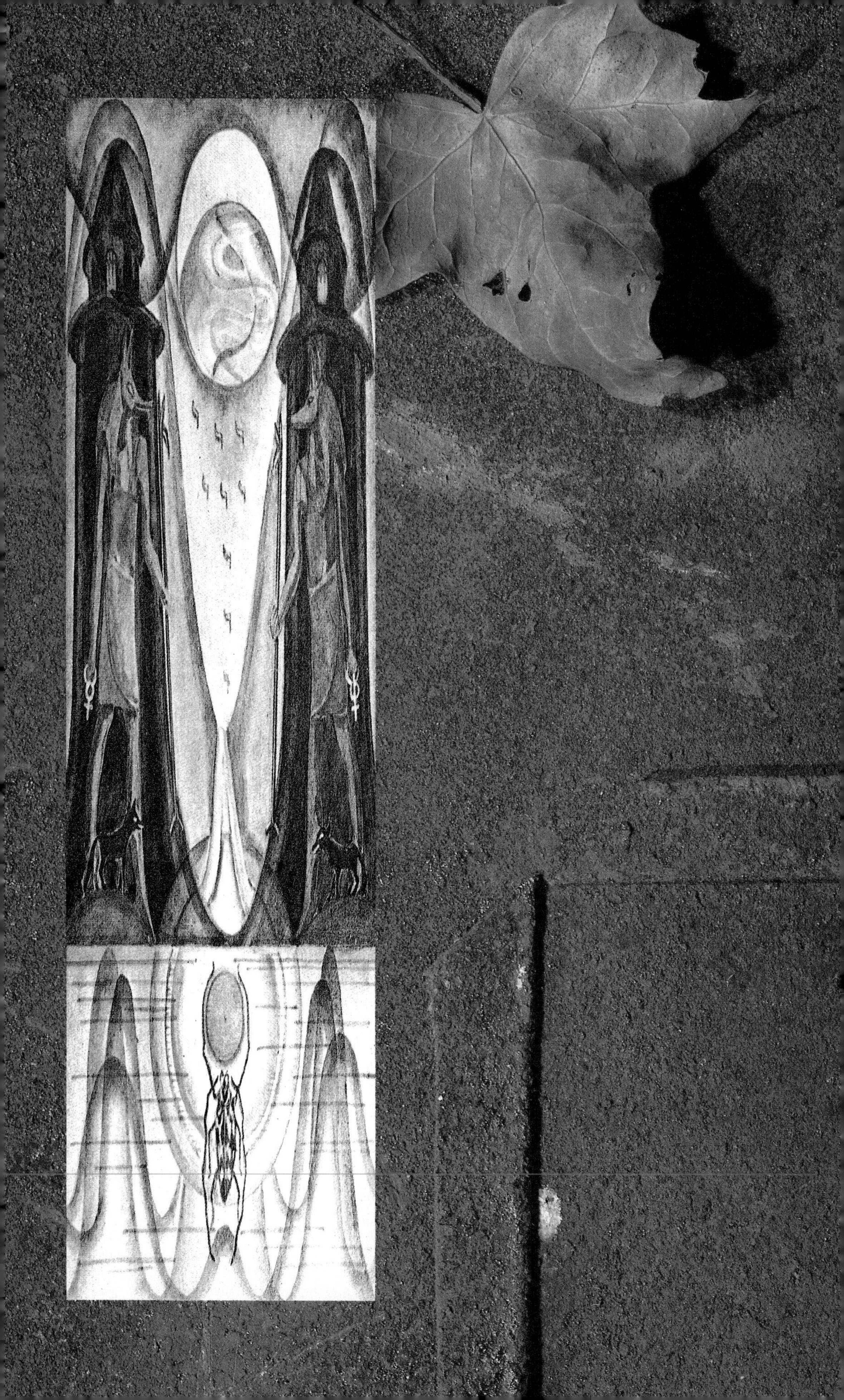

And is not that a Mother's gentle hand that withdraws your curtains,

And a Mother's sweet voice that summons you to rise?

To rise and forget, in the bright sunlight,

the ugly dreams that frightened you so when all was dark -

LEWIS CARROLL
'Alice's Adventures in Wonderland'

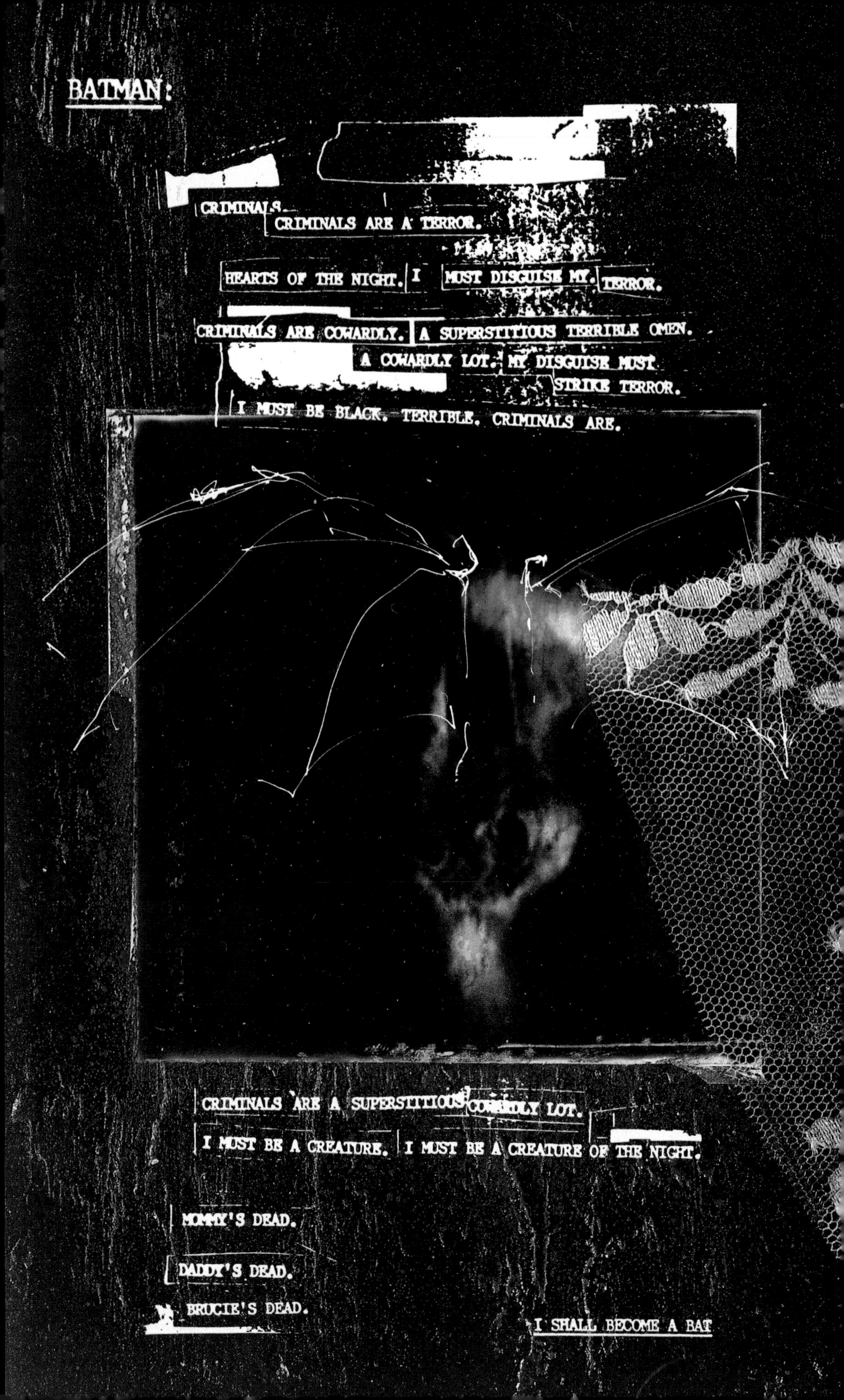
BATMAN:
CRIMINALS.
CRIMINALS ARE A TERROR.
HEARTS OF THE NIGHT. I MUST DISGUISE MY. TERROR.
CRIMINALS ARE COWARDLY. A SUPERSTITIOUS TERRIBLE OMEN.
A COWARDLY LOT. MY DISGUISE MUST STRIKE TERROR.
I MUST BE BLACK. TERRIBLE. CRIMINALS ARE.
CRIMINALS ARE A SUPERSTITIOUS COWARDLY LOT.
I MUST BE A CREATURE. I MUST BE A CREATURE OF THE NIGHT.
MOMMY'S DEAD.
DADDY'S DEAD.
BRUCIE'S DEAD.
I SHALL BECOME A BAT

JOKER:

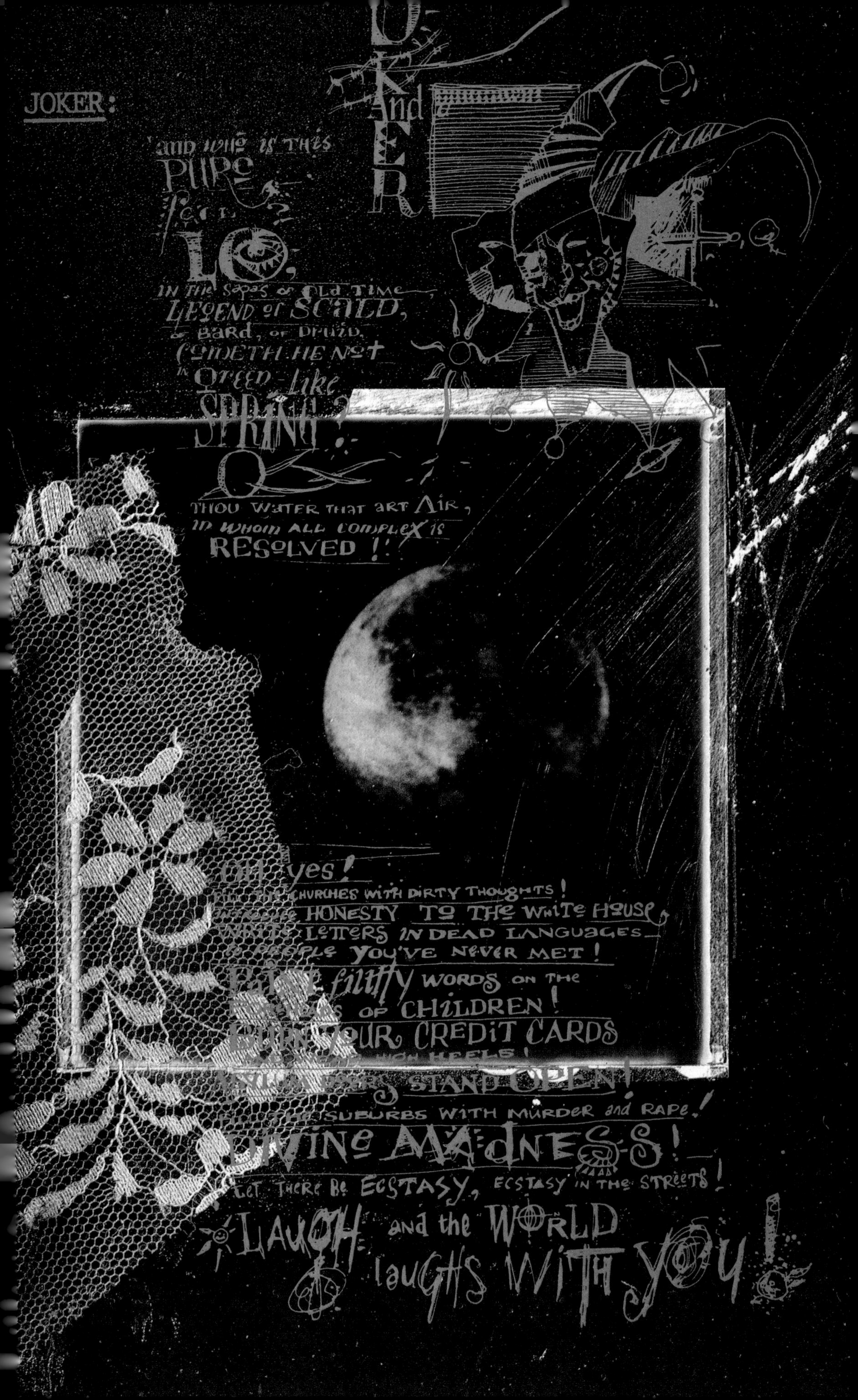
And who is this
Pure fool?
Lo,
in the sagas of old time,
Legend of Scald,
of Bard, of Druid,
Cometh he not
in green-like
Spring?
O
thou water that art Air,
in whom all complex is
RESOLVED !!
Oh yes!
churches with dirty thoughts!
HONESTY TO THE WHITE HOUSE
WRITE LETTERS IN DEAD LANGUAGES
to people you've never met!
filthy words on the
of CHILDREN!
Burn your CREDIT CARDS
high heels!
stand open!
suburbs with murder and rape!
DIVINE MADNESS!
Let there be ECSTASY, ECSTASY in the streets!
LAUGH and the WORLD
laughs WITH YOU!

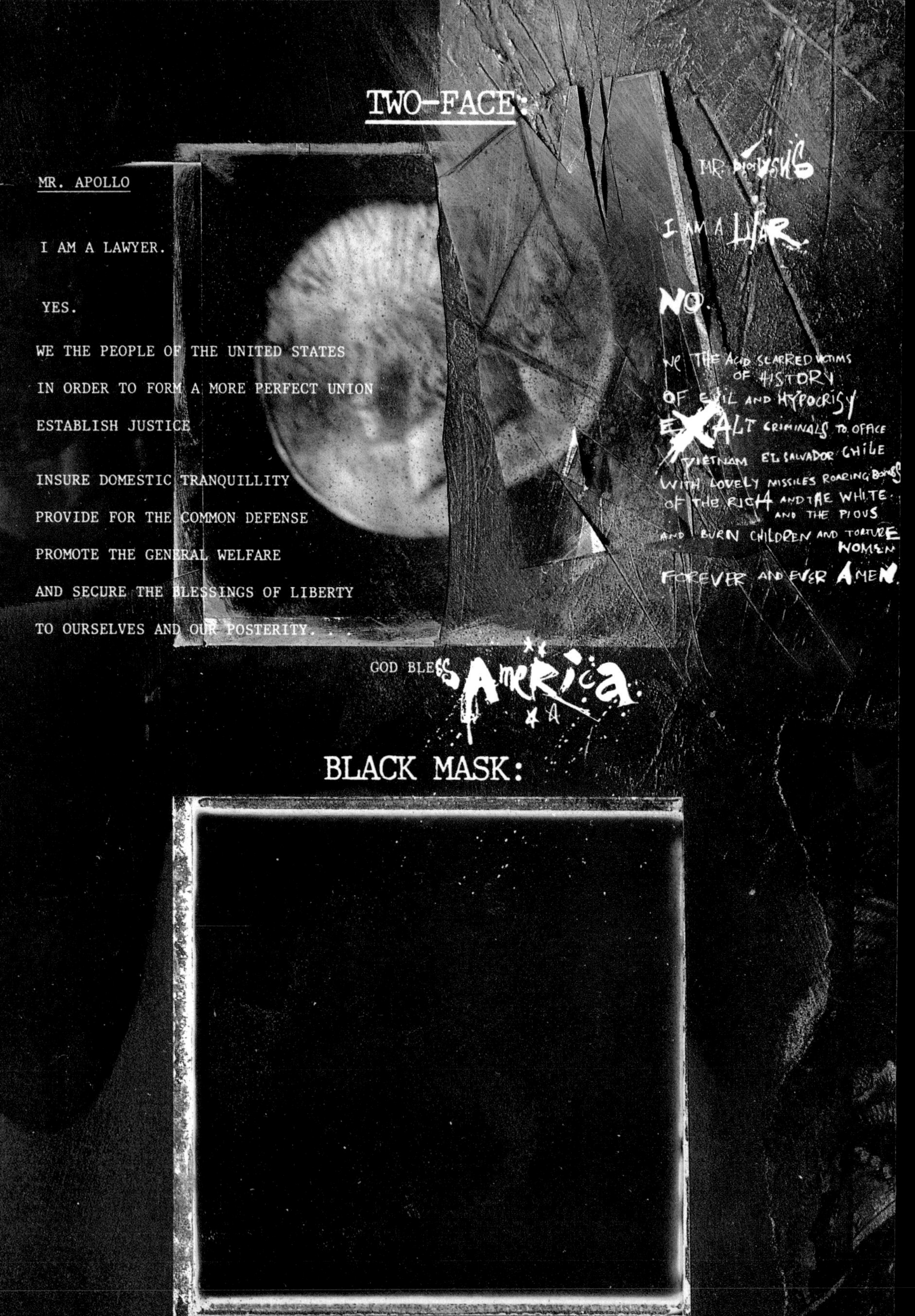
TWO-FACE:
MR. APOLLO
I AM A LAWYER.
YES.
WE THE PEOPLE OF THE UNITED STATES
IN ORDER TO FORM A MORE PERFECT UNION
ESTABLISH JUSTICE
INSURE DOMESTIC TRANQUILLITY
PROVIDE FOR THE COMMON DEFENSE
PROMOTE THE GENERAL WELFARE
AND SECURE THE BLESSINGS OF LIBERTY
TO OURSELVES AND OUR POSTERITY. . .
MR. DIONYSUS
I AM A LIAR.
NO.
WE THE ACID SCARRED VICTIMS OF HISTORY
OF EVIL AND HYPOCRISY
EXALT CRIMINALS TO OFFICE
VIETNAM EL SALVADOR CHILE
WITH LOVELY MISSILES ROARING BOMBS
OF THE RICH AND THE WHITE AND THE PIOUS
AND BURN CHILDREN AND TORTURE WOMEN
FOREVER AND EVER AMEN.
GOD BLESS America
BLACK MASK:

MAD HATTER:

I should say I'm very much elevener than any of the people who put me here. As a matter of fact, I could leave any time I wanted. It's only a doll's house after all.

Anyway, I don't mind. I like dolls.

particularly the live ones.

CROC:

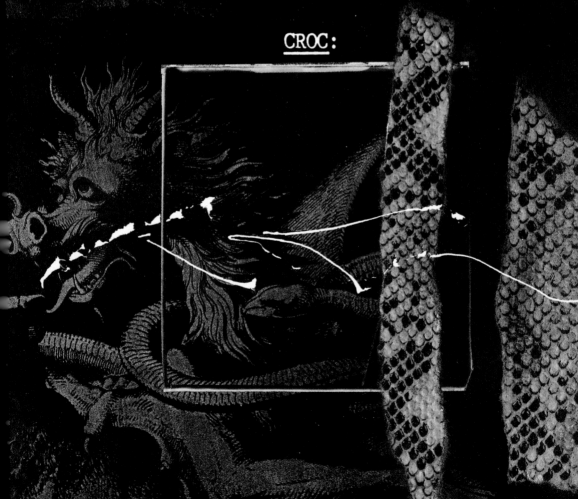

DOCTOR DESTINY:

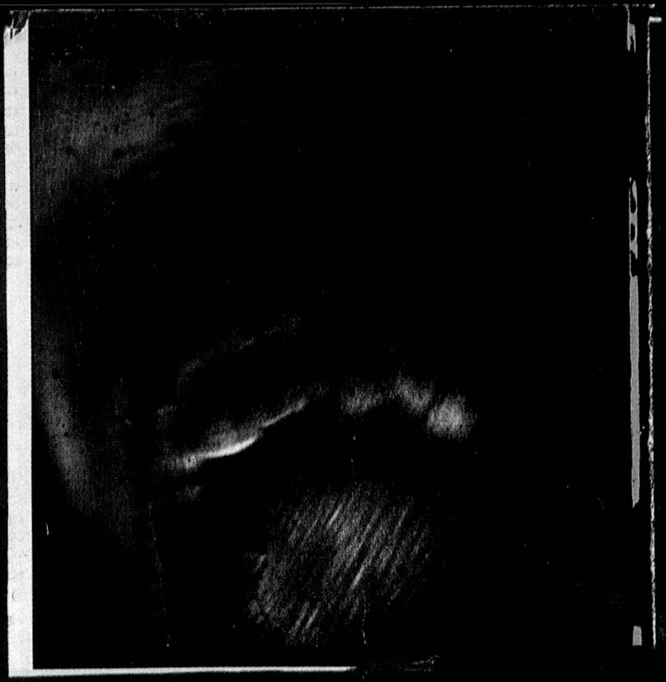

in dreams I walk with you...

MAXIE ZEUS:

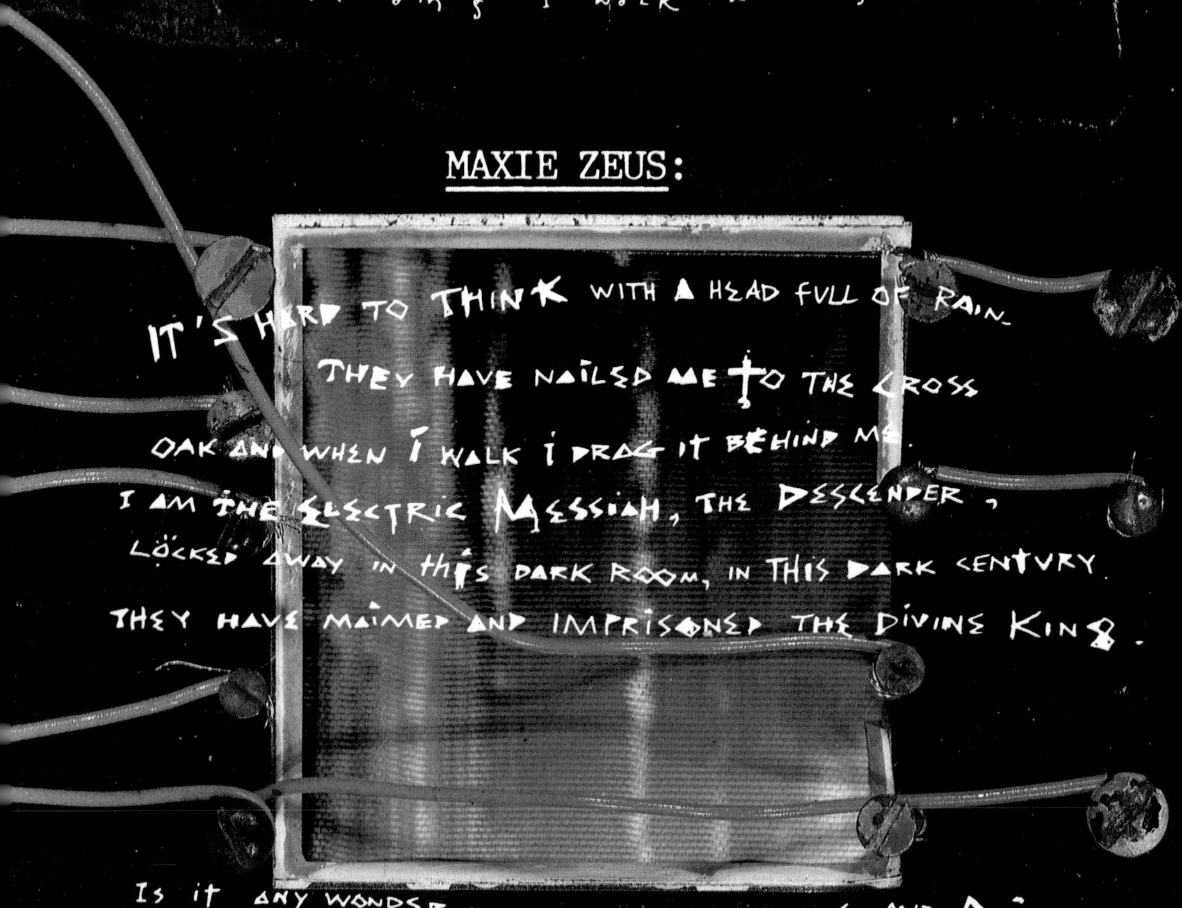

IT'S HARD TO THINK WITH A HEAD FULL OF RAIN.
THEY HAVE NAILED ME TO THE CROSS
OAK AND WHEN I WALK I DRAG IT BEHIND ME.
I AM THE ELECTRIC MESSIAH, THE DESCENDER,
LOCKED AWAY IN THIS DARK ROOM, IN THIS DARK CENTURY.
THEY HAVE MAIMED AND IMPRISONED THE DIVINE KING.

Is it ANY WONDER THE WORLD SICKENS AND DIES?

CLAYFACE:

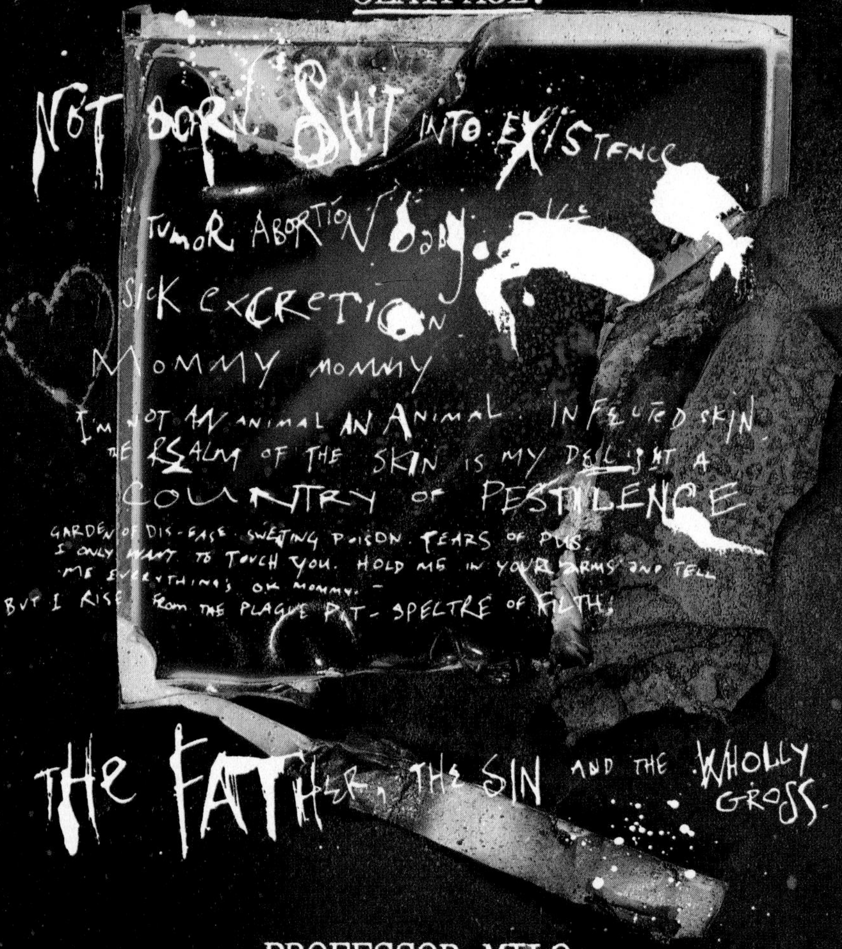
NOT BORN SHIT INTO EXISTENCE
TUMOR ABORTION baby.
SICK EXCRETION
MOMMY MOMMY
I'M NOT AN ANIMAL AN ANIMAL. INFECTED SKIN.
THE REALM OF THE SKIN IS MY DELIGHT A
COUNTRY OF PESTILENCE
GARDEN OF DIS-EASE. SWEATING POISON. TEARS OF PUS.
I ONLY WANT TO TOUCH YOU. HOLD ME IN YOUR ARMS AND TELL
ME EVERYTHING'S OK MOMMY. -
BUT I RISE FROM THE PLAGUE PIT - SPECTRE OF FILTH.
THE FATHER, THE SIN AND THE WHOLLY GROSS.

PROFESSOR MILO:

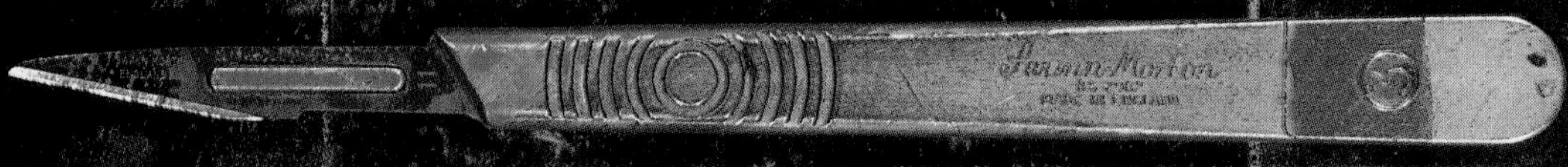

I DON'T KNOW HOW MANY TIMES I HAVE TO SAY THIS.
I AM SANE. I AM PERFECTLY AND COMPLETELY SANE.
I SHOULDN'T BE IN HERE AT ALL.
THERE'S BEEN A TERRIBLE MISTAKE.

GRANT MORRISON began his comics career in 1978, with contributions to the short-lived experimental comics magazine *Near Myths*. This promising start was immediately followed by eight years of poverty and unemployment. In 1986, however, he found himself working for Britain's *2000 AD*, for whom he wrote the successful *Zenith* series.

He is currently writing *Animal Man* and *Doom Patrol* for DC, *St. Swithin's Day* for Trident Comics and the controversial *New Adventures of Hitler* for *Cut* magazine. Future plans include a comic biography of Andy Warhol and a graphic novel entitled *Sick Buildings*.

In his secret identity, he is an award–winning playwright and also plays rhythm guitar and sings with indie noise band The Fauves.

He lives and works and sleeps occasionally in Glasgow, Scotland.

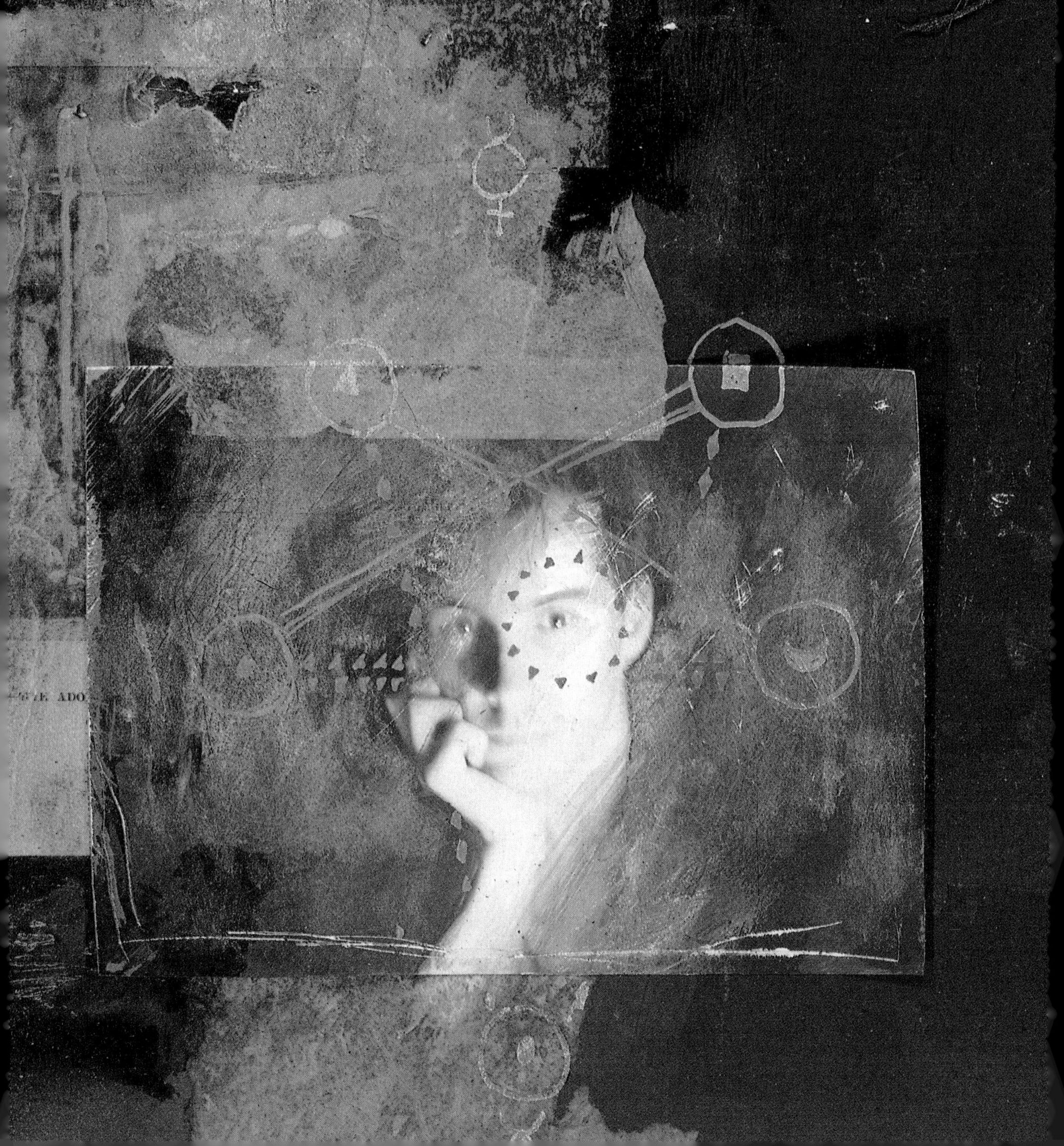

Dave McKean lives and works in Surrey, England, with his partner, Clare, and a piano. He studied design, illustration and film at Berkshire College of Art and Design for four years, where he subsequently returned to teach audio visuals and film for a year and a half. Dave has illustrated two comics, both with writer Neil Gaiman. *Violent Cases* was published by Escape in 1987 and has won three Eagle and Mekon awards. *Black Orchid* was published by DC in 1988 and was nominated for an Eisner and a Harvey award.

Dave is also working with Gaiman on *Signal to Noise*, a continuing story running in *The Face* magazine; *Black Cocktail*, an illustrated novel by Jonathan Carroll; numerous book covers; and various other works.

He has written and performed music soundtracks for TV commercials and video and played at the Bracknell Jazz Festival in 1986.

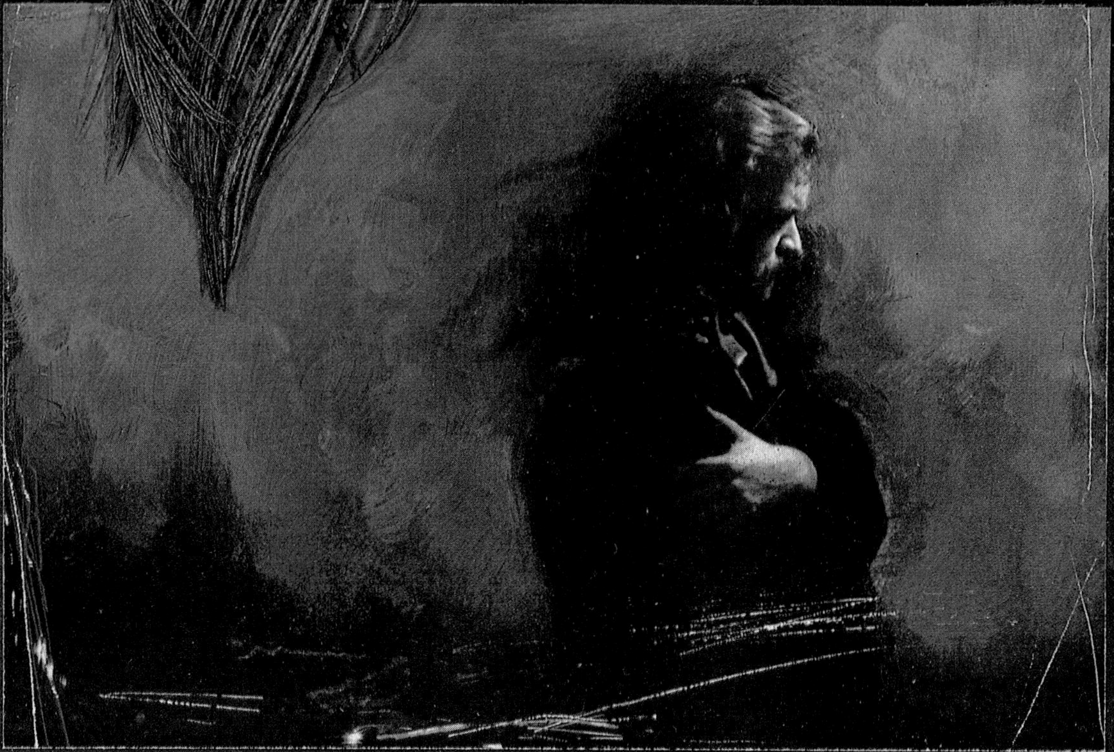

Thanks to Judy Cartwright, Jim Clements, Neil Jones, Neil Gaiman, Clare and Delia Haythornthwaite, Ron Tiner, Mark Nevelow, Mary Dalton, Keith Harris, Dick Jude, Andrew and Christopher Waring, Len Wein, Rolie Green, Tony Stochmal and all at Splash of Paint Design.

GRANT MORRISON
DAVE McKEAN